HIGHER
English

Jane Cooper

Materials for formal assessment practice written by:

Ann Bridges: Textual Analysis (pages 148–152 plus
Answer guide, pages 200–214)

Colin Eckford: Close Reading (pages 65–71 plus
Answer guide, pages 177–199)

HODDER
GIBSON

The Publishers would like to thank the following for permission to reproduce copyright material:

Photo credits
Page 4 (all) Used by permission of The Random House Group Ltd.; Page 61 © Gary/Fotolia.com; Page 73 © TSPL/Writer Pictures; Page 92 (top to bottom) © Image Source/Alamy, © J. Fredric May/Getty Images, © Mary Evans/Classic Stock/H. Armstrong Roberts; Page 93 ©2006 John Hedgecoe/ Topfoto; Page 98 © ClassicStock/Alamy; Page 123 © ullsteinbild/TopFoto; Page 124 (both) © Penguin Group Ltd.

Acknowledgements
Introductory instructions, past paper questions and marking instructions reproduced by permission of SQA.
Extract from *Mortal Causes* copyright © 1994 Ian Rankin. Reproduced with kind permission of Orion Books, an imprint of The Orion Publishing Group, London; Extract from *The Big Over Easy* by Jasper Fforde, Copyright © Jasper Fforde, 2005, reproduced by permission of Hodder and Stoughton Limited; Extract from *Touching the Void* by Joe Simpson, published by Jonathan Cape. Reprinted by permission of The Random House Group Ltd.; Extract from *Once in a House on Fire* by Andrea Ashworth, published by Pan Macmillan, London, copyright © Andrea Ashworth, 1998; Extract from *Hugh Fearlessly Eats It All* by Hugh Fearnley-Whittingstall, reproduced with kind permission of Bloomsbury Publishing Plc; Extract from "Big Brother is closing in" (retitled "A Dangerous Assumption") copyright Sam Taylor; Extract from "The Big Question: What do new discoveries tell us about Stonehenge" by Steve Connor copyright The Independent, 24/09/2008; Extract from "Leave these stones their eternal secrets" (retitled "The Theories Pile Up") by Robin McKie copyright Guardian News & Media Ltd 2008; 'Incident' from *The Poems of Norman MacCaig* by Norman MacCaig is reproduced by permission of Polygon, an imprint of Birlinn Ltd (www.birlinn.co.uk); 'Afternoons' from *Collected Poems* by Philip Larkin, published by Faber and Faber Ltd, reproduced with kind permission of Faber and Faber Ltd; 'All the Little Loved Ones' from *Selected Stories* by Dilys Rose ISBN 978-1842820773 reproduced courtesy of Luath Press; *Shooting An Elephant* from *Shooting An Elephant And Other Essays* by George Orwell (Copyright © George Orwell, 1936) by permission of Bill Hamilton as the Literary Executor of the Estate of the Late Sonia Brownell Orwell and Secker & Warburg Ltd.; 'Work and Play' from *Collected Poems* by Ted Hughes, published by Faber and Faber Ltd, reproduced with kind permission of Faber and Faber Ltd; Reproduced with permission of Herald & Times Group. The Herald, "Is Paranoid Parenting the Greatest Danger to our Kids?" by Melanie Reid, 26/02/2001; Extract of 489 words from "Impact! The Threat of Comets and Asteroids" by Verschur, Gerrit (1996), by permission of Oxford University Press, Inc; Extracts from "The Shape of Things to Come" © The Economist Newspaper Limited, London 2010; Extracts from "Despite Google, we still need good libraries" by George Kerevan published by the Scotsman, 15/12/2004, © The Scotsman Publications Ltd; Extracts from "Yes, I will let Mr Prescott build in my backyard" copyright Richard Morrison / The Times / nisyndication; Extracts from "If eco-snobs had their way, none of us would go anywhere" by Janet Daley, published by The Telegraph, 08/01/2007 © Telegraph Media Group Limited 2007; Extract from "Is it okay to fly?" by Leo Hickman copyright Guardian News & Media Ltd 2006; Extract from "Cities on the Edge of Chaos" by Deyan Sudjic copyright Guardian News & Media Ltd 2008.

Extracts on p.33 taken/adapted from the following sources: 1) http.//deathpenaltycuurriculum.org; 2) www.heraldscotland.com; 3) www.bbc.co.uk/news; 4) www.suite101.com; 5) www.coursework.info.

Every effort has been made to trace all copyright holders, but if any have been inadvertently overlooked the Publishers will be pleased to make the necessary arrangements at the first opportunity.

Although every effort has been made to ensure that website addresses are correct at time of going to press, Hodder Gibson cannot be held responsible for the content of any website mentioned in this book. It is sometimes possible to find a relocated web page by typing in the address of the home page for a website in the URL window of your browser.

Hachette UK's policy is to use papers that are natural, renewable and recyclable products and made from wood grown in sustainable forests. The logging and manufacturing processes are expected to conform to the environmental regulations of the country of origin.

Orders: please contact Bookpoint Ltd, 130 Milton Park, Abingdon, Oxon OX14 4SB. Telephone: (44) 01235 827720. Fax: (44) 01235 400454. Lines are open 9.00–5.00, Monday to Saturday, with a 24-hour message answering service. Visit our website at www.hoddereducation.co.uk. Hodder Gibson can be contacted direct on: Tel: 0141 848 1609; Fax: 0141 889 6315; email: hoddergibson@hodder.co.uk

© Jane Cooper 2011
First published in 2011 by
Hodder Gibson, an imprint of Hodder Education,
An Hachette UK Company
2a Christie Street
Paisley PA1 1NB

Impression number   5 4 3 2 1
Year   2014 2013 2012 2011

Cover photo © Scott Kemper/Alamy
Illustrations by Moira Munro and Tech-Set Limited
Typeset in 12/14 Bembo by Tech-Set Limited
Printed in Italy

A catalogue record for this title is available from the British Library

ISBN: 978 1444 124354

CONTENTS

Introduction	The Higher English Course	iv
Chapter 1	Writing for the NAB and the Folio	1
Chapter 2	Close Reading	42
Chapter 3	Poetry: 'Incident'	72
Chapter 4	Poetry: 'Porphyria's Lover'	82
Chapter 5	Poetry: 'Afternoons'	92
Chapter 6	Prose: 'All the Little Loved Ones'	102
Chapter 7	Prose: 'Shooting an Elephant'	118
Chapter 8	The Critical Essay	133
Chapter 9	Textual Analysis	148
Chapter 10	Answers to Close Reading Questions	153
Chapter 11	Answers to Textual Analysis Questions	200

INTRODUCTION
The Higher English Course

The Higher course gives you many opportunities to display your English skills. You will be assessed by NABs you sit in class, by sending away a folio of your writing, and also by an exam at the end of the course.

You can do the NABs, which you must pass before you can go on to the exam, in any order, and your teacher will decide when you are ready to try them. They are:

- **Textual Analysis**, in which you are given an unfamiliar short piece of literature and have to analyse the writer's skills and techniques.

- **Close Reading**, in which you read a short passage of non-fiction and answer questions on it.

- **Writing**, in which you plan and produce one written piece.

The Writing Folio will contain two pieces of writing and gets sent away to the SQA in April, shortly before your exam. The two pieces in it must be of different genres.

Once you have passed all the NABs and sent away your Folio you'll be ready for the exam, which will be in mid May. There are two exam papers:

- **Close Reading**, in which you'll read two non-fiction passages on a similar subject and answer questions on them.

- **The Critical Essay**, in which you write two essays about literature texts you have studied in class.

This book contains a complete Higher English course, including three poems and two short prose texts you can study to prepare for the Critical Essay exam. (Your teacher may also use other literature texts, perhaps a play or a novel.) You will also want to do lots of exam practice by using past papers, but everything else you need is here.

Updates and syllabus changes: important note to teachers and students from the publisher

Please remember that syllabus arrangements change from time to time. We make every effort to update our textbooks as soon as possible when this happens, but – especially if you are using an old copy of this book – it is always advisable to check whether there have been any alterations to the arrangements since this book was printed. You can check the latest arrangements at the SQA website (www.sqa.org.uk), and you can also check for any specific updates to this book at www.hoddereducation.co.uk/higherenglish.

We make every effort to ensure accuracy of content, but if you discover any mistakes please let us know as soon as possible – see contact details on back cover.

CHAPTER 1
Writing for the NAB and the Folio

Higher writing is tested in two ways:

1 You will sit a NAB in school.

2 In April of your exam year, you will send off a Folio of two pieces to be externally marked. The mark you get for these counts as 20 per cent of your overall Higher mark. The two pieces must be from different genres of writing. One of them can be a piece you have also used to pass your NAB, or you can submit two different pieces.

The reason this chapter comes at the start of the book is that it may take you most of your Higher year to get that Folio together. You may wish to try the different sorts of writing taught here at different times, and produce a number of different first drafts before you decide, with help from your teacher, which two are best and should be redrafted for the Folio.

What the markers are looking for

Whenever your work is marked, both for the NAB and the Folio, you are being tested on four different areas of your writing skill: **content, structure, expression** and **technical accuracy**. You should display strengths in every area, and a severe weakness in any one of them could lead to your failing this task.

- Your **content** should be relevant to your chosen task and genre. It should be suitable for the audience who will read it. There should be some depth and complexity to your work, which should be well developed.
- Your piece should have good **structure**. The structure should suit your chosen task and genre and should suit your audience. Your chosen structure will help your writing have impact.

- In your **expression** you should use the techniques we expect to find in your chosen genre of writing. (You will find guidelines later in this chapter about these.) You need to choose effective words and vary the types of sentences you use. The reader should be aware of following a point of view in what you write, and your style and tone should help to put this across.
- **Technical accuracy** is how well you use the English language. This includes your paragraphing, spelling, grammar and punctuation, which should all be consistently accurate. You cannot pass if your work is not technically accurate.

Warning

The next few pages are going to contain lots of information about the course requirements for writing. Don't panic. You don't have to try to memorise all of this. As you read it over, just make sure you understand everything. You can check back at these pages at any time to make sure that you are following the rules and guidelines properly.

What you can write

Your Folio should contain two pieces in two different genres. One piece should be what the SQA calls 'creative', which actually means that you can produce any one of these types of writing to fulfil the requirements for this genre:

- a personal reflective essay
- a piece of prose: story or novel extract

- a poem or set of linked poems
- a drama script.

Later in this chapter you will learn about how to write in the first two of these styles, reflective and prose fiction.

The second Folio piece should be what the SQA calls 'discursive', which actually means that you can produce any one of these types of writing to fulfil the requirements for this genre:

- a persuasive essay
- an argumentative essay
- a report.

Later in this chapter you will learn about how to write in the first two of these styles, persuasive and argumentative.

Remember, since you can use your Writing NAB as a Folio piece, whatever you write for the NAB ought to fit these Folio criteria as well.

Length

Your Folio pieces should each be between 650 and 1,300 words long (though poems can be shorter). If your piece is too short it's very unlikely to pass because it's unlikely to be the sort of developed piece that Higher markers want to see. If your piece is too long, marks will be taken off.

Your title, any footnotes, and any bibliography or list of sources are not counted. If your piece contains quotations these are regarded as part of the word count.

Authenticity

Because your Folio is worth 20 per cent of your marks, quite a sizeable chunk of the entire Higher course, it's vital that the SQA can be sure that every student is working in the same way and under the same conditions, so that marking can be fair. Your Folio has to be your own work, and at Higher level you are not allowed to have too much support or detailed input from your teacher.

What you can do
Be given teaching that extends your knowledge, understanding and appreciation of a range of genres.

Use printed or electronic sources to find background information or ideas.

Use a dictionary, spellchecker or thesaurus.

Discuss your ideas with your teacher as part of your planning.

Be given written comments on your first draft, and discuss that draft with your teacher.

Be given broad suggestions for how to improve your first draft.

What you can't do
Rely heavily on ideas or wording that you found in a printed or electronic source.

What your teacher can't do
Give you detailed advice about how to restructure or reword your first draft.

Pick out and correct mistakes in your expression or your technical accuracy.

Tell you that you must write about a certain genre or topic that he or she has chosen.

Give you detailed notes, or a specific plan, or a model so detailed that you wouldn't be coming up with your own structure.

This might all sound very detailed and strict. Remember that you can check back at these rules at any point in your work, and remember that their overall purpose is to get you to do what you should want to do anyway – to use your own ideas to write your own piece that shows your own abilities.

Sources

You'll probably need to refer to outside sources as you write your discursive piece. These must be acknowledged.

- If you have used a newspaper or magazine article you must name the writer and give the publication date.
- If you use information from the internet you must give the name of the site and the specific page address.

- If you quote from a book you should give the title and publication date.
- Any quotations should be inside quotation marks.
- You **absolutely must not, ever**, copy and paste, or retype, exact wording from a website or from anywhere else.

Drafting and redrafting

All real writing is drafted and redrafted. However, because your Higher Folio is a test of how well you can write, and to make sure that everyone is being tested fairly, you are not allowed to keep endlessly polishing your work.

Your teacher should keep a note of your title and ideas, and keep your plan, your first draft and a copy of your final version safely at school. The SQA might ask to see these.

Your teacher can write comments and suggestions on your first draft, and can discuss these with you, but cannot mark mistakes in detail. It's up to you to be able to correct these. You should not normally have more than two goes at writing any particular piece.

You will need to sign a declaration to say that your Folio is your own work. The two pieces that go into that Folio should be produced under conditions that help to ensure that the work is your own. In practice, the easiest way to do this is to write your first draft of each piece in class.

Your teacher will compare that draft to any later versions to make sure that the work, while it improves and develops, is without a doubt still your own.

Presentation

Your Folio pieces should be typed, and printed in black ink on just one side of the paper. Use a clear standard font of 12 point size. Your text should have a straight margin on the left side. Margins should be 2 cm wide all round the page and you should use double line-spacing, with a double return for new paragraphs. The poor marker may have several hundred Folio pieces to read and all these guidelines make your work clear and easy to follow.

Well done! You've made it through pages of rules and guidelines. Did you understand it all as you read it? Remember that you can refer back to these pages at any time. In fact you should keep coming back to these pages and double-checking that you are following the rules.

Now that we've got through all this, let's move on to the fun part, the writing itself.

At the start of the chapter we saw that the SQA wants you to write in two different main genres, **creative** and **discursive**, and that these break down into seven types of writing altogether. There isn't space in this book to deal with all of these, but we will look at the four that most students are most likely to want to write: **prose fiction** and **personal reflective writing** from the creative genre; and **argumentative** and **persuasive** writing from the discursive genre.

Prose fiction

The wide genre of prose fiction includes all short stories and novels. However, we can often tell that the fiction we are reading belongs to a more particular genre. For example, Andy McNab, Lee Child and James Patterson all write books that belong to the thriller genre. Each genre has its own rules and conventions (the way things usually happen) and these can be very helpful for writers.

Midsomer Murders, Rebus, Taggart, CSI, The Wire, A Touch Of Frost and *Lewis*.

Don't panic. You're not going to be asked to write a whole novel. You're just going to write the first chapter.

Now try this

Work with a partner or small group. Make a list of answers to this question:

- What do you think a writer needs to do in the first chapter of a novel? (Don't think specifically about detective novels for the moment, just think about what every novel writer should do at the start of their book.)

Next, share your answers with the whole class and build up a bigger list.

Now try this

Work with a partner or small group. Make a list of all the fiction genres you can think of.

Next, share your answers with the whole class and build up a bigger list.

Now try this

Work with a partner or small group. Make a list of answers to this question:

- What particular things do you think a writer needs to do in the first chapter of a detective novel?

Next, share your answers with the whole class and build up a bigger list.

In this chapter, we are going to find out about one particular fiction genre – **the detective novel.** You may have heard of Ian Rankin, Quintin Jardine, Val McDermid and Henning Mankell, who write in this genre. The makers of TV programmes love this genre too. Think of

Read the following text. It's just the first two pages of a book, not the whole chapter.

BEWARE OF THE DOGWALKERS

'We should just round up all the dogwalkers.'
'Ma'am?'
'The dogwalkers. Haven't you noticed it's always them who finds one of these? Very
5 suspicious if you ask me.'
'Quite, Ma'am. Anyway, what would you like me to do?' Perhaps this was just the DCI's little joke. It was PC Harry Stevens' first murder, but he'd heard that officers who saw this kind of thing
10 all the time developed a sort of black humour, a coping mechanism.

'Bring me the dogwalker,' said DCI Heather Barnes wearily. 'Just the one dogwalker. The one who found her.'
15 'Certainly Ma'am.' Stevens began scrambling up the slope away from the burn and towards the footpath at the top where a shaky-looking middle-aged woman was sitting on a fallen log. She was clutching her spaniel as if it might bring
20 her some comfort – unlikely as the dog was too busy yapping at the growing crowd. How could a crowd form in a place like this? Stevens liked

cities, bars, and shops. To him this pathway at
the edge of a village might as well have been the
25 Gobi desert, but a crowd was forming nonetheless.
Already he could see three other uniforms, two
bio-suited members of the MO's team and a local
TV news crew. News crews were bad news.

Barnes knew this too. 'And get rid of that
30 camera crew!' Stevens heard her yell as he
approached the dog lady.

The body was lying, as in Heather's memory
they always seemed to, half naked and half buried.
The dog had scurried through the leaves in its
35 excitement and she couldn't be sure how much it
might have disturbed the scene. The MO's men
should be able to tell her. 'I'm sorry,' she said to
the dead girl. 'I will find out who did this.' It was
what she always said to the dead.

40 At the top of the slope Harry Stevens was
wishing he felt more authoritative. 'I must ask
you to step back and cease filming. You'll have an
opportunity to ask the DCI any questions you like
at a proper briefing later.' The few minutes he'd
45 spent with the dead girl seemed to have made him
smaller and quieter and the news crew weren't
really paying him much attention.

'Just a couple minutes. Yeah? Local colour?
Early reactions?' The reporter was wearing a
50 slightly too shiny suit under his slightly too red
anorak. His wellingtons worried Stevens most

of all. The man was keen. Any minute now he
might head off down the slope towards the boss.

Impatient at last with waiting for the walker
55 to be brought to her, Heather Barnes was on her
way back up the slope, having left the body with
the men in the white suits. She made straight for
the reporter. 'Mr Morton. You have an amazing
instinct for these sorry scenes.'

60 'Just doing my job, Heather. People have
a right to know when there's a maniac on the
loose.'

'*Mister* Morton,' she said firmly. 'We are at
the very early stages of what will be a complex
65 investigation ...'

'So you're saying you won't be able to find
this guy quickly?'

'I'm saying,' she said through gritted teeth,
'that it is far too early for you to be using words
70 like loose and maniac, or even assuming that we
are looking for a guy.'

'So you have no leads whatsoever? Viewers
will find that very disturbing.'

'A discovery has been made, Mr Morton. At
75 this stage I am unprepared to say more.'

'But it's a girl, isn't it?' persisted the reporter.
'And it looks from up here as if she's only half
dressed.'

'And your point is?'

80 'It's February, so presumably you're not
thinking that she came out here for a wee
sunbathe and just lay down to die?'

Heather had had enough. 'Mr Morton, you
are not helping. In fact you are actually stopping
85 me at this moment from doing my job at all. I
need to interview the woman who found the
body.'

'So you're at least prepared to confirm that
the girl's dead then? Not just sleeping?'

90 'Enough, Morton.'

As she walked off, the reporter turned to his
cameraman. 'Anything we can use?'

'Not much. But I did get a little sound clip
earlier on when I was setting up the levels.
95 Something odd that the DCI said to her PC. You
should take a listen.'

Do you want to add anything to your list of what you think a detective novelist needs to do in his or
her first chapter?

Read the rest of Chapter 1 of *Beware of the Dogwalkers.*

Heather was in the incident room when she saw that night's news. It started well. The staged press conference was clear, brisk. She could see herself putting across the facts: a dead body,
5 probably that of a girl in her late teens, had been found by a local person. Early indications were that the victim had been lying there for less than twelve hours. Residents were asked to report anything that might be significant to
10 the investigation. Police were especially hoping to hear from anyone who could help them to identify the deceased.

All of that was fine. The next item was more of a problem. A number of animal welfare groups,
15 the Kennel Club, and the local chapter of the Association of Professional Dogwalkers and Pet-sitters had all joined together to issue a strongly worded statement. They utterly condemned the suggestion that the killer might have been a
20 dogwalker.

This called for an exceptionally strong coffee. The pot that held the proper stuff was empty, as usual. Nowhere in the exhaustive incident manual did it say who was in charge of the coffee pot, so it
25 was always empty. Heather reached into her desk drawer and found a jar with about half an inch of granules solidified at the bottom. Poking them with a fork – there was no sign either of a spoon – did no good. Sighing, Heather tipped boiling
30 water straight from the kettle into the jar, screwed the lid on, and was shaking it vigorously when the Super strode in.

'Now Heather!'

'Sir?'

35 'The wife's furious. I've just had her on the phone. She can't believe what you said about dogwalkers. You know how fond she is of wee Angus and Hamish.'

'With respect, Sir …'

40 'DCI Barnes, people only say that when they're about to say something very disrespectful, and you know that I hold my dear wife in the highest regard.'

'Yes Sir, and I'm sure you're very fond of
45 wee Angus and Hamish too, bless their wee white tails, but wouldn't it be more appropriate for your wife to be furious about the fact that somebody has killed a teenage girl and dumped her body like a piece of old meat?'

50 'Just so, Heather. Anything in that jar for me?' The Super, having delivered his message and done his domestic duty, was now back to his usual avuncular self.

'Not really, Sir, not unless you like tar with
55 your shortbread.'

'Better come to my office then. I've got a pot of Colombian on the go.'

Superintendent Bruce Henderson's office was legendary. His dog-loving wife, Olive, was famed
60 for keeping him well under her thumb, but she was a lovely home-baker. Bruce's office was both a haven from her iron rule, and a source of delicious aromas that sometimes reached as far as the holding cells. Heather accepted a mug of
65 Colombian, a brownie and a small cheese scone. Apparently Olive was practising for the Women's Guild annual bake-off.

'So what do we have, Heather?'

'Pretty much what you heard me say at the
70 news conference, Sir. There's a dead girl but we don't know who she is. No ID, no match to any current missing person's report. MO's team think she was killed somewhere else and dumped there shortly after she died. We didn't
75 tell them that.'

'Anything else you didn't tell them? Do you know how she died?'

'Blunt force trauma to the head. Hit two or three times but the first blow was probably
80 enough to kill her. Stripped afterwards, probably in an attempt to remove killer's DNA, forensics,

stuff like that. No sign of anything sexual.'

'That's good.' Henderson took a deep bite from his brownie. A walnut piece dropped onto his
85 napkin. 'So what can we do about the dog thing?'

Heather sighed. 'I didn't know they were listening, Sir. I was down the bottom of the slope with Harry Stevens. He was looking a bit green. His first body, you see. I thought a wee joke might
90 help. Bloody directional microphones.'

'Absolutely. But we'll have to do something, just to calm them down and get the attention back on the real story. We've no clues and we need the public to help, not to be told by that idiot Morton
95 that we're about to round up all the pet owners and submit them to the Chinese water torture.'

'I suppose I could make a statement. Say how much we appreciate the fact that the dog-walking community have always helped us with our
100 enquiries.'

Henderson sucked in his teeth, his current mouthful of coffee, and a number of deliciously chocolatey crumbs. 'I don't think that's quite the way to put it. Isn't helping us with our enquiries
105 what people do when we arrest them and ask them really hard questions because we've got a strong suspicion that they actually might have killed someone and dumped the body?'

'Yes, Sir.'
110 'Yes, Heather. I think some kind of gesture might be called for.'

* * * * *

She felt stupid. The force's media team had suggested she'd 'play more sympathetically with the public' if she wasn't alone when filmed. 'I
115 won't be alone,' she'd insisted. 'I'll have two West Highland terriers, that idiot Peter Morton and his fat cameraman. Plus I've just been told to expect

some guy who used to present *Blue Peter* and a team from the dog channel!'

120 They'd made her take Harry Stevens too. He'd been sent home to put on something that wasn't uniform, but it was obvious to everyone that the whole thing was staged. Heather's office suit looked wrong on the footpath and
125 wrong beside Harry's designer jeans. Angus and Hamish clearly had no respect for her authority and were winding themselves around her ankles. Olive had handed them over with a long list of instructions and a stern look and was now
130 hovering just out of shot.

They'd chosen a neutral location of course, a country park. All the footpaths radiated from what had once been a rich Victorian's country lodge and was now a nature interpretation
135 centre and ranger station.

They'd been walking for about ten minutes when the path they were on turned towards a burn and the ground grew wet and slimy. Morton and his cameraman, slithering along
140 behind them, were not happy. 'Slow down, can't you? I'm sure we've got enough footage now.'

'But, Peter,' she grinned, 'I think we're far enough from the road to let these wee guys off their leads.' Bending down she unhooked
145 the two little white dogs, who darted off immediately in quite opposite directions. Within moments she'd lost sight of Angus in the undergrowth by the water. She gave Stevens a look.

150 'Yes, Ma'am.'

He was back horribly soon. 'Ma'am, I think you'd better come and take a look.'

The film crew caught up with them just as Heather was reaching for her mobile. Beside her
155 lay another half-naked girl. Another body.

Now try this

Discuss the answers to these questions:

- What has the writer done in this first chapter to make you want to read on into Chapter 2?
- What do you think is going to happen in Chapter 2?
- What do you think is going to happen in the rest of the novel?

You should have noticed that the writer is doing more than just setting the plot – the crime story – in motion. She's also establishing characters, and letting us see the relationships between them. Because the story mostly sticks to Heather's point of view, we can tell that she is the main character, and someone we are supposed to like and sympathise with. We see that she has a difficult relationship with the reporter, but a mostly good one with her own boss, Superintendent Henderson, and that she and her PC, Stevens, aren't quite used to working together yet.

People often ask writers where they get their ideas from. The writer of *Beware of the Dogwalkers* got the idea from a country walk, when she realised that she was in the kind of place where dogwalkers always seemed to find bodies. You might be worried that you'll have trouble coming up with an idea of your own, especially when so many other people have written detective novels before you. To prove that ideas can come from anywhere, it's time to play a game.

Now try this

Close your book. This game will only work if you don't know what comes next. As long as your teacher has a copy of the book and can tell everyone in the class what to do, it'll work out fine. Go on, close your book.

The only person reading this now should be the teacher. This exercise uses randomly chosen words to set up the plot of a crime story in which there is a suspicious death. The use of random words in this is actually very structured, so it's important that you take your students through this task in order, and that they follow the instructions carefully.

First put your students into pairs and get them to choose two random words. It works best if the words they choose are nouns. Make sure every pair has time to choose their two nouns before you explain the next step.

Then explain the following: the two words they have chosen are to be used to create the scene or setting of a crime story. (For example, if they chose the words *tiger* and *stain*, the set-up could be that a man was found dead just outside the tiger cage in a zoo with a strange green stain on his shirt.)

Give them a few minutes to work their scenario out. At this stage they do not have to decide exactly how the victim died.

Next get your pairs of students to choose a further three random nouns. Give them plenty time to do this before you go on to the final step.

Now tell them that these words are the clues. They must now use these words to construct a reasonable hypothesis, using these clues to explain how the suspicious death took place and who might have caused it. (For example, if the second set of words was *rhino*, *corn*, *chicken*, the explanation could be that the man was on his way to take a bucket of corn to the chickens when he was charged by an escaped rhino. The green stain came from a pen in his pocket that burst when he was crushed by the charging beast.)

Get your students to share their answers with the class, first of all saying what their words were, then explaining what scenarios or solutions they came up with. Lastly, tell them they can open their books again!

I hope you can see that ideas can come from anywhere, and that the oddest things can sometimes get you going on a story. Let's look a little more specifically now at one particular element of your chapter – the crime scene.

You'll find one of these in the first few pages of nearly every detective novel, or before the first advert break in any TV crime drama. Certain elements – what we might call genre markers – come up again and again:

- The senior detective arrives to find other police force staff already at work.
- The senior detective usually has a more junior colleague.
- The setting is described to create atmosphere.
- There is a detailed, possibly gruesome, description of the victim's body.
- A police doctor or pathologist is at work.
- The detective starts noticing clues, asking questions and drawing conclusions.

As you read the following two crime scenes, look for the above elements.

The first crime scene comes from one of Ian Rankin's Edinburgh-set novels about Inspector John Rebus. During the Edinburgh Festival, something nasty has been found under the Royal Mile.

'You know where we are?' the constable asked.

'Mary King's Close,' said Rebus. Not that he'd ever been down here, not exactly. But he'd been in similar old buried streets beneath the High Street.

5 He knew of Mary King's Close.

There were ducts and pipes, runs of electric cable. Signs of renovation were all around. Rebus pointed to an arc lamp. 'Can we plug that in?'

The constable thought they could. Rebus

10 looked round. At the end of the hallway he could see a wooden toilet, its seat raised. The next door along led to a long vaulted room, the walls whitewashed, the floor earthen.

'That's the wine shop,' the constable said. 'The

15 butcher's is next door.'

So it was. In its ceiling were a great many iron hooks, short and blackened but obviously used at one time for hanging up meat.

Meat still hung from one of them.

20 It was the lifeless body of a young man. His hair was dark and slick, stuck to his forehead and neck. His hands had been tied and the rope slipped over a hook, so that he hung stretched with his knuckles near the ceiling and his toes

25 barely touching the ground. His ankles had been tied together too. There was blood everywhere, a fact made all too plain as the arc lamp suddenly came on, sweeping light and shadows across the walls and roof. There was the faint smell of decay,

30 but no flies, thank God. Dr Galloway swallowed hard. Rebus tried to steady his own heart.

Though it was against regulations he leaned forward and touched the young man's hair. It was still slightly damp. He'd probably died on

35 Friday night and was meant to hang here over the weekend, time enough for any trail, any clues, to grow as cold as his bones.

'What do you reckon, sir?'

'Gunshots.' Rebus looked to where the blood

40 had sprayed the wall. 'Something high velocity. Head, elbows, knees and ankles. He's been six-packed.'

From *Mortal Causes* by Ian Rankin

This second crime scene is deliberately bizarre. In this novel, nursery rhyme characters are real people, mostly living quiet lives in the suburbs. Should any 'nurseries' become involved in crime, either as victims or suspects, Detective Inspector Jack Spratt and his Nursery Crime Division investigate them. In the following extract, Humpty Dumpty has suffered a fatal fall.

The yard was shaped as an oblong, fifteen feet wide and about thirty feet long, surrounded by a high brick wall with crumbling mortar. Most of the yard was filled with junk – broken bicycles,

5 old furniture, a mattress or two. But at one end, where the dustbins were spilling their rubbish on the ground, large pieces of eggshell told of a recent and violent death. Jack knew who the victim was immediately, and had suspected that

10 something like this might happen for a number of years. Humpty Dumpty. The fall guy. If this wasn't under the jurisdiction of the Nursery Crime Division, Jack didn't know what was. Mrs Singh, the pathologist, was kneeling next to the shattered

15 remains dictating notes into a tape recorder. She waved a greeting to him as he walked over but did not stop what she was doing. She indicated to a photographer areas of particular interest to her, the flash going off occasionally and looking

20 inordinately bright in the dull closeness of the yard.

Humpty's ovoid body had fragmented almost completely and was scattered among the dustbins and rubbish at the far end of the yard. The
25 previous night's heavy rain had washed away his liquid centre, but even so there was still enough to give off an unmistakable eggy smell. Jack noted a thin and hairless leg – still with a shoe and sock – attached to a small area of eggshell draped with
30 tattered sheets of translucent membrane. The biggest piece of shell contained Humpty's large features and was jammed between two dustbins. His face was a pale white except for the nose, which was covered in unsightly red gin blossoms.

35 One of the eyes was open, revealing a milky-white unseeing eye, and a crack ran across his face. He had been wearing a tuxedo with a cravat or a cummerbund – it was impossible to say which. The trauma was quite severe and
40 to an untrained eye his body might have been dismissed as a heap of broken eggshell and a bundle of damp clothing.
Jack kneeled down to get a closer look. 'Do we know why he's all dressed up?'
45 Mary consulted her notebook.

From *The Big Over Easy* by Jasper Fforde

Now try this

Discuss the following questions with a partner, a group or the class:

- Did the writers use all the genre markers you expected?
- Did the writers use any ideas or techniques that surprised you?
- Which did you prefer, and why?

Now try this

At this stage, it's a good idea to also watch at least the first twenty minutes of a TV detective drama. There's almost certainly something suitable on TV this week, or you might be able to persuade your teacher to let you watch something together as a class. You should watch until you get at least as far as a 'scene of the crime' moment like those on the previous pages.

We're going to leave the detective novel on one side for a little while, and look at some more general writing skills that will help to bring your chapter to life.

First, we're going to look at a skill that's often summed up in the words: **show, don't tell**. To make that clear, have a look at the following sentences.

> I came into the room. I saw Alan. I greeted him and sat down in a chair.

Now look at these sentences.

> I stormed into the room. I glared at Alan. I grunted at him and flung myself into a chair.

How does the speaker feel about Alan? Angry of course. But notice, he never tells us, 'I felt angry with Alan.' Instead, by changing the simple verbs like *came*, *saw*, *greeted* and *sat* into more expressive ones like *stormed*, *glared*, *grunted* and *flung*, the narrator shows us the emotion.

Now try this

Go back to the first basic set of three sentences beginning, 'I came into the room …' Rewrite them to show the following emotions:

- The narrator is afraid of Alan.
- The narrator finds Alan very attractive.
- The narrator is surprised to find Alan there.

As you can see, the difference between showing and telling often comes from choosing interesting vocabulary. By using the right words to put across how characters move, act, appear or speak, we can show what they are like, or how they are feeling.

Now try this

Copy and complete the following table. It'll help you create a bank of words and phrases.

	How might the character speak?	What might their face look like?	How might the character move?
angry			stamping slamming storming grabbing
sad	stuttering sighing moaning		
happy			
scared		white faced eyes wide mouth tight	

Now try this

One more task on showing, not telling. This one will take us back towards the detective novel. Write a paragraph to describe, in as much detail as possible, a desk in a police station. The way you describe the desk, the things you put on it and how everything has been set out should start to show the life and character of the detective who works at that desk. For example, if there are photographs of children on the desk, we can guess that the detective is probably a parent. Lots of dirty coffee cups and an empty painkiller box suggest one kind of person, a nearly-empty desk with a ticked 'to do' list on it suggests quite another.

Don't use any characters, action or speech in your writing, just description. When you've written

your piece, swap with a partner and see what you can work out about each other's detectives.

Looking at a real example

You are going to see a piece of detective fiction produced by a real student.

Now try this

First of all just read through the piece of writing. You may wish to do this aloud around the class, or you might want to read it on your own.

Found face down beside the canal – the traditional place but with far from traditional injuries.

'Could I just say one thing, Constable?' DI
5 Caroline White enquired lightly.

'What?'

'Just what exactly is a football doing at our corpse's feet?' It was not, she predicted, the work of a particularly aggravated referee.

*****

10 It was a scorcher of a day: the sun blazed down on the grass, heat causing a shimmering haze over the pitch. A group of lads were playing footie when one of them took an overly-exuberant free kick, hammering the ball over the
15 crossbar. The offending striker raced after it as it rolled down the embankment and out of sight towards the canal.

Helpfully, by the time the striker got there, someone had stopped the ball with a foot.
20 Unfortunately, the owner of the said appendage was in no fit state to pass it back.

The boy raced down, trampling through the undergrowth and caught sight of his quarry. He stared transfixed at his other find as a wave
25 of smells filled his nostrils. The deceased was baking in the summer sun and the stench of death mingled with the overture of murky canal water.

He turned sharply and made his own
30 contribution to the assorted bouquet of pungent aromas by thoroughly disseminating his lunch on the grass.

*****

'Ah,' White replied. That explained the football and the vomit. She could discount football-
35 related violence as the cause of death.

The scene was even worse than the last Rangers match she had policed. Blood stained the summer green grass, trickling from the rigid cadaver's right hand where the young
40 man's thumb had been messily severed. More blood flowed copiously from a number of stab wounds to the back and from the head where the left ear should have resided. The aforementioned ear lay several feet from its
45 habitual and far more comfortable resting place. White assumed that constituted a serious hearing impairment.

She briefly considered doing the same thing to the superintendent. After all, it was
50 he who had called her in on her day off to clear up this mess.

Forensics officers drifted like spectres through the gruesome scene, photographed evidence from all angles and tagged and
55 bagged the severed ear – although 'tagging' the exhibit seemed a trifle unnecessary in her professional opinion. It was unarguably an ear.

'Caroline!' William James, the pathologist,
60 greeted her cheerfully, as though they were talking over drinks and not over a mutilated corpse. 'DI White,' he amended, seeing the look that had crossed her subordinate, DS Draper's, face. 'I didn't know you were working today.'
65 'I wasn't,' she riposted.

He didn't enquire any further. 'Try and not step on my blood,' he said and led them round to make a clearer inspection of the body.

Bending down to a crouch beside the body
70 she surveyed the remains. There were multiple contusions to the head and neck and the back was thoroughly lacerated where a knife had slashed through soft tissue and the fabric of his now tattered shirt.

75 The marks on the back of his hands and the trail – partially trampled by the boy who had made the discovery – alluded to the hypothesis that he had been killed somewhere else and then dragged here; but that begged
80 the question, why hadn't the body been shoved into the canal?

'When did he cop it?' she asked, rising quickly and fighting the urge to retch. DS Draper thought he glimpsed a shiver pass down
85 his superior's spine, a crack in her unflappable persona.

'He copped it, as you so eloquently put

it, in the early morning at a conservative estimate,' James replied with a half smile.

90   Hearing a commotion, White hurried up the embankment towards the perimeter cordon – a police line, after all, exerted its own curious gravitational pull – and ducked under the tape one of the PCs gallantly lifted for her.

95   The local rag had deployed a reporter to quiz them on their find, but as their man jockeyed for position he was elbowed aside by the collective muscle of a BBC news crew and the correspondent who worked all the morbid

100 cases, lucky devil. She wondered briefly how he had offended the upper echelons so badly that he always got lumbered with the grisly finds. Then again, perhaps he enjoyed them.

    She swallowed. Press interviews were in her

105 top three for room 101, just next to informing next of kin and the evil of bureaucratic paperwork.

    She was expertly vague and merely confirmed that the body found was a victim of a

110 'violent attack'. She omitted the grislier details and refrained from uttering that special phrase, 'treating the death as suspicious'. 'Suspicious' was too ironic, Orwellian even. It could hardly have been more suspicious if the body had been

115 found in the middle of a crop circle, smoking a cigar and lying on an Axminster carpet. Having appeased the nosy hacks for the time being, she returned to the scene.

    DS Draper hurried towards her. 'We found his

120 wallet. The poor sod is one Alex Blackwell.'

'Driving licence?'

'Nope. He's a card-carrying member of the Green Party,' Draper replied.

'So Jeremy Clarkson probably bumped him

125 off ...'

'D'you think it could be politically motivated? He's probably in town for the by-election.'

    She considered the question. Alright,

130 the Tories were fair game, and Labour was understandable, but only a highly frustrated individual would go for a Liberal, and a Green? That was just sadistic.

    As she opened her mouth to reply the phone

135 rang. She hastily stabbed the answer button. 'Yes?'

'Sorry, DI White, but a body has been found. It's nasty: missing finger, severed ear.'

'I know,' she replied, harassed at the waste

140 of her time. 'I'm looking at it.'

'What?'

'I'm already there, at the canal by the playing field.'

'No, this one's on the industrial estate.'

145 'Tell me it's not a Green Party activist?'

'No. It's a Labour one.'

    The sheer enormity of the task hit her. Hundreds of activists would be flooding into town for the upcoming by-election and

150 someone with questionable morals seemed to have a bit of a grudge against the democratic process. 'Bugger.'

Now try this

Now that you have read the story once, you are going to analyse it in more detail. Consider these questions.

1 Did the writer use the genre markers you expected?

2 Did the writer do anything that surprised you?

3 Write a couple of sentences to show what made it a **good** piece of writing.

4 Suggest two things the writer could have done that would have made the story work **even better**.

Planning your own first chapter

You need to plan, in quite a lot of detail, two main aspects of your story. If you've planned stories in the past, what you probably did was plan the **plot** of your story, the events that would happen in it. We'll get around to that later. First you need to plan, and get to know, your main **character**. It's time to create your detective.

Now try this

Using the following list of questions and prompts, make a list of details that show that you know, and have carefully thought about, your main detective character.

- male or female?
- age?
- appearance?
- home/family situation?
- main personality traits?
- any unusual quirks, habits, hobbies?
- what is this person's background?
- what motivates them to do the job?
- does this person always stick to the rules?
- does your character work well with others, or prefer to go it alone?
- how does this person cope with the stresses of the job?

Once you have answered all these questions, you should know your character well, and if you know them well, you can write well about them. **Be careful!** That doesn't mean that you will actually use all these details in your writing. After all, you're only writing the first chapter of a novel. You should never end up writing something like:

> Heather could never forget her first case. She hadn't been able to catch the killer and she'd never forgiven herself. Now she felt she owed it even more to every victim to find the killer.

Writing that would be a horrible example of telling when you should be showing. Instead, knowing that a failed case is what motivates Heather, the writer of *Beware of the Dogwalkers* writes:

> 'I'm sorry,' she said to the dead girl. 'I will find out who did this.' It was what she always said to the dead.

Once you know your **character**, it's time to start thinking about your **plot**.

Now try this

First of all, choose one of the following rough shapes for your chapter. Each has three steps, and each includes a crime scene.

POSSIBLE STRUCTURE 1

Your detective arrives at the scene.

The crime scene is examined and the detective gets information about the case from other characters.

The story cuts to the detective following up some sort of lead.

POSSIBLE STRUCTURE 2

Your detective arrives at the scene.

The crime scene is examined and the detective gets information about the case from other characters.

The detective leaves the scene with no real leads and facing a very baffling case. At the very end of the chapter, a clue or lead does come up.

POSSIBLE STRUCTURE 3

The novel starts with somebody being attacked and killed. We may know who the victim is, but the identity of the attacker is not revealed.

Your detective arrives at the crime scene.

The crime scene is examined.

POSSIBLE STRUCTURE 4

The novel starts with someone (perhaps a member of the public) finding a body.

The novel cuts to your detective arriving at the crime scene.

The crime scene is examined.

POSSIBLE STRUCTURE 5

The novel starts with a description of a member of the public doing something quite normal.

The novel cuts to your detective arriving at the crime scene.

The crime scene is examined, and the reader now realises that the body being examined is that of the ordinary person they saw at the start of the chapter.

You should now have the very rough outline of the three main stages in your opening chapter and you should know your main detective character really well.

Now try this

Spend about half an hour planning your first chapter carefully, bearing in mind everything you've worked out so far. Your plan might use headings, might be a bullet-pointed list, or might be a mind map or spider plan.

As you plan your chapter, think about whose point of view you will follow. A senior detective? A more junior officer? A witness or other member of the public?

Make sure your chapter is going to end in a way that makes the reader wish there was

going to be a Chapter 2. You might use a full-scale cliffhanger, where you shock your reader into turning the page, or you might use a gentler hook like having your detective heading off somewhere so that we feel we want to go along too.

When your plan is finished, pair up with another student and explain your plans to each other. Don't be afraid to ask each other questions or to help your partner fix things that don't quite work yet.

Just before you write your story, here's some final advice:

1   Make sure you use lots of dialogue in your chapter. If your characters don't speak to each other, they will never seem as if they are alive, and our story will feel completely flat and dull. Not only does speech give your story life, but

the way characters speak and the words they use reveal lots about them.

2   British police detectives are known by their titles (Detective Constable, Detective Sergeant, Detective Inspector and Detective Chief Inspector, often abbreviated to DC, DS, DI, or DCI) and never just called 'Detective' as

American characters would be. So, when you first introduce a character you would call them 'PC Harry Stevens' or 'DCI Heather Barnes'. After that you might call that person Heather if you want readers to sympathise with her or Barnes if you want her to feel like a more distant character.

3   British police tend to work in teams with a clear leader and a reasonably strong sense of rank. The head of a murder investigation would be at least a DI, or even a DCI. Unlike the detectives you may have seen in American films or dramas, British police don't really have partners.

4   Detectives are in a police division called CID. They wear smart plain clothes. Uniformed police have different titles. It's likely that your crime scene would have a number of uniformed PCs at it, taking statements and securing the site.

Now try this

It's now time to write your piece.

When you've written it, read your work over before you hand it in to your teacher. Think about the four areas you will be assessed on and ask yourself the following questions:

CONTENT
- Have I stuck to my task?
- Have I developed my ideas in some depth?

STRUCTURE
- Is my work clear to follow?
- Have I used structural devices like cliffhangers, flashbacks and cuts to give my work impact?
- Have I made the reader believe, and wish, that there could be a second chapter?

EXPRESSION
- Have I followed the conventions of the detective genre?
- Have I used good vocabulary and different sorts of sentences?
- Have I followed a clear point of view?

TECHNICAL ACCURACY
- Are my spelling, grammar and punctuation all accurate?

Once you have checked over your work, hand it in to your teacher. He or she will mark it and give you feedback and suggestions for ways to improve it.

Personal Reflective Writing

This is a genre of writing that many students do very well in. It is also one that you have probably worked on earlier in your school career.

Now try this

Divide the class into two halves, and then divide each half into small groups of three people. Work in these groups for five minutes.

All the groups in one half of the class should list all the reasons why they think people do well at Personal Reflective Writing. All the groups in the other half of the class should list the particular features that we look for in a piece of Personal Reflective Writing.

Each group should share their answers with the rest of the class.

Genuine reflection

When you have worked on personal writing before, you probably concentrated most on bringing the experience to life. Your reflection might have been quite individual – looking back at what the experience meant to you and to those close to you.

Now that you're working at Higher level, your reflection has to go further. It might help if you think of the piece of writing like this:

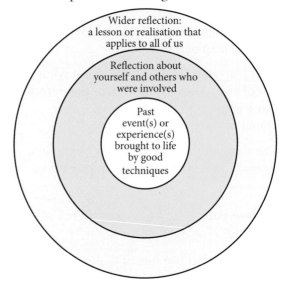

Wider reflection: a lesson or realisation that applies to all of us

Reflection about yourself and others who were involved

Past event(s) or experience(s) brought to life by good techniques

The best way to show you an example of what we mean by this is to look at a piece written by a Higher candidate.

Now try this

Read this piece called 'The Crowd'. As you do so, pay especially close attention to the ideas in the last two paragraphs about how being part of a crowd affects our behaviour.

THE CROWD

It was raining. I turned through the dark, deserted streets alone. My feet were soaking and my jeans were saturated as far as my knees so that my legs were numb with cold.
5 Rain trickled down my neck, making me shiver, and I shoved bare hands further into the deep pockets of my black canvas jacket. Suddenly I noticed, out of the corner of my eye, a group of youths down a narrow side
10 street. I froze. Had they seen me? Slowly, I crept closer and slid silently behind a bin. No. They hadn't seen me. I was certain of that. I cautiously poked my head out the tiniest little bit from my hiding place and peered
15 through the darkness.

Smoke from their cigarettes was suspended in the air around them like morning mist. I could see only their vague outlines in the dim orange light. There must have been at least
20 twenty, twenty-five even. I couldn't tell for sure. One of them, bottle in hand, bent down and picked something up off the ground. He launched the small object, which I assumed was a stone, at the upstairs window of one of
25 the flats which looked out onto the dull street.

The stone flew undeterred through the icy night air and hit the window with a sharp click. Thankfully it bounced off and landed

safely back on the ground. Next, the entire
30 mob began to pelt stones at the window and eventually, after withstanding an incredible attack, it shattered, scattering hundreds of sharp shards of glass all over the glistening pavement. An angry muffled
35 cry could be heard from within the flat and the youths jeered and ran away before anyone had the chance to confront them or, worse still, identify them.

I too left. I set off back on my long walk,
40 pretending to be totally oblivious to what had only just happened, temporarily erasing the event from my memory till I was safely back home. Never mess with the crowd.

I couldn't sleep that night. I understood. I
45 finally understood everything. I understood why I had just walked away. I understood why the youths had behaved as they did. I understood it all. I suddenly remembered that overwhelming feeling, that wonderful
50 sense of belonging when you discover you are no longer an individual but just one minuscule part of what makes up that intricate, complex, powerful body – the crowd. All your principles and convictions
55 suddenly shrink to insignificance and you lose a sense of who you are. Our whole personality evaporates into nothing. That is how I felt that day at Dungavel Detention Centre.

60 The protest against the imprisonment of asylum seekers at Dungavel had not even begun and already I had an immense feeling of elation. That atmosphere was tense, almost electric. The sound of the dry
65 drums resounded through the barren valley. Everyone was screaming and all over the barbed-wire-topped ex-prison fence were pinned thousands of banners and leaflets creating a beautiful, colourful collage

70 round the Centre. I gripped my mum's hand as tightly as I could. We all gathered round a platform on which the orators made their speeches. The crowd chanted and cheered and clapped and I felt so united with everyone else

75 that I began to cry. Tears streamed down my face – I had never experienced such a powerful sense of belonging in my entire life and at that moment I was ready to do anything. The crowd controlled me and I know, without any

80 doubt, that I would have followed it whatever it chose to do, wherever it chose to go. I chanted when the crowd chanted; I cheered when the crowd cheered; I clapped when the crowd clapped.

85 I understood then why a crowd sometimes behaves in a way in which anyone who is not part of it is unable to understand. Crowds are dangerous. They change people. They consume unique individuals into a homogeneous

90 mass. Although I knew that the youths' behaviour was not justified because they were part of a crowd, I understood that they had been unable to escape the clutches of the power of the crowd. I understood why I

95 had been such a coward, why I had chosen to deny what I had seen and run away. I had been scared because, next to the crowd, I was nothing. To challenge the crowd is potentially lethal.

100 We often see crowds behaving badly in protests, at football matches, even in our everyday lives on the streets and we reassure ourselves that, no matter what, we will never behave as badly as the crowd. We will never

105 become so involved that we will lose complete control over our own selves. Can we really be so sure?

We'll return to that piece, and the idea of wide and genuine reflection, again as we work through this chapter. For the moment, just keep in mind that this is the kind of thing you are aiming to do.

Choosing what to write about

It shouldn't be too hard for you to choose a topic. After all, you know yourself better than anyone else does. You are unique, interesting and well worth writing about.

And you have to choose your own topic. Not only is your teacher not allowed to give you an exact subject to write about, in this case your teacher just can't. Only you have lived your life and you are the only person in the world who has had your particular set of experiences. You are the only person in history who ever had the exact set of family and friends that you have. Your brain is the only one in the entire universe to hold your set of memories, thoughts and feelings.

Now try this

Stop and think. Is there an experience you have had which matters to you very much, one that you'd like to write about in your Personal Reflective Essay? Remember that you must be able to get that wider reflection out of it, the kind that applies to us all. If you can think of such an experience, make a note of it now. If not, read the next section and follow the prompts.

Narrowing down your ideas

If you don't already have a subject in mind, then it may help you to think very quickly about a lot of different experiences you may have had, and see if any of them is suitable for a longer piece.

Now try this

You'll see one question which splits into seven parts. Can you write just one paragraph for each option below?

What is the **worst** thing that has ever happened to you?

hardest

happiest

saddest

most frightening

strangest

most confusing

Now try this

Can you write just one paragraph for each of these eleven options below?

Which event or time in your life has most shaped you?

made you grow up or mature?

most changed your family?

was the biggest challenge for you?

was when you experienced great loss?

was when you experienced great success?

was when you experienced failure?

was when you had to take responsibility?

made you feel most isolated?

showed you the best of people/someone?

showed you the worst of people/someone?

Now try this

Now you are going to think about these eight ways a person could make an impact on your life. Again, can you write just one paragraph for each option below?

Which person has most influenced you?

has most helped you?

has most hurt you?

do you miss most?

have you been in most conflict with?

have you had the most complicated relationship with?

have you had a very changeable relationship with?

are you most glad to be rid of?

Now try this

You should now have perhaps as many as twenty-six short paragraphs in front of you. Read them over. Which one could you write about in depth in your Personal Reflective Essay? Remember, you need an idea that will lead you on into the wider kind of reflection we already saw in 'The Crowd'.

Although you won't be writing your essay for a while, it's a good idea to choose your topic now, so that as you work through the rest of this chapter you are doing it with your subject in mind. If you're still really stumped, go home and look through some photographs to see if that sparks anything off.

Good writing techniques

Thoughts and feelings

Your Personal Reflective Essay will really come to life when you include your thoughts and feelings. No one else knows these. Only you can tell the reader about them.

To show you what I mean, let's look at an example from a book called *Touching the Void*. The writer, Joe Simpson, was climbing in Peru when he broke his leg. In this extract his climbing partner is about to begin lowering the injured Simpson down the mountain on a rope.

> I lay on my chest immediately beneath Simon, and edged down until all my weight was on the rope. Initially I couldn't commit myself to letting my feet hang free of the snow. If it
> 5 crumbled we would be falling instantaneously. Simon nodded at me and grinned. Encouraged by his confidence I lifted my feet and began to slide down. It worked!
> He let the rope out smoothly in a steady
> 10 descent. I lay against the snow holding an axe in each hand ready to dig them in the moment I felt a fall begin. Occasionally the crampons on my right boot snagged in the snow and jarred my leg. I tried not to cry out but failed. I didn't
> 15 want Simon to stop.
> In a surprisingly short time he did stop. I looked up and saw that he had receded far from me, and I could make out only his head and shoulders. He shouted something but I couldn't
> 20 make it out until three sharp tugs explained it. I was astounded at the speed at which I had descended 150 feet. Astounded and pleased as punch. I wanted to giggle. In a short time my mood had swung from despair to wild
> 25 optimism, and death rushed back to being a vague possibility rather than the inevitable fact. The rope went slack as I hopped on to my good leg. I was acutely aware that while Simon was changing the knot over we were at our most
> 30 vulnerable. If I fell, I would drop a whole rope's length before it came tight on to him, and he would be whipped off the mountain by the impact. I dug my axes in and stayed motionless.
>
> From *Touching the Void* by Joe Simpson

Now try this

Simpson is obviously feeling a mixture of emotions, some positive, some negative. Copy and complete the following table to help you explore the emotions in the extract. You should be able to find a wide range of emotions.

Emotion	Evidence	Positive or negative
hesitation	'Initially I couldn't commit myself to letting my feet hang free of the snow.'	negative

Interestingly, people often write extremely well about hard experiences. If we go through sad, difficult or tragic events we are strongly aware of how we feel at the time. Sad events affect and shape us. We have to keep working with and processing the memories, thoughts and feelings that go with these events.

Now try this

Go back to the piece of reflective writing by the student, the one that was printed on pages 17–18. Pick out that writer's thoughts and feelings.

Details and description

Because your memories are important to you, when you bring them to mind they will be full of tiny details, things you noticed at the time. Many of these details might not be very important in themselves, but they are important in your writing because they bring that memory to life.

To let you see what I mean, here's a piece from the start of *Touching the Void*, before Joe Simpson breaks his leg.

> I was lying in my sleeping bag, staring at the light filtering through the red and green fabric of the dome tent. Simon was snoring loudly, occasionally twitching in his dream world. We
> 5 could have been anywhere. There is a peculiar anonymity about being in tents. Once the zip is closed and the outside world barred from sight,

all sense of location disappears. The sounds of rustling, of fabric flapping in the wind, or
10 of rainfall, the feel of hard lumps under the groundsheet, the smell of rancid socks and sweat – these are universals, as comforting as the warmth of a down sleeping bag.

I felt a homely affection for the warm
15 security of the tent and reluctantly wormed out of my bag to face the prospect of lighting the stove. It had snowed a little during the night, and the grass crunched frostily under my feet as I padded over to the cooking rock. There was
20 no sign of Richard stirring as I passed his tiny one-man tent, half collapsed and whitened with hoar-frost.

From *Touching the Void* by Joe Simpson

This short passage is stuffed with tiny details. Simpson manages to use nearly all of his senses to bring the description to life.

Now try this

First **list** your five senses. Then **re-read** the Joe Simpson passage above. Next, **note down** the details that fit each sense. Which sense has the writer not used in this extract?

It's easy to use your sense of sight as you describe what you remember in detail, but Simpson's example is a good reminder to bring in as many of our other senses as is appropriate.

Now try this

Read this third extract from *Touching the Void*. Although Joe's accident hasn't happened yet, he and Simon have already had a difficult time, being caught in a storm just after reaching the summit of the mountain. They've spent the night in a cave Joe dug in the snow. As you read, make a list of the small details that make it seem vivid and convincing. Again, look for his use of different senses.

I had the stove burning away cheerfully by my side, and could look beyond it through a hole in the snow cave. The early morning sun etched the ridge lines with shadows and danced blue
5 shadings down the edges of the mountain face. For the first time in the last four days the tense concentration in my body relaxed. The anxious struggles of the previous night had been forgotten.
10 It was cramped in the snow hole. Simon was still asleep, lying on his side close by me, facing away. His hips and shoulders pressed up against my side, and I could feel his body warmth seeping through my sleeping bag. I moved
15 carefully to avoid waking him and felt myself smiling. I knew it would be a good day.

I dressed and geared up first, before climbing out of the cave. Simon was slow getting ready, and it wasn't until he joined
20 me outside that I remembered his frostbite. My good humour vanished to be replaced by worry when he showed his fingers to me. One fingertip was blackened and three other fingers were white and wooden in appearance.

From *Touching the Void* by Joe Simpson

Did you notice that, as well as the descriptive detail you were looking for, Simpson again uses a mixture of positive and negative emotions in his writing?

Now try this

Go back to the piece called 'The Crowd'. Pick out the details that bring it to life. Look especially for any use of different senses.

Using dialogue

Something else you can do to bring this genre of writing to life is to put speech into it. Just as dialogue makes stories vivid, it does the same for Personal Reflective Writing. Don't worry if you can't remember the exact words you and other people said, you can make up something which seems close enough.

The following extract comes from a book called *Once in a House on Fire*, in which Andrea Ashworth describes a stormy and difficult childhood. She had two angry and abusive stepfathers, and the man she calls 'Dad' in this section is the second of these.

When it came to Parents' Evening I was glad I had said nothing to make my teachers look down on Mum and Dad. Shame simmered in my veins, mingling with fiery pride, when I walked into the hall
5 between them. Dad's neck was locked in a tie. My mother had applied a home perm; the curls were still coiled tight. My mother looked pretty but petrified.

'You both look fantastic,' I insisted. But there was no way they were going to step across the hall
10 to meet Tamsyn's mother and father or any of the teachers. It was as if I were the parent and they were naughty children, hiding from the grown-ups.

'We weren't going to light up,' Dad whispered when I caught him and my mother rolling
15 cigarettes behind a pillar in the hall: 'It's for when we get out of here.'

Miss Craig strode up and thrust out her hand to shake Dad's.

'Ahowd'yerdo?' He nearly choked over the
20 aitch. The roll-up machine disappeared.

Miss Craig held my mother's hand for longer, looking her in the eye. 'I hope you realize what talent you've got on your hands.' She made it sound the opposite of a compliment. 'Andrea's a
25 very gifted girl.'

Miss Craig urged them to send me to a good sixth-form college, to see that I read the papers – the broadsheets, she explained in a condescending voice, such as the *Guardian*, *The*
30 *Independent*, *The Times*, not the tabloids, like *The Sun* and the *Mirror*. Not even the *Daily Express*, she made clear, when my mother wondered. Above all, they must ensure that I did my homework in quiet and peaceful surroundings.

35 'Your daughter is university material,' she said, before moving off to shake more hands. 'It would be criminal to let her abilities go to waste.'

'Snooty bitch!' Dad ground the gear stick into reverse, screeching out of the school car
40 park. 'What've you been telling her, eh?'

'Nothing, Dad,' I swore.

'Miss Craig's always a bit high and mighty,' I tried to reassure my mother, who was still smarting from the snide tone and innuendoes.
45 'Everyone says so.'

I sat between my parents in the cab of our truck, my heart jiggling along, secretly memorizing everything Miss Craig had said. I had a chance – we jolted over bumps in the road
50 – I had a chance. To get somewhere.

From *Once in a House on Fire*
by Andrea Ashworth

Notice that Ashworth doesn't use all the dialogue that she could use. The paragraph that begins, 'Miss Craig urged them,' reports a section of conversation that would have been much longer if the writer had conveyed it in dialogue. By choosing only certain parts to tell with speech, the writer focuses on the most important aspects of her memory: her parents' reaction to being in her school, and her realisation that her intelligence might be a passport to a new kind of life.

Now try this

Just to show why the version with dialogue is better, try to rewrite this piece so that we get all the same information, but without any of the characters speaking.

Now try this

Think about the piece that you are planning to write. Where could you use speech to bring it to life?

Using storytelling techniques

Earlier in this chapter, when you were preparing to write your piece of prose fiction, we looked at the technique of showing, not telling. This is just one of many storytelling techniques (and the dialogue that you just worked on above is another) that will help make your Personal Reflective Writing better.

Now try this

First, go round the class and give everybody a letter A or B. All the letter A students should go back again and re-read the piece of writing called 'The Crowd', which was printed on pages 17–18. All the letter B students should go back again and re-read the three extracts by Joe Simpson and the one by Andrea Ashworth.

As you re-read your piece(s), look for and note down evidence of the writer using any of these techniques:

> dialogue   showing not telling   imagery
> starting at a moment of action   flashback
> short sentence or paragraph for impact
> minor sentence   repetition
> jump cut to a different scene or action
> use of incident or anecdote

Also, think of one technique you think your writer could have used but did not. When could he or she have used that technique? How would this have improved the piece of writing?

Now find someone with the other letter, who has read the other piece(s) – not someone who sits near you in class. Share what you found with each other.

Being personally reflective

It's significant that this task is called Personal **Reflective** Writing. To be able to pass, you need to write **reflectively**. This is something that only mature and insightful writers are able to do. At Higher level you need to be able to reflect in a personal sense, but also more widely.

Reflecting in a personal sense really means two things.

Firstly it means **examining yourself**. If you stand in front of a mirror you can examine yourself pretty thoroughly by looking at your reflection. Every spot and blemish will be visible, but you'll also be able to see all your good features and everything that you like about yourself.

If you apply this idea to your writing it means that you might question and criticise yourself. On the other hand, you might realise that you handled the situation well. You may realise that certain experiences have shaped you and made you into the person you are, just as growing up changes the way your face looks in the mirror.

The second meaning of reflection is **looking back**. Think of the rear-view mirror in a car. The driver can keep his or her eyes on the road ahead, while using the mirror to see what is happening behind.

Often events in our lives make much more sense once they are over and we are older and wiser.

Perhaps when something happened to you it was a really terrible experience, but now you realise that you benefited from it in some way. Events may be confusing when they happen, but when you look back on them they may make more sense.

As well as reflecting on yourself you can reflect on others. You may also be aware of how events and experiences have affected other people as well as you. It may be that you disagreed with someone at the time, but you now realise they did the right thing. On the other hand, when we are young we sometimes accept the things adults do without question, but as we grow up we are not so sure about their motives.

Below is a list of reflective phrases. Any of these phrases can be used to begin a reflective sentence or a reflective paragraph.

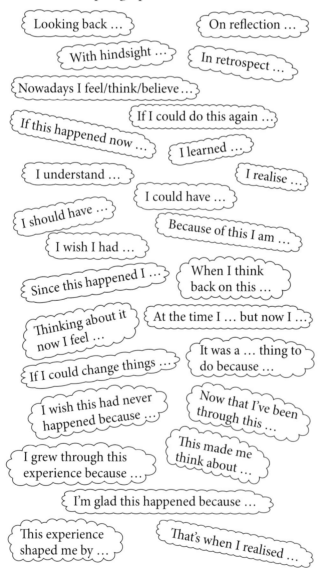

Although it says that these phrases will help you to start reflective sentences and paragraphs, your writing will actually be more subtle, and therefore better, if you don't use them at the very start, so that you're not being too blatant.

> Despite the loss of her friendship, I grew through this experience because …

is better than

> I grew through this experience because, although I lost a friend I …

and

> I was unable to admit to anyone that I was in the wrong, but on reflection …

is better than

> On reflection, I realise I was in the wrong …

Now try this

Go back to the subject that you thought of earlier, the topic you have chosen to write about. Spend some time making notes on how you could use this experience for personal reflection. What lessons have your experiences taught you about yourself and those around you? How have these experiences shaped and changed you?

Being more widely reflective

When tackling this kind of task at Higher level, you need to take your reflection wider still. You need to show that your experiences have taught you something about life, about society, or about people in general.

Look at this extract from the piece you saw earlier. The writer, having watched a gang of youths stone a window, begins considering how we are affected by being part of a crowd:

> All your principles and convictions suddenly shrink to insignificance and you lose a sense of who you are. Our whole personality evaporates into nothing.

Most of the writer's wide reflection comes near the end of the piece, after the anecdote of the protest at Dungavel.

> Crowds are dangerous. They change people. They consume unique individuals into a homogeneous mass. Although I knew that the youths' behaviour was not justified because
> 5 they were part of a crowd, I understood that they had been unable to escape the clutches of the power of the crowd. I understood why I had been such a coward, why I had chosen to deny what I had seen and run away. I had
> 10 been scared because, next to the crowd, I was nothing. To challenge the crowd is potentially lethal.
> We often see crowds behaving badly in protests, at football matches, even in our
> 15 everyday lives on the streets and we reassure ourselves that, no matter what, we will never behave as badly as the crowd. We will never become so involved that we will lose complete control over our own selves. Can we really be
> 20 so sure?

The writer considers how crowds, and crowd behaviour, can affect us all, and ends the piece by challenging us to think, and to relate this reflection to our own values and our own actions.

Now try this

In your own words, sum up this writer's wider reflection. What did the writer learn?

Here's another extract from Joe Simpson's *Touching the Void*. Again this comes from the early part of the book. Joe and his climbing partner Simon have just reached the summit of a mountain in the Peruvian Andes called Siula Grande.

Now try this

As you read, look for and note down:
- any times when Simpson is being personally reflective and examining himself
- any times when Simpson reflects in a way that lets him take a wider look at human nature.

> We took the customary summit photos and ate some chocolate. I felt the usual anticlimax. What now? It was a vicious cycle. If you succeed with one dream, you come back to
> 5 square one and it's not long before you're conjuring up another, slightly harder, a bit more ambitious. I didn't like the thought of where it might be leading me. As if, in some strange way, the very nature of the game
> 10 was controlling me, taking me towards a logical but frightening conclusion. It always unsettled me, this moment of reaching the summit, this sudden stillness and quiet, which gave me time to wonder at what I was
> 15 doing and sense a niggling doubt that perhaps I was inexorably losing control – was I here purely for pleasure or was it egotism? Did I really want to come back for more? But these moments were also good times, and I knew
> 20 that the feelings would pass. Then I could excuse them as morbid pessimistic fears that had no sound basis.

From *Touching the Void*
by Joe Simpson

Now try this

Go back to the subject that you thought of earlier, the topic you have chosen to write about. Spend some time making notes on how you could use this experience for wider reflection. What lessons have your experiences taught you about life, about society, or about people in general?

Looking at a real example

You are going to see another piece of Personal Reflective Writing produced by a student.

Now try this

First of all just read through the piece of writing. You may wish to do this aloud around the class, or you might want to read it on your own.

At first glance our family – mum, dad, daughter and son – appears as normal as any other but it is, in fact, quite different. My brother is adopted.

5 It took a number of attempts before we were able to finalise this arrangement. Before my brother, Euan, there were two other foster brothers, Richard and Ian, who were unable to remain a part

10 of our family life.

Richard came to us when he was six years old. Sadly, like many adoption cases, Richard had been mistreated. My first impression was of a distant child.

15 Although he wasn't really part of our family, he wasn't not a part of it. He seemed more like the family pet than a brother but I accepted it all the same.

He adjusted surprisingly well

20 considering: perhaps this was a result of his young age. Although Richard remained with us for four years I don't remember much about our relationship, but he was particularly

25 close to my father who had always wanted a son. I can recall the silence in our house when his mother took him back, a silence broken by my father saying he'd always be welcome

30 in our home.

Richard had, for some strange reason, believed it was his fault his mother had left him and so jumped at the chance to return to her. Six months

35 later he was again rejected, thrown out of the house, his belongings sold and his bank account emptied – his mother kept all the proceeds. The offer of help that my father had given

40 Richard could not be taken up – we had another 'brother' by then and Richard soon became little more than a memory.

As I look back on these events, I

45 realise the influence and the pain that his mother had inflicted upon him. Because of these, Richard could never have allowed himself to become part of our family.

50 The other 'brother' was a boy called Ian who was nine when he came to us. Ian made the biggest impression on me in the three years he lived with us – I was older then and was able to

55 remember more. Like Richard, Ian had been in care. Unlike Richard, this had been since he was two. It took some time to realise the full extent to which this 'care' had

60 affected his life.

Suddenly I had the protection of an older brother. Wherever he went I followed, with the intensity of a besotted fan. For me, Ian was more

65 than just a foster brother. We grew close as we shared our childhood and it was this that hurt so much when Ian left.

My mother said she could no longer

70 cope with him because he was 'just an empty shell,' and showed no emotion. According to her, Ian hid a cold-hearted nature behind a mask of childhood innocence. I don't

75 remember seeing this side of him at all. I look back on the day that he was taken away and I recall the tears that he cried. I think perhaps that Ian never truly realised how

80 much he had until he was taken away. I imagine the pain my mother must have felt as she watched him go and realised that it was her who had decided his fate. If I sound

85 bitter I don't mean to because I'm not, but I just think it was wrong to have given up so easily: perhaps it is because of this that there are so many foster children still in care

90 while childless couples pursue some idea of a 'perfect' family.

When Ian left, our family drew into itself for a time, but my father still had his dream of having a boy

95 and so, once again, we contacted the social services. This time we got a toddler, eighteen months old, called Euan. His young age was perhaps a

100 blessing as it enabled him to adjust well. He doesn't remember anything now about his previous life, and so he isn't curious about his real parents, or about the reasons for his separation from them.

105 At first, because of the large age gap between us, it seemed like Euan was more my own child than a brother and I took an active part in teaching him to read and write and 110 telling him what I knew about life. I remember certain events during his early childhood that a mother usually remembers, such as his first day at school and his first tooth falling 115 out. I think that my position in the family as only child after Ian left gave me more responsibility, and it was this that contributed to the feeling of protectiveness when Euan 120 came along.

I think that he has had a lot of pressure placed on him by my parents to be better than Ian and Richard and I believe that their 125 expectations are too great for such a young child. The problems that Ian and Richard faced have nothing to do with Euan's life and it is in this sense that I believe the past should be 130 forgotten and we should all look to the future.

As Euan has settled in to the family, I have begun to think about the role of the social services and the 135 awe-inspiring power that they hold. They literally decide on the fate of the child in care. The social services have the power to make or break a family according to their whims 140 while the child plays piggy in the middle. This often ends with the foster family, hurt and having been rejected once too often, giving up hope and watching as the social 145 worker drives off down the road with their dream in the back seat.

Rejecting Ian was a cruel thing to do, especially to a child who had been in care all his life, and after 150 reflecting I believe that it would have been handled differently had my parents been his real parents. I think that parents who have difficulties with foster children tend to give up 155 more easily than they would if it had actually been their own child and it is because of this that there are so many children languishing in care today.

160 It seems, now, that our family has come to the end of its emotional drama and the search for a little boy is over. It is through this search that I have become strangely older and 165 wiser and I am able to stand back from my life, and look at how it has affected me and my family. I wonder, if my parents had realised what they would have to go through 170 to fulfil their dream, would they still have pursued it?

However, through all of this one thing remains true – a family is not the people with whom you are born 175 but the relationships you form with them and how you, yourself, make it work. At times I feel nostalgic and wonder what happened to my other 'brothers'. Maybe one day I'll know.

Now try this

Now that you have read this Personal Reflective Essay once, you are going to analyse it in more detail. The easiest way to do this is to have a photocopy of it in front of you. You'll also need pens and pencils. If you have a variety of colours, that's even better. You may wish to work with a partner.

You'll need to use the following symbols:

1 Every time you find the writer sharing **thoughts** draw a **think cloud** beside this in the margin.

2 Every time you find the writer sharing **feelings** draw a **heart** beside this in the margin.

3 Every time you find the writer using **detail or description** draw an **eye** beside this in the margin.

4 Every time you find the writer using **dialogue** draw a **speech bubble** beside this in the margin.

5 Every time you find the writer using **a storytelling technique** draw an **open book** beside this in the margin. Write the name of the technique on the pages of the book.

6 Every time you find the writer **being reflective** draw a mirror in the margin. If you think the writer is **reflecting more widely**, put a capital **W** on the centre of the mirror.

7 Write a couple of sentences to explain what made it a **good** piece of writing.

8 Suggest two things the writer could have done that would have made the work **even better**.

By the way, if you'd like to look at one more example of a Personal Reflective Essay before you plan and write your own, there is another example in Chapter 7 of this book, the essay 'Shooting

an Elephant' by George Orwell. He uses all the skills of Personal Reflective Writing. He brings an incident to life in detail; tells us about his own thoughts and feelings at the time; reflects on his own behaviour and that of others around him; and reflects more widely on the nature of empires. All of this makes his piece an excellent example of the Personal Reflective Essay.

Planning your Personal Reflective piece

You've had a chance now to look at two long pieces of Personal Reflective Writing produced by Higher students, and at a number of shorter extracts from published books. Reading and examining all these pieces has shown you that you need to use all these genre features:

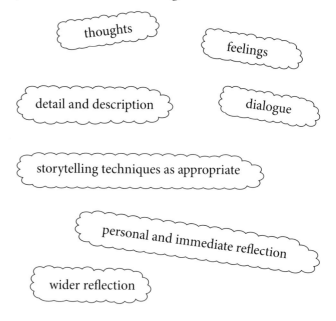

Now try this

You'll need a photocopy of the blank plan on the following page. You should have lots of ideas by now, so ask your teacher if you can a have a copy in A3 size.

Use the prompts and shapes to help you plan your piece of Personal Reflective Writing. The shapes are those you used to annotate the piece about fostering and adoption, but they are bigger this time so that you can write your ideas on them.

What event or experiences are you going to write about?

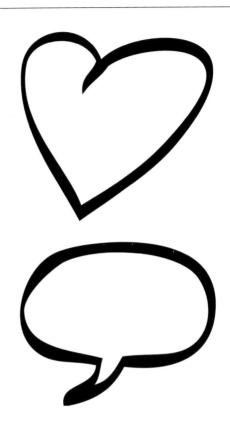

Which storytelling techniques will you use, and at which points in your writing?

PERSONAL REFLECTION

WIDER REFLECTION

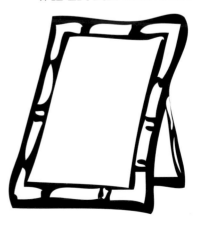

Using your plan to help you, explain your ideas to another student. Your teacher may also want to see and discuss your plan. Remember that he or she also has to keep a copy of that plan in case the SQA asks to see it at any point.

It's now time to follow your plan and write your piece.

When you've written it, read your work over before you hand it in to your teacher. Think about the four areas you will be assessed on, which were explained at the start of this chapter, and ask yourself if you've met all the criteria.

Your teacher will read your work and add comments so that you can discuss the piece and improve it.

What we've done so far

So far in this chapter we have found out about the rules and guidelines for Higher Writing. We found out about the genre that the SQA calls **Creative Writing**. This covers four sorts of piece:

- a Personal Reflective Essay
- a piece of prose: story or novel extract
- a poem or set of linked poems
- a drama script

and we learned in detail about the first two.

Now it's time to go on to the other major genre, which the SQA calls **Discursive Writing**. Remember that in your Folio, you need one piece from the Creative genre, and one from the Discursive.

Discursive Writing

The second Folio piece should be what the SQA calls **Discursive**, which actually means that you can produce any one of these types of writing to fulfil the requirements for this genre:

- a persuasive essay
- an argumentative essay
- a report.

We're going to work on the first two of these in detail.

In **argumentative** writing you explore an issue or question. Both sides of the subject are explored, and you will usually come to a conclusion at the end, while still allowing the reader to decide for himself or herself.

In **persuasive** writing you start with a clear belief or strongly held point of view. In this kind of piece, you will try to use evidence and language to make the reader agree with you.

You can't really decide whether your piece will be argumentative or persuasive until you've chosen a subject, so let's deal with that issue first.

Subjects to avoid

Some topics come up again and again. Your teacher, and the SQA marker, have probably read all the arguments about **euthanasia**, **abortion** and **capital punishment** many times before, and will quickly notice if you miss out anything they expect to find, or if there is any important aspect of the argument which you don't explore carefully enough.

Unless you are truly an expert, or really feel that you have something striking and original to say, steer clear of writing about these subjects. And, if you really want to tackle one of these issues, it's best to do it in a two-sided, argumentative way. Otherwise you'll sound like an extremist.

Choosing a topic

Whether your writing ends up being argumentative or persuasive, you need to pick a topic about which people have strong opinions. It should also be a topic in which you have a genuine interest: the SQA mark scheme for this task says your writing should be 'characterised by a clear sense of engagement with the ideas/issues' and that you should show a 'strong understanding' of these ideas and issues. The SQA also says that the line of thought in your writing should be 'clear and sustained'. You'll only manage all of this if you pick a topic you care about.

So how do you choose a subject? You could:

- ask yourself which subjects you are interested in or care about: these will often be tied in to the things you choose to spend your time on

- visit your school library: some publishers produce special series of books where each book contains articles on one controversial subject. Without even reading the books themselves at this stage, just finding out which subjects they deal with might help you think of a topic.

- watch TV news programmes, read newspapers and use news websites

- ask your teacher which topics his or her students have written about successfully in the past.

Now try this

You shouldn't go any further, or spend any time on research, until you know that your teacher thinks your topic is a good one. Once you have chosen a topic, write it down and give a note of it to your teacher.

If you know already which approach you want to take – two-sided argumentative or one-sided persuasive – write this down along with your subject. If you're not sure which approach to take yet, don't worry. It will become much clearer after you've done your detailed research.

Researching

Whether your piece of writing is one-sided or two-sided, and no matter how much you think you already know about the subject, you need to do some research. Everything you eventually write will be based on this and it's time well spent.

Your first port of call will probably be the internet. You could visit the websites of charities and pressure groups who have an interest in your topic. If, for example, you are writing about development issues you could visit the sites of organisations like Oxfam or Christian Aid.

Many newspapers have excellent websites. These can be very useful if your topic has been in the headlines recently, and often give real-life examples

you can use. One very good site is **www.guardian. co.uk**, which makes no charge and is easy to search.

You need to take far greater care with the online encyclopaedia **www.wikipedia.org**, because it is written by the people who use it. This means that though the contributors are genuinely interested in their subjects, some of what they write can be quite biased. You shouldn't use Wikipedia as your only source, and you should check anything you find there against other sources to make sure it is accurate.

If you don't know which sites you want to use, you'll need to begin by using a search engine such as Google. Try to use only one or two keywords for your search. The search engine doesn't know what you are thinking, or why you are looking these words up, so be as precise as you can about what you want.

If you're using a phrase, put double quotation marks round it. Let's suppose you are writing an argumentative essay on whether NASA faked the 1969 moon landing. Looking for **"moon landing"** will find web pages using that complete phrase. This might be just what you want to know:

> One suspicious detail in the supposed photographs of the **moon landing** is that the US flag appears to be flying straight and proud when, as the moon has neither atmosphere nor a breeze, it should be dangling limply from its pole.

If you type the same two words without quotation marks you will get all the pages that have the word *moon* and the word *landing* anywhere on the same page. This isn't so helpful:

> As the plane was **landing** I saw a beautiful full **moon** shining over the city.

This is a good time to go back to your school library or local library and ask the staff for advice about the most suitable sources of information on your topic. One thing you will find there is an encyclopaedia. These can be very good on established factual information, but as huge books like this take many years to write and put together, they are not great sources for material on current controversial topics. For that, you may be better going back to the internet.

Depending on your topic, you might also speak to people about their own experiences. If you are writing about the rights and wrongs of organic food and you know a farmer, speak to him. If you are arguing that young people nowadays are put under far too much pressure to achieve at school, ask a teacher what she thinks.

By the way, and just in case you think you don't, or in case you think your topic doesn't call for it, everyone needs to do research. Even the most personal persuasive essay will only persuade, will only convince the reader, if what you write is supported by facts, statistics, experiences and anecdotes.

Using your own words

There was one very important note of advice in the guidelines at the start of the chapter: you **absolutely must not, ever**, copy and paste from a website or from anywhere else.

You are allowed to get ideas and information from sources, but you can't use someone else's words and pass them off as your own. This is called **plagiarism** and if the examiners think that you have cheated in this way the consequences can be very serious. You could fail English. You could also have all your other exam papers and course work pulled out and re-marked as they look for further rule-breaking.

To help you avoid accidentally falling into plagiarism, here's a useful piece of advice to follow during the research stage:

 **Warning**

It's OK to read, underline or highlight someone else's words, but **whenever you make a note,**

do that in your own words. It doesn't matter if you type the words, or hand write them, **whenever you put words on a page, they should be your own**.

I hope all these warnings get the point across. The advice is only useful, of course, if you know how to put something into your own words. This skill is called **paraphrasing**. It's worth practising because it won't just be useful to you in your Discursive Writing. You also need to be able to do this as you answer all the **U** for Understanding questions in the Close Reading NAB and exam, where lifting words straight from the text will mean you get no marks, even if you have found the right information.

There's a third reason for making sure that you can paraphrase all the ideas and information you find. You're not just avoiding plagiarism, and you're not just practising a skill you'll use elsewhere too. You're also making sure you understand what you have read. The best way to prove that you really grasp something is to be able to explain it yourself in a different way.

Look at this sentence found by a student who decided to research global climate change:

> The overwhelming consensus among climate change scientists is that human activities are responsible for much of the climate change we're seeing.
> (www.nerc.ac.uk)

The student needed to put this in his own words, which he did like this:

> Those who research this subject believe our own actions are the main cause of the climate change we are experiencing. They are in almost complete agreement about this.

This student used a lot of different tactics as he paraphrased.

First, he changed some important words or expressions.

Now try this

You will see a list of expressions from the original sentence. What did he change each one into?

- overwhelming consensus
- climate change scientists
- human activities
- responsible for
- much of the
- we're seeing.

Secondly, he changed the number of sentences from one to two. Thirdly, he put the two ideas in the original sentence the other way round. All of this shows that he has understood and can process the information.

What he didn't change was the phrase 'climate change' itself. Because that is his subject, and that is what his whole essay is about, he can keep using those words.

Now try this

Here are five more extracts students found while researching different topics. Remembering the techniques above, paraphrase each extract. The subject of each extract is given for you at the start.

1 [The death penalty] Those who believe that deterrence justifies the execution of certain offenders bear the burden of proving that the death penalty is in fact a deterrent.

2 [Raising the legal age for buying alcohol] In the US, the age to drink legally is twenty-one. However, it is naive to assume that there is no drinking problem. University students attend house parties where binge drinking is the norm. They lack the protection that would come from being in a bar or nightclub. In addition, attending such parties usually requires transport, which is a key reason why so many American students drink and drive.

3 [Having a curfew for teenagers] It is impossible to solve anti-social behaviour by using repression. If the British government enforces this law, rebellious teenagers will

merely become convinced that society is actually against them.

4 [The pros and cons of same-sex schooling] Thirty years ago, the popular belief about same-sex education was that it upheld outdated stereotypes about gender, such as women should study nursing and men should study engineering. Experts at that time believed that coeducation dispelled those gender myths.

5 [Whether footballers are overpaid] Football has become an industry, and its employees – the players – have taken their places alongside the world's elite of movie and rock stars. Across the planet, football has slowly grown to become the world's biggest and most widely followed sport. It is only natural, therefore, that some of the huge profit that the football league makes each year finds its way into the hands of its key assets: the players.

Citing your sources

Another of the authenticity guidelines we saw at the start of the chapter was about being able to show where your information came from. As you research, take a note of all these things. You will need to list them in a **bibliography** at the end of your essay:

- the writer and publication date of newspaper or magazine articles
- the website name and specific page address for any information found on the internet
- the title and publication date of any books referred to.

Now try this

If you haven't already told your teacher whether your essay will be two-sided argumentative or one-sided persuasive, now is the time to do so. Read over your notes, and consider which approach you are going to take. These prompts should help you decide:

- If you find your topic interesting, but you're genuinely not sure what your stance on it is, or if you think it's a highly complex issue without an easy answer, you should go for the two-sided argumentative approach.
- If you've developed a genuine opinion on the subject, and if you think you can put it across in a way that makes you sound engaged and committed without seeming to be a raving zealot, go for the persuasive approach.
- If the best writing style for you is to be measured and formal, then you should probably go for argumentative writing.
- If you know that you can write in a lively and witty way, you could try persuasive writing.
- Finally, more weighty subjects suit the argumentative genre better, while odder, less serious or more quirky subjects can benefit from a persuasive approach.

Using your research to support opinions

Once you have collected your information, you should try to find a way to make each fact or idea you have found support an opinion. Facts can be proved. They are true and nobody can argue against them.

> Pizza is made by placing cheese, tomato sauce, and perhaps other toppings on a bread base.

Opinions are more personal. They are what people think, and different people can have different opinions about the same thing.

> Never mind the calendar, central heating and public sanitation, the best thing Italy ever gave the world was pizza.

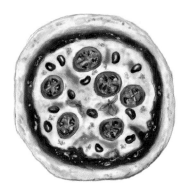

In **persuasive** writing, organise the facts to support what you believe. In **argumentative** writing, organise them to support the two different sides of the argument.

Here's an example from a student who is writing persuasively about his belief that footballers are overpaid.

> **Fact/example from research**
> The typical Premiership footballer earns £60,000 a week. The salary for a newly qualified nurse is less than £20,000 a year.
>
> **How does this support my opinion?**
> The fact that some footballers can earn over 150 times as much as nurses, who do a valuable and difficult job that requires years of training, shows they are overpaid.

Now try this

Look through the notes you gathered during your research. Remember, these should be in your own words by now. Organise your material as shown above, picking out the useful facts and working out how each one could be used to support an opinion.

A good writer will be able to 'spin' facts to support their opinion. Two newspapers could have two very different opening sentences at the start of their front-page stories:

A tram scheme that will turn the city centre into a building site and cause years of traffic chaos was revealed today.	A tram scheme that will provide rapid, low-carbon public transport and cut journey times across the city was revealed today.

They're both reporting the same story, but they have spun the facts to suit their opinion.

Being able to bend facts towards the direction you want to go is especially useful in persuasive writing, when you are trying to make your readers agree with you.

Planning two-sided, argumentative pieces

In these essays you should show that you understand the arguments on both sides. At the end you can give your opinion, and your readers can decide on theirs.

There are two ways you can structure these essays. We'll look very quickly at the simple structure first. It would be better, though, if you used the complex structure, and we'll go into that in more detail. The **simple structure** works like this:

Step 1 A one-paragraph introduction to the topic:

> Although Britain abolished the death penalty in the 1960s, there are frequent pleas for its reintroduction, usually after the details of some grisly multiple murder are splashed across the tabloids.

Step 2 A link sentence, explaining which side of the argument you will begin with.

> Those who advocate the return of capital punishment have many firmly held beliefs.

Step 3 Now take all of the points on one side of the argument. Each point should be in a separate paragraph, and these points should be backed up with facts, observations or personal experiences. Use **topic sentences** and the **PEE structure**. (You will find out more about these soon: see pages 37–38.) Start with the strongest, most convincing arguments and work your way down to the weaker ones. You should aim to have at least three or four paragraphs on the first side of the argument.

Step 4 Write a link sentence showing that you are about to switch to the other side of the argument.

> Those on the other side of the argument are just as passionate in their belief that there would be no benefit in executing even our most notorious criminals.

Step 5 Now do the same on this side of the argument as you did at Step 3, working again from the stronger points down to weaker ones.

Step 6 Finally, in your conclusion, briefly sum up what you have written. Now say which side you agree with and why. Show which arguments convinced you, or refer to an experience in your life or the life of someone you know which has convinced you that a particular side is right. You may wish to leave the reader with something to think about.

> It is clear that both sides have strong arguments. Having examined them, I feel that on the whole we will not create a better Britain by killing our criminals. Any system that says it is wrong to kill people, but then tries to prove that by killing, is misguided.

By the way, we've used the example of an essay on the death penalty deliberately because you shouldn't be writing about it. It was on our short list of overworked topics earlier in the chapter.

The **more complex structure** for two-sided pieces makes you look more skilled at handling your material. It works like this:

The introduction and conclusion are the same as they are in a simply structured essay. However, in the main body of the essay, you begin with the strongest argument from one side of the argument. Then, in the next paragraph, you work through a point on the opposite side that contradicts what you have just written about. Each of these paragraphs will use **topic sentences** and the **PEE structure**, which will be explained later in this chapter.

To illustrate this, let's imagine an essay on another of those overworked and therefore banned topics, euthanasia. Here's a point from the pro-euthanasia side of the argument:

Perhaps the strongest argument for allowing terminally ill patients to choose to die is that this will prevent great suffering. Not only can people in the final stages of a long illness experience terrible pain, they may also suffer the indignity of being unable to take care of their own most basic needs. The right to die could spare them all of this.

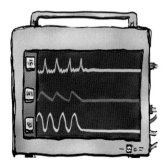

Now here's the answering point from the anti-euthanasia side.

However, this assumes that dying patients are somehow not being properly cared for. This is not true. Modern advances in pain control mean that even the last days of life can be made comfortable, allowing patients to spend longer with their loved ones. Many say that we should not demand the right to choose when we die, but the right to die with dignity.

Then take the second strongest point from the first side of the argument. Explain it, and then challenge it by making another point from the opposite side to contradict it. Keep going, following this pattern.

You may find that some of your points cannot be paired up in this way. You can deal with them just before you start your conclusion. All the remaining points can be rolled into two short paragraphs, one for the ideas which support one side of the argument, for example:

There are other valid reasons why many people think that we should allow the ill to choose when to end their lives …

and the other for the evidence that concludes the other side of the argument, for example:

Those who are against this also have further important points to make …

Now try this

If you know that you are going to write an argumentative essay, decide now which of the two structures would be best for you to use.

Structuring persuasive writing

Organising this kind of piece is very similar, but simpler. In persuasive writing you don't have to switch from one part of the argument to the other, because you are always trying to defend your own point of view.

Step 1 A one-paragraph introduction to the topic. Make clear straight away what you believe about the subject. Use your wit and passion to grab the reader's attention from the start.

Our supermarkets, corner shops, even our petrol stations are filling with brightly coloured celebrity magazines. We seem to have become so used to them that we never question their place in our lives. However, I firmly believe Britain would be a better place if we gathered up every copy of *Heat, Hello, OK, Grazia* and all their shiny little clones and dumped them in a recycling facility. Somewhere offshore. The mid-Atlantic should do it.

Step 2 Using the points you've planned, set out your argument. Each point should be in a separate paragraph, and these points should be backed up with facts, observations or personal experiences. Use **topic sentences** and the **PEE structure** whenever you can. (You will find out

more about these soon.) Start with the strongest, most convincing arguments and work your way down to the weaker ones.

> What's most striking about these magazines is their overwhelming similarity. The same faces crop up week after week, and a trawl of any given week's offerings will throw up (and that vomit reference is deliberate) perhaps five or six versions of the same story about the same botoxed fembot having boozy second thoughts during her tacky, Sahara-themed hen night. With so few characters to go round, and so little of interest to say about them, do we really need more than a dozen weekly magazines all trying and failing to say it?

Although you are always defending your own position in this kind of writing, your argument will be stronger if you can show that you understand the other side's position and can disprove it.

> Some readers will defend these tatty comics, and the creatures they tirelessly report on, by saying that they bring celebrities down to Earth. What *Heat, Grazia, More, OK* and the others do for us is show that celebrities are nothing different. They are just like little old us. But they aren't. In real life divorce is a heartbreak not easily cured by taking a dozen friends on a get-over-him holiday in the Maldives. When real people lose or gain half a stone in weight they buy a new pair of jeans. They do not get papped in their bikini and splashed across the front page. Real women do not marry three times before their thirtieth birthday and get a different paper to pay for every tasteless set of nuptials.

Step 3 You may find that some of your points are not strong enough to be dealt with in their own separate paragraph. If you still feel they are valuable and want to use them, then you can deal with them just before you start your conclusion. All the remaining points can be rolled into one short paragraph:

> As if all of this is not enough, we also have to remember …

Step 4 Finally, in your conclusion, briefly sum up what you have written. End with a strong, clear statement that shows again why you believe you are right. You may also want to challenge the reader to think or respond.

> Sweeping the celebrity magazines from the shelves would make the world a better place. We'd fill our minds with higher thoughts, we'd have a much clearer view of what normal adult behaviour looks like, and we might even read more books. Do you really need to know how much a TV presenter weighs?

Structuring your paragraphs

As well as structuring and ordering your whole essay, you need to have a clear structure in each paragraph. The best way to do this is to use **topic sentences**, and **the PEE pattern**. You will also learn to use these when writing Critical Essays about the literature you've read, but they apply just as much here.

Topic sentences

A topic sentence is called this for two reasons.

1 It refers to the topic of the essay.

2 It introduces the topic of its paragraph.

The topic sentence is usually the first in the paragraph. Look at the following paragraph from our writer on the death penalty. The topic sentence has been underlined. The words that tie that sentence into the topic of the whole essay are in bold.

> Some wish to see the **death penalty reintroduced as a punishment for murder because they see it as a way of making the punishment fit the crime.** If someone is guilty of taking a life, they argue, that person should then forfeit his own life. Any other punishment is too merciful, too lenient in the harsh light of what the criminal has done. This argument is strongly advocated by some Christian commentators, as they believe it fits the biblical principle of 'an eye for an eye'.

Using PEE

If you are writing an argumentative essay, then within each paragraph of your essay, apart from the introduction and conclusion, you should try to use the **PEE** structure. You may not be able to use this structure quite so often in persuasive writing, but should still do so whenever you can. It goes like this:

P – Make a **POINT** that is relevant to the topic of your essay. This point is the topic sentence at the start of the paragraph.

> One reason why celebrity magazines should be terminated is because this would actually make the lives of celebrities better and happier.

E – Give **EVIDENCE** to back up the point you are making. This should be a fact you found out during your research, something you have noticed, or something you have experienced yourself.

> A flick through just three of these, all published in the last week, revealed a total of thirty-two photographs which had obviously been taken by paparazzi photographers without the subject's permission, and at times clearly without even their knowledge.

E – **EXPLAIN** this. If you are writing to persuade, show how it adds to your argument. If you are doing a piece of argumentative writing, show how the point and evidence contribute to this side of the topic.

> It can do no good for anyone's mental health to know that they are being constantly stalked, and that even to put the bin out or nip to the shops for a pint of milk is regarded as an invitation to invade their privacy.

Direction markers

Certain words and phrases signal the direction of the argument in a piece of discursive writing, or emphasise the writer's point of view in persuasive writing. Most of these words and phrases appear at the start of a paragraph or sentence.

Now try this

You may wish to work with a partner or small group. Look at these four headings:

- These expressions move the argument forwards.
- These expressions let the argument change direction.
- These expressions allow the writer to sum up.
- These expressions show the writer is sure he is right.

Now look at the expressions below. Each one fits best under one of those headings. Get a piece of A4 paper and divide it into four large boxes. Put each heading at the top of a different box. Underneath the heading, list the expressions that fit there. Check any new words with a dictionary as you go.

nonetheless   at the same time   second(ly)
on the contrary   without question
rather   in addition   although
obviously   likewise   and   furthermore
in contrast   conversely   alternatively
instead
without a doubt   on the other hand   as a result
whereas   significantly   in retrospect
undeniably   surely
unquestionably   without question   indubitably
therefore   consequently
definitely   in conclusion   third(ly)
thus   however   first(ly)   because
otherwise   next
moreover   despite   accordingly
but   equally
yet   similarly   to sum up   on the whole
also   in brief
nevertheless   to balance this
absolutely   in spite of   finally
what is more   certainly   in other words

Now try this

Still working with your partner, see how many words or phrases you can think of to add to each list.

Some other useful words

If you want to refer to another argument so you can knock it down, two useful words are *claim* and *allege*. They hint that you do not believe something the other side says.

> The footballer **claims** to be a dedicated family man and a devoted father to his two young sons.

> Her enemies **allege** that she reached her current position after unusually fast promotion through the company, a firm in which she has a very close relationship with the chairman, Sir Antony Blackadder. She, however, **claims** that Blackadder merely recognised her potential and mentored her to help her fulfil it.

What is the writer suggesting about the footballer and the businesswoman mentioned above?

Some words are useful if you can't prove something for sure. These words are also useful for suggestions and rumours. These words include *reported*, *rumoured*, *believed*, *could*, *likely*, *would* and *may point to*. For example, here's a piece of gossip that may have very few provable facts behind it:

> It is **believed** that troubled TV presenter Sonia Summers **could** again be struggling with the addiction problems originally **reported** earlier this year. It is **rumoured** that her use of alcohol and painkillers **could** have risen once again to the worrying heights that allegedly led her to seek treatment in January. It is **likely** that ITV bosses, who pay her £1million a year to present *A Healthy Mind in a Healthy Body* **would** be very unhappy if she were facing such issues. The TV star's close friends are **reported** to be very concerned. Summers's non-appearance at last week's celebrity half-marathon **may point to** continuing problems with substance misuse.

Some particular techniques for persuasive writing

Persuasive writing tends to use certain techniques. Some of the most common are:

- **repetition** of words or phrases
- dramatic-sounding **short sentences**
- including the reader by using **'we'** and related words
- asking **rhetorical questions** – which do not need an answer but make the reader think
- using what's called **'the rule of three'** – doing something three times over. This might be three examples, three rhetorical questions, three uses of the same word or phrase, and so on.
- use of an anecdote or personal experience to justify why the writer holds a certain opinion
- an **appeal to the reader's emotions**, or **emotive language** which stirs up the reader's feelings
- offering the reader a **vision** of success or achievement.

Now try this

Read the following text. It is by the food writer and TV presenter Hugh Fearnley-Whittingstall. He's taking the perhaps unexpected stance of persuading people that it's better for animals if we are *not* vegetarian.

As you read the piece, look for examples of each technique being used.

VEGETARIANS WITH TEETH

'How do you know stegosaurus is a vegetarian?' asked Oscar.

'You can tell from his teeth,' I said, feigning confidence in my hazy paleontological
5 recollection. 'Dinosaur experts think they weren't the right teeth for eating meat.'

'But Ned's got the right teeth for eating meat, and he's a vegetarian too,' said Oscar.

Good point, I thought.

10 'Well, Ned has a choice, because he's a human being. Animals either are vegetarians, or they're not.'

'I'm a shoe-man bean. Does that mean I can choice?'

15 'Yes,' I said.

'Well, I'm going to choice to eat meat then.'

'Why's that?' I asked.

'Because I like it.'

'Me too,' I said.

20 What I didn't say to Oscar is that I have been thinking a fair bit recently about the whole vegetarian/carnivore thing. Why exactly do I eat meat? I don't think it's particularly good for me (partial as I am to the fattier cuts). I abhor the way
25 most of it is produced. And, much as I enjoy eating it, I don't imagine life without it would be completely unbearable. So you see, I am not an untroubled carnivore. So why haven't I become a vegetarian?

Well, I guess there's my image to think of.
30 Connoisseur of obscure body parts. Enthusiastic muncher of small furry animals. But honestly, I'd give it all up – even the bacon – if I was properly convinced it was the right thing to do. Recently, I've been considering the matter in some depth
35 for a book I'm working on. Soon I hope to have resolved the matter to the satisfaction of my own conscience – one way or another.

But in the meantime, there's one thing I'd like a bit of help with. And perhaps there's a
40 vegetarian out there who can oblige. (Or more likely, a vegan, because what vegans understand, to their credit, is that the dairy industry is the meat industry – or at least the beef industry.)

My questions are these: what would the
45 vegetarian Utopia look like? And would anyone seriously want to live there? How would vegetarians set about dismantling the mixed farming system? What would happen to all the farm animals?

One possible response is that because killing
50 animals is simply wrong, a moral absolute, questions like mine are irrelevant (as well as irritating). But that really isn't good enough. Because if enough of us were genuinely persuaded of the wrongness of killing animals
55 for food (which is presumably what vegetarians would like to happen) we could then choose democratically to live in a meat-free society and these questions would become very real.

Would vegetarians be in favour of the
60 mass slaughter of farm animals, to accelerate the arable revolution? And if so, would the carnivorous minority be allowed a last supper of the slaughtered corpses? Presumably the answer is 'no' on both counts.

65 More likely, the WPTVB (Working Party for the Transition to a Vegetarian Britain) will favour a gradual scaling down of stocking, to a point where small populations of a wide range of breeds are managed, by man, in 'Tame
70 Life Parks'. Here they are well looked after and preserved for their educational and historic interest. Meanwhile the countryside is turned over to the cultivation of fruit and vegetables – grown, of course, without the aid of animal
75 manures, and therefore with the input of huge quantities of chemical fertilisers.

But the matter cannot quite rest there. What happens when the sheep and cows get a bit long in the tooth? Or short in the tooth, as is the problem
80 with ageing livestock. They can't feed properly, and quickly lose condition. In the absence of predators to finish them off, they will die a lingering and stressful death. Will the vegetarians allow human, and humane, intervention? Can we 'put them
85 out of their misery'? And, incidentally, do we incinerate their carcasses? Feed them to our pets? To the worms? Or, as a sop, to those appalling carnivores, for an occasional 'treat'?

I guess what it boils down to is this. All
90 animals must live some kind of life, and die some kind of death. And having died, they will be eaten, whether it's by a maggot, a crow, or a person.

The carnivore's position, and mine until you persuade me otherwise, is that the best, most
95 morally acceptable way to co-exist with our dependent, domesticated livestock is to take

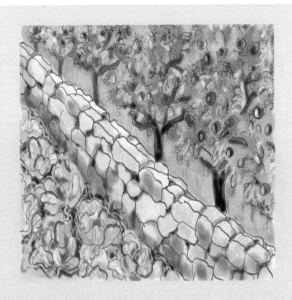

care of them when they are alive, ensure that they have a quick and, in relative terms at least, stress-free death. And then eat them.

100   I accept entirely that, through industrial farming practice, we are guilty of a gross abuse of our responsibility of care, and a treatment of farm animals that is often morally without defence. But surely reform, and not abstinence,
105   is the answer?

If you're a sheep, the question of who ends up eating you when you're dead is the very least of your worries. And, in the long run, you'd probably rather be a sheep than a stegosaurus.

'Vegetarians with Teeth', published in
Hugh Fearlessly Eats It All,
by Hugh Fearnley-Whittingstall

Now try this

First, share your answers with the rest of the class. Next, give examples of any other techniques you found Fearnley-Whittingstall using to make his argument effective.

Now try this

It's time to plan your piece. (You may already have done quite a lot of planning after the research phase if you organised your material into what the facts were, and how each fact could be used to support an argument.) Look back at all the material you gathered from your research. Double-check that you did put everything you found into your own words. Following all the advice this chapter has given you, prepare a paragraph plan for your piece. Remember, you have a choice of simpler or more complex structures if you are writing an argumentative essay.

Now try this

It's now time to write your piece. Don't forget the bibliography of your sources at the end. When you've written it, read your work over before you hand it in to your teacher. Think about the four areas you will be assessed on, which were explained at the start of this chapter, and ask yourself if you've met all the criteria.

Your teacher will read your work and add comments so that you can discuss the piece and improve it.

CHAPTER 2 Close Reading

The first of the two exams you will sit in May is a test of your skills in Close Reading. You also have to pass a Close Reading NAB in class. That means you'll probably be working on these skills throughout the year, which is why this chapter is near the start of the book.

If you are really serious about passing, you need to expand your experience of language and ideas now.

- Try to regularly read a good newspaper like the *Guardian*, *The Scotsman*, *The Herald*, *The Independent* or *The Times*. Don't just read the news stories near the front, but also the feature articles and opinion pieces in the later pages.

- Expand your knowledge of language, and of how people debate and argue about their ideas, by watching TV programmes such as *Newsnight*.

- Fill your head with ideas by listening to *Today*, the morning news programme on BBC Radio 4, and by listening to other programmes on that station.

If you encounter unfamiliar words see if you can work them out from the context, or look them up. You will not be able to take a dictionary into the exam, so it's important to work on building up your vocabulary.

Now try this

Find a partner. Every pair of students will need a Higher Close Reading past paper, and a Standard Grade Credit Close Reading past paper. Make sure you have both the text and the questions in each case. It's best if the papers are as recent as possible.

First of all, have a look at the front of the Higher paper.

- How much more time do you get for the Higher task?
- Are there any special warnings or advice to pay attention to?

Next, spend time reading and looking at the passages in each paper.

- How are the passages similar?
- How are they different in:
  - length
  - layout
  - genre of writing
  - vocabulary
  - style of writing?
- What makes the Higher text more difficult?

Now look at the way the questions are laid out on the page.

- Are there any similarities at all?
- What are the differences in layout? Think about:
  - use of headings or sections
  - use of bold
  - number of marks given
  - where you write your answers
- What makes the Higher layout more of a challenge?

Now read the wording of the questions.

- What similarities do you find between papers at both levels?
- What are the differences?
- What makes the Higher questions more difficult?

Some basics about the paper

Higher Close Reading tasks are always based on non-fiction, usually a piece of journalism or an extract from a book. The examiners usually pick passages on controversial topics, or subjects that people have strong opinions about.

In the Close Reading NAB there is one passage, on which you have to answer 30 marks' worth of questions. You get an hour for this task.

In the exam there will be two passages, both dealing with the same topic but perhaps taking different points of view on the subject. The second passage tends to be a little shorter than the first. You have to answer 50 marks' worth of questions and get an hour and three quarters to do this. There will be about 25 to 30 marks' worth of questions on the first passage, slightly fewer questions, around 15 to 20 marks' worth, on the second passage, and a question at the end which is worth about 5 marks and asks you to compare the two passages in some way.

When you read the questions you will notice that each has a letter at the end beside the number of marks available: **U**, **A** or **E**.

- **U** questions test your **understanding** of the passages, your ability to follow the ideas and argument and grasp **what** the writers say.
- **A** questions test your **analysis** of the passages, your ability to explain **how** the writers convey their points of view, and how the language techniques they use contribute to the impact of their writing.
- **E** questions ask for your **evaluation** of the writing, your assessment of **how effectively** the writers have achieved their purpose.

Throughout this chapter you will find explanations of how to tackle certain types of questions. There will be worked examples for you to look at, and questions from SQA past papers for you to try. At the end of the chapter are two larger opportunities for practice, one worth 30 marks like the NAB and one which is, like the exam, worth 50 marks.

You will need more practice than this. Your teacher will probably get you to work through lots of whole past papers, and you can also buy books of these to work through by yourself. There are also other textbooks you can buy, such as *Higher English Close Reading* by Ann Bridges and Colin Eckford, and *Higher English Close Reading Preparation* by Colin Eckford.

The most important thing you can do, the rule above all other rules, is **answer the question**. Read it carefully, find out what the markers want you to do, and do it. **Answer the question.** This chapter will teach you more about how to do this, but what you have to do, at all times is **just answer the question!**

Some basics about tackling the questions

As you are practising the different types of questions explained in this chapter, try to keep these two bits of advice in mind at all times.

First, don't rehash the wording of the question in your answer. If the question says:

> How does the writer's word choice show her disapproval of the beliefs of the 'experts' to whom she has just referred?

Don't start your answer like this:

> The writer's word choice shows her disapproval of the beliefs of the 'experts' to whom she has just referred by …

You're just wasting time rewriting all those words. The examiners know what's in the question; they want to see if you can answer it. Try an answer like this instead:

> Her use of 'so-called' before the word 'experts' suggests she is unsure of their expertise. Her description of their beliefs as 'outlandish' shows she thinks their opinions are bizarre rather than convincing.

Secondly, try to use either headings or bullet points to organise longer answers. This will make it much easier for the marker to follow what you are saying. Also, if you are answering a complex question, using bullet points or headings will help you keep track of your work and make sure that you have done everything you were asked to do.

For example, if a question asks you to

> **Give four reasons the writer presents for …**

you could number the parts of your answer from 1 to 4, or use four bullet points.

Similarly, if a question begins with

> **Show how the writer uses imagery and word choice to …**

then you should organise the first part of your answer under the heading IMAGERY and the next part under the heading WORD CHOICE.

U for understanding questions

Using your own words

On the front of the question paper you will see this wording, which will be in bold to indicate how important the message is:

> **When answering questions coded 'U – Understanding', use your own words as far as is reasonably possible and do not simply repeat the wording of the passage.**

You will also see a reminder of this instruction above the questions on each passage. The instruction applies to all of the **U** questions, but the individual questions themselves will not say anything about using your own words.

This is very important. The **U** questions are, by and large, the easiest ones in the exam. However, they are also the foundation on which the rest of your success in the task depends. If you don't understand the passage, you'll never be able to analyse or evaluate it. The only way to show that you truly understand something, that it has been through your brain and that you have processed the information, is to be able to explain it in your own words.

There's more advice about the skill of paraphrasing – putting things into your own words – in Chapter 8, but because it's so important we will also take time to work on it here.

Now try this

Look at this sentence from the start of a Higher exam passage about the future of cities:

> In a world changing faster now than ever before, the dispossessed and the ambitious are flooding into cities swollen out of all recognition.

A student needed to put this into his own words, which he did like this:

> The pace of change in the world is faster than it has ever been. Cities are growing so fast that they can hardly be recognised as those who have lost their homes, and those who are highly determined, pour into them.

This student used a lot of different tactics as he paraphrased. First, he changed some important words or expressions.

Here is a list of expressions from the original sentence. What did he change each one into?

> world changing faster now than ever
> dispossessed
> ambitious
> flooding
> swollen out of all recognition

Secondly, the student changed the number of sentences from one to two. Thirdly, he put the ideas in the original sentence in a slightly different order. All of this shows that he has understood and can process the information.

What he didn't change was the word *cities* itself. Because that is the subject, and is what the whole passage is about, he can keep using that key word.

Now try this

You're going to see the first three paragraphs of that Higher passage about changing cities. Several sections in the article have been underlined. **Rewrite** each one in your own words. You don't have to change every single word, and you may find that some long sentences can be reworded better as two or even three shorter ones.

In a world changing faster now than ever before, the dispossessed and the ambitious are flooding into cities swollen out of all recognition. Poor cities are struggling to cope. Rich cities are reconfiguring themselves at breakneck speed. **(1)** China has created an industrial powerhouse from what were fishing villages in the 1970s. Lagos and Dhaka attract a thousand new arrivals every day. **(2)** In Britain, central London's population has started to grow again after fifty years of decline. **(3)** We have more big cities now than at any time in our history. In 1900, only sixteen had a population of one million; now it's more than 400. Not only are there more of them, they are larger than ever. In 1851, London had two million people. **(4)** It was the largest city in the world by a long way, twice the size of Paris, its nearest rival. That version of London would seem like a village now. **(5)** By the official definition, London has getting on for eight million people, but in practical terms it's a city of 18 million, straggling most of the way from Ipswich to Bournemouth in an unforgiving rush of business parks and designer outlets, gated housing and logistics depots.

Having invented the modern city, nineteenth-century Britain promptly reeled back in horror at what it had done. To the Victorians exploring the cholera-ridden back alleys of London's East End, the city was a hideous tumour sucking the life out of the countryside and creating in its place a vast polluted landscape of squalor, disease and crime. **(6)** In their eyes, the city was a place to be feared, controlled and, if possible, eliminated.

Now try this

Using your own words, answer this Higher exam question about the middle paragraph of the extract:

> **Q1** Explain two ways in which 'That version of London would seem like a village now.' **2 U**

Remember, you could number or bullet point the two parts of your answer.

Questions about your understanding of the writer's ideas

If you don't understand the writer's ideas in the passage, you'll get nowhere. Some of the **U** for Understanding questions therefore just ask you to show that you follow what the writer is saying. Remember – demonstrating that means using your own words, though the question itself won't say that.

Look at this extract from a passage in which the writer complains that we have become far too protective of children, and too ready to listen to those who think children are in danger:

I am tired of these prophets of death and injury. I do not need the Royal Society for the Prevention of Accidents to tell me that children should wear helmets while sledging, because I am incensed at the thought of the hundreds of kids whose parents will now ban them from sledging on the five-million-to-one chance that they might hit a tree. I mourn also for the kids who will never know the delight of cycling with the wind in their hair, or climbing trees, or exploring hidden places. Growing up devoid of freedom, decision-making, and the opportunity to learn from taking their own risks, our children are becoming trapped, neurotic, and as genetically weakened as battery hens.

Imagine you were asked this question:

Why, according to the writer, are modern children in danger of becoming 'as genetically weakened as battery hens'? 2 U

The key words in the passage that show the writer's ideas are, 'Growing up devoid of freedom, decision-making, and the opportunity to learn from taking their own risks'. You could paraphrase the writer's words with an answer like this:

Children have lost their liberty. They don't make choices for themselves or try anything hazardous.

Now try this

Answer these questions from Higher past papers. The first extract comes from the same passage about our paranoid overprotection of children.

> Teachers are giving up teaching, and youth organisations are dying because they cannot find adults prepared to run them. Everywhere good, inspirational people are turning their backs on children because they are terrified of the children and their parents turning on them, accusing them of all manner of wrongdoing. They can no longer operate, they say, in a climate of suspicion and fear.

Q2 Why, according to the writer, are teachers and youth workers 'turning their backs on children'? 2 U

The next comes from a passage about the danger of comets and asteroids hitting Earth.

> The discovery that a comet impact triggered the disappearance of the dinosaurs as well as more than half the species that lived 65 million years ago may have been the most significant scientific breakthrough of the twentieth century. Brilliant detective work on the part of hundreds of scientists in analysing clues extracted from the study of fossils, and by counting the objects in near-earth space, has allowed the dinosaur mass-extinction mystery to be solved. As a result we have new insight into the nature of life on Earth.

Q3 According to the first sentence, what important discovery has been made about comet impact? 2 U

The next extract comes from later in the same passage. Use numbers or bullets to organise your answer.

> Once we appreciate that impact catastrophes have shaped life as we know it, and that such events will happen again in the future, how will this awareness alter the way we see ourselves in the cosmic context? Will we let nature take its course and trust to luck that our species will survive the next violent collision? Or will we confront the forces that may yet influence the destiny of all life on Earth?

Q4 According to the writer, what two possible courses of action are open to us with regard to future 'impact catastrophes'? 2 U

In the next passage, the writer considers why so many people are now obese.

> Evolution is mostly to blame. It has designed mankind to cope with deprivation, not plenty. People are perfectly tuned to store energy in good years to see them through lean ones. But when bad times never come, they are stuck with that energy, stored around their expanding bellies.

Q5 'Evolution is to blame.' How does the writer go on to explain this statement? 2 U

Q2 and Q4 extracts: from "Impact! The Threat of Comets and Asteroids" by Verschur, Gerrit (1996). By permission of Oxford University Press, Inc.
Q5 extract: from "The Shape of Things to Come" © The Economist Newspaper Limited, London 2010.

Now try this continued

In the next passage, the writer is discussing the importance of public libraries. Watch out for the words 'by close reference' in the question. They tell you that you need to pick up on very specific details from the text, and that you can get away with using brief, very precise quotations, as long as you mostly explain in your own words.

My love affair with libraries started early in the Drumchapel housing scheme in the Fifties. For the 60,000 exiles packed off from slum housing to the city's outer fringe, Glasgow Council neglected the shops and amenities but somehow remembered to put in a public library – actually a wooden shed. That library was split in two – an adult section and a children's section. This was an early taste of forbidden fruit. Much useful human reproductive knowledge was gained from certain books examined surreptitiously in the adult biology section.

Q6 In your opinion, does the writer think Glasgow Council gave the library in Drumchapel a high priority? Justify your answer by close reference to the lines. **2 U/E**

To finish off this section with a question worth more marks, here's another extract from the passage on libraries. Use numbers or bullets in your answer.

It may well be that public demand and technical change mean that we no longer need the dense neighbourhood network of local libraries of yore. But our culture, local and universal, does demand strategically situated libraries where one can find the material that is too expensive for the ordinary person to buy, or too complex to find online. Such facilities are worth funding publicly because the return in informed citizenship and civic pride is far in excess of money spent.

Libraries also have that undervalued resource – the trained librarian. The ultimate Achilles' heel of the internet is that it presents every page of information as being equally valid, which is of course nonsense. The internet is cluttered with false information, or just plain junk. The library, with its collection honed and developed by experts, is a guarantee of the quality and veracity of the information contained therein, something that Google can never provide.

Q7 Give four reasons the writer presents in these lines in favour of maintaining traditional public libraries. **4 U**

Context questions

Sometimes the examiners ask you to work out from the context what a word or expression means. They think you probably won't know the given word but should be able to work it out from what surrounds it. If you do happen to know the word, that's a bonus.

These questions are usually worth two marks and there is a two-step method for dealing with them. First, you need to **give the meaning** of the word or expression. You won't get any marks at all if you don't clearly give this meaning. Then, you **explain how the clues in the context helped you work out the meaning**. Do this by quoting the words that gave you clues, then explaining briefly how they showed the meaning.

Look at this extract from the text on cities that you've seen already:

By the official definition, London has getting on for eight million people, but in practical terms it's a city of 18 million, straggling most of the way from Ipswich to Bournemouth in an unforgiving rush of business parks and designer outlets, gated housing and logistics depots.

Imagine you were asked this question:

Show how the context helps the reader to arrive at the meaning of the word 'straggling' in line 3.

You could answer like this.

'Straggling' means spreading out over some distance. This can be understood from the context which refers to London spreading 'from Ipswich to Bournemouth' as this is a wide area extending to the east of England and to its south coast.

It will help if you learn this script for answering these questions:

'_____' means _____.

This can be understood from the context which refers to _____ as this _____.

Now try this

Answer these questions from Higher past papers. The first is once again from the passage on our overprotection of children. Use the script to help you answer.

> If you read a wonderful new book by sociologist Frank Furedi – *Paranoid Parenting* – you will see the story of a teacher who quit the profession after a school trip was cancelled. Some parents were worried the trip would involve their children in a 45-minute journey in a private car. Would the cars be roadworthy? Were the drivers experienced? Were these non-smoking cars?

Q8 How does the story told in the paragraph help you to understand the meaning of the word 'paranoid'? **2 U**

The next extract comes from the passage on the damage an asteroid impact could do to our planet.

> Others are, however, convinced that it is only a matter of time before we face Armageddon. Liberal Democrat MP and sky-watcher Lembit Opik says: 'I have said for years that the chance of an asteroid having an impact which could wipe out most of the human race is 100 per cent.' He has raised his worries in the Commons, successfully campaigned for an all-party task force to assess the potential risk, and helped set up the Spaceguard UK facility to track near-Earth objects. He admits: 'It does sound like a science fiction story and I may sound like one of those guys who walk up and down with a sandwich board saying the end of the world is nigh. But the end is nigh.'

Q9 Show how these lines help you understand the meaning of the word 'Armageddon'. **2 U**

This extract is from the passage about the value of public libraries.

> Libraries have another function still, which the internet cannot fulfil. Libraries, like museums, are custodians of knowledge – and should be funded as such. It has become the fashion in recent decades to turn our great national libraries and museums into entertainment centres, with audio-visuals, interactive displays and gimmicks. While I have some enthusiasm for popularising esoteric knowledge, it cannot always be reduced to the level of a child's view of the universe. We have a duty to future generations to invest in the custodians of our culture, in particular its literature and manuscripts.

Q10 The writer twice calls libraries 'custodians'. What does this mean and how does its context help you to arrive at this meaning? **2 U**

Now try this continued

The next extract comes from a passage which questions whether we are going to bring on the end of the world because of the pollution we cause.

It is certainly possible that the premises advanced by environmental campaigners are sound: that we are in mortal danger from global warming and that this is a result of human activity. Yet when I listen to ecological warnings such as these, I am reminded of a doomsday scenario from the past.

In his 'Essay on the Principle of Population', published in 1798, Thomas Malthus demonstrated, in what appeared to be indisputable, mathematical terms, that population growth would exceed the limits of food supply by the middle of the nineteenth century. Only plague, war or natural disaster would be capable of sufficiently reducing the numbers of people to avert mass starvation within roughly fifty years. This account of the world's inevitable fate (known as the 'Malthusian catastrophe') was as much part of accepted thinking among intellectuals then as are the environmental lobby's warnings today.

Q11 What does the phrase 'doomsday scenario' mean and how does the context help you to arrive at this meaning?   **2 U**

This extract is once again from the passage on protective parents.

It seems the childcare pendulum has swung: the principal threat to children is no longer neglectful parents, but excessively protective ones who are always worrying about germs. Frank Furedi, reader in sociology at the University of Kent, has written a book, *Paranoid Parenting*, in which he explores the causes and far-reaching consequences of too much cosseting. 'It is always important to recall that our obsession with children's safety is likely to be more damaging to them than any risks that they are likely to meet in their daily encounter with the world,' Furedi writes.

Q12 How does the context in which it is used help you to understand the meaning of the word 'cosseting'?   **2 U**

Link questions

You might get a question about how a certain sentence or a specific paragraph acts as a link in the passage. The examiners have usually decided already that the sentence or paragraph **is** a link; now they want you to explain **how** it carries out its linking function.

There is a method for answering these questions. The basic formula is:

Quote + link back; quote + link forward

You begin with a short quotation from the linking sentence, then explain what ideas this links back to. Next, use a different short quotation from the link sentence, then explain what ideas this introduces and links forward to.

Use this structure for your answer:

The words … (quote from link sentence) refer back to the idea of … (give the idea) which was mentioned … (say where).

The words … (quote from link sentence) introduce the idea of … (give the idea) which comes up in … (say where).

It's easier to understand this if we look at a worked example. This extract comes from a passage about the current fascination with rural life, and whether this actually says anything to us about our history and heritage.

Then there is the proliferation of action groups dedicated to stopping construction of roads, airports, railway lines, factories, shopping centres and houses in rural areas, while multifarious organisations have become accustomed to expending their time and energies in monitoring and reporting on the state of grassland, water, trees, moorlands, uplands, lowlands, birds' eggs, wildflowers, badgers, historical sites and countless other aspects of the landscape and its inhabitants.

It might be thought – indeed it is widely assumed – that it must be good for the countryside to be returned to the central position it enjoyed in British life long ago. Yet there is a particularly worrying aspect of the new rural mania that suggests it might finally do the countryside more harm than good.

This is the identification, in the current clamour, of the countryside in general and the landscape in particular with the past – the insistence on the part of those who claim to have the best intentions of ruralism at heart that their aim is to protect what they glibly refer to as 'our heritage'. This wildly overused term is seriously misleading, not least because nobody ever seems to have asked what it means.

By referring to specific words and phrases, show how the middle paragraph above performs a linking function at this stage in the writer's argument. 2 A

The words 'returned to the central position' refer back to the aims of the action groups which were mentioned in the first paragraph. The words 'worrying aspect' introduce the idea of the writer's concerns which come up in the third and last paragraph.

Now try this

Here's a past paper question for you to try. The extract is from the passage that questions whether, particularly by flying, we are creating pollution that could destroy our environment.

Is your journey really necessary? Who would have thought that, in the absence of world war and in the midst of unprecedented prosperity, politicians would be telling us not to travel? Just as working people have begun to enjoy the freedoms that the better-off have known for generations – the experience of other cultures, other cuisines, other climates – they are threatened with having those liberating possibilities priced out of their reach.

And when I hear politicians – most of them comfortably off – trying to deny enlightenment and pleasure to 'working class' people, I reach for my megaphone. Maybe Tommy Tattoo and his mates do use cheap flights to the sunshine as an extension of their binge-drinking opportunities, but for thousands of people whose parents would never have ventured beyond Blackpool or Rothesay, air travel has been a social revelation.

So, before we all give the eco-lobby's anti-flying agenda the unconditional benefit of the doubt, can we just review their strategy as a whole?

Remember, it is not just air travel that the green tax lobby is trying to control: it is a restriction on any mobility. Clamping down on one form of movement, as the glib reformers have discovered, simply creates intolerable pressure on the others. Londoners, for example, had just become accustomed to the idea that they would have to pay an £8 congestion charge to drive into their own city when they discovered that the fares on commuter rail and underground services had been hiked up with the intention of driving away customers from the public transport system – now grossly overcrowded as a result of people having been forced off the roads by the congestion charge.

Q13 Referring to specific words and phrases, show how the sentence 'So, before … as a whole?' performs a linking function in the writer's argument. 2 U

There are so many other types of **U** for Understanding question you could be asked that it's not possible to go into them all here. Just remember the key points: answer the question; don't rehash the question in your answer; use bullet points, numbers or headings to organise long answers. Make sure you understand all the advice so far before moving on to the next section.

A for Analysis questions

Most of the marks available in any Close Reading task come from **A** for Analysis questions. These also tend to be the hardest questions to answer. Furthermore, individual questions can be worth a lot of marks – while most **U** questions are for just 1 or 2 marks, **A** questions are quite often worth 4 marks.

Word choice questions

First, a warning. You'll often find the word 'language' used in a question. You might be told to:

> Show how the writer's use of language …

or asked:

> How does the writer's language … ?

When the examiners ask you about language **they do not mean just word choice**. Any answer to a question about language might include word choice, but should include an analysis of the use of other language techniques – such as sentence structure, imagery, tone, alliteration and so on – as well.

So, when you really are being asked about word choice, what's going on?

We know that any word a writer uses has been chosen in some sense. Word choice questions are about words that have been chosen very carefully, for particular reasons, or to suggest particular meanings.

Most words have two levels of meaning, a simple **denotation**, and a more complex, deeper **connotation**.

For example, the words *stormed*, *sauntered* and *swaggered* all have the same denotation. They all tell us that a person walked, moving along by

putting one foot in front of the other. However, they all have different connotations, telling us different things about how the person walked. *Stormed* suggests anger, *sauntered* tells us the person was relaxed and carefree, *swaggered* implies that the walker is perhaps rather arrogant.

When you are asked a word choice question, the examiners want you to examine the connotations of the words.

Now try this

You will see pairs or trios of words. In each group the words have the same basic denotation but different connotations. For each group, work out the denotation they share, and the different connotations of the individual words.

plump	obese	fat
elderly	mature	ancient
drunk	inebriated	tipsy
complex	intricate	
question	enquiry	
fanatic	believer	fundamentalist
partner	lover	beloved
announced	stated	broadcast

When you answer a word choice question, you need to **quote** the words you think are significant, then go into their **connotations**, all the time making sure you answer what the question has actually asked you. Look at the worked example, which is based on a passage in which the writer has just explained that her son's primary school had banned sweets, crisps and chocolate.

> After school and in the playground, away from the teachers' eyes, sweets and chocolates were traded. They became the marks of rebellion and the statements of independence. Eating foods they suspected the grown-ups would rather they didn't made those foods ever so much more enticing. They weren't just food but food plus attitude.

Show how the writer's word choice makes clear the children's attitude to the school ban.   **2 A**

The word 'enticing' suggests that the children found the forbidden food tempting and exciting. The phrase 'not just food but' implies the sweets became a symbol of their fight against the school's authority.

Now try this

Answer these questions from Higher past papers. We'll do the first one in detail. It comes from the passage about our fascination with the countryside. Here's the extract:

> One faction has cried constantly that the countryside is in mortal danger from greedy developers whose only motive is profit; another has kept roaring that farmers are killing every wild thing in sight and threatening the very soil on which we stand through overuse of machinery and chemicals; still another has been continually heard ululating over a decline in the bird population, or the loss of hedgerows, or the disappearance of marshland, or the appearance of coniferous forest.

Now answer the question. You'll be able to answer it six times over, with less and less help each time.

Q14 Show how word choice emphasises the strong feelings of those who believe the countryside is under threat. **2 A**

A The words 'cried constantly' suggest that ...

B The words 'mortal danger' suggest ...

C The word 'greedy' suggests ...

Now find three more examples of word choice to examine in that paragraph.

The extracts for questions 15 and 16 come from the passage on the value of public libraries.

> The internet search engine Google, with whom I spend more time than with my loved ones, is planning to put the contents of the world's great university libraries online, including the Bodleian in Oxford and those of Harvard and Stanford in America. Part of me is ecstatic at the thought of all that information at my fingertips; another part of me is nostalgic, because I think physical libraries, book-lined and cathedral-quiet, are a cherished part of civilisation we lose at our cultural peril.

Q15 How does the writer's word choice help to convey his view of the importance of 'physical libraries'? Refer to two examples in your answer. **2 A**

> Libraries also have that undervalued resource – the trained librarian. The ultimate Achilles' heel of the internet is that it presents every page of information as being equally valid, which is of course nonsense. The internet is cluttered with false information, or just plain junk. The library, with its collection honed and developed by experts, is a guarantee of the quality and veracity of the information contained therein, something that Google can never provide.

Q16 Show how the writer's word choice emphasises the contrast between his attitude to libraries and his attitude to the internet. 2 A

The extract for question 17 is from the passage about our fascination with the countryside, in which the writer discusses the views of different pressure groups.

> Yet if you sweep away the apoplectic froth and the self-interested posturing and look at the reality, the threat to the countryside recedes dramatically. Yes, we do occupy a crowded little island. But what makes it seem crowded is that 98 per cent of us live on 7 per cent of the land. Britain is still overwhelmingly green. Just 11 per cent of our nation is classified as urban.

Q17 Show how the writer's word choice emphasises his view that the threat to the countryside is less serious than the English middle classes suggest. **2 A**

Now read this extract from the passage on whether we should restrict air travel to save the environment.

> Is your journey really necessary? Who would have thought that, in the absence of world war and in the midst of unprecedented prosperity, politicians would be telling us not to travel? Just as working people have begun to enjoy the freedoms that the better-off have known for generations – the experience of other cultures, other cuisines, other climates – they are threatened with having those liberating possibilities priced out of their reach.
>
> And when I hear politicians – most of them comfortably off – trying to deny enlightenment and pleasure to 'working class' people, I reach for my megaphone. Maybe Tommy Tattoo and his mates do use cheap flights to the sunshine as an extension of their binge-drinking opportunities, but for thousands of people whose parents would never have ventured beyond Blackpool or Rothesay, air travel has been a social revelation.

Q18 Show how the writer's word choice conveys the strength of her commitment to air travel for all. **2 A**

As well as looking at the denotations, and especially at the connotations and suggested ideas, of the words the writer uses, you may sometimes notice that the word choice belongs to a certain type of language.

Now try this

Work with a partner or in a small group. You will see the names of certain types of language. For each language type, first explain in your own words what the term means, then give at least three examples. The first one has been done for you.

Language type	Definition	Examples
emotive language	language designed to shock, or to get an emotional response from the reader	shocking terrible horrific
formal register		
informal register		
hyperbole		
slang		
dialect		
jargon		

Writers might also use some of the words you met in the Writing chapter. Words like *certainly*, *surely*, *undoubtedly*, for example, would give an impression that the writer was very sure of his or her opinion.

Not only is word choice important in its own right, the words that writers choose also help them to create the **tone** of their writing. We'll look at that area now.

Tone questions

It's easy to understand what we mean by **tone** if we think of a speaking voice. When you hear someone speaking, you can tell if they are angry, confused, excited or afraid. These tones in the speaking voice are created by factors like the volume, the speed of speech, and how fluently or haltingly the words come out.

It's a little harder at first to see how we can identify tone in written English, when there are no sounds, only words, but skilled writers can create a tone by word choice alone.

When you are asked a question about tone, you may have to do as many as four different things:

1 Identify a tone – you have to do this if the examiners don't name a tone, but you usually get no marks for doing so.

2 Quote words which create that tone – again you have to do this but will probably get no marks for doing so.

3 Explain how the words you have quoted create the tone – this is where you begin to earn marks.

4 Answer any other aspect of the particular question you are tackling.

At the top of the next column there's another extract from the passage about our fascination with rural life. After it you'll be given a little help to have your first go at a tone question.

Then there is the proliferation of action groups dedicated to stopping construction of roads, airports, railway lines, factories, shopping centres and houses in rural areas, while multifarious organisations have become accustomed to expending their time and energies in monitoring and reporting on the state of grassland, water, trees, moorlands, uplands, lowlands, birds' eggs, wildflowers, badgers, historical sites and countless other aspects of the landscape and its inhabitants.

Q19 Show how the writer's use of tone in these lines conveys his disapproval of the 'action groups'.　　　　　　**2 A**

The writer creates a _____ tone. He does this by using the words '_____' which are (repeat the tone) _____ because they suggest ...

I am fed up listening to scaremongers about the E. coli virus, telling me my child should never visit a farm or come into contact with animals. I am weary of organisations that are dedicated to promulgating the idea that threats and dangers to children lurk everywhere. I am sick of charities who on the one hand attack overprotective parents and at the same time say children should never be left unsupervised in public places.

Q20 Identify the writer's tone and explain how it is conveyed.　　　　**3 A**

The next extract discusses how comet and asteroid impacts shaped evolution on Earth.

Survivors of essentially random impact catastrophes – cosmic accidents – were those creatures who just happened to be 'lucky' enough to find themselves alive after the dust settled. It doesn't matter how well a creature may have been able to survive in a particular environment before an event – being thumped on the head by a large object from space during the event is not conducive to a long and happy existence.

Q21 Explain how the writer creates a slightly humorous tone. **2 A**

In this extract, the writer is discussing rising property values, and housebuilding in the countryside.

I write these sentences with the heavy heart of a class traitor, for I am a middle-class, middle-aged property owner who has smugly watched his own house soar in value as more and more young househunters desperately chase fewer and fewer properties. I am inordinately proud of my view across the green belt (from an upstairs window admittedly because of the motorway flyover in between). And I intend to spend the weekend rambling across the rural England I have loved since boyhood.

Q22 Show how the writer's use of language in these lines creates a self-mocking tone. **2 A**

The next extract comes from the passage about the pollution that may be caused by air travel.

The only solution – and I am just waiting for the politicians to recommend it explicitly – is for none of us to go anywhere. Stay at home and save the planet. But that would be a craven retreat from all the social, professional and cultural interactions that unrestricted mobility makes possible – and which, since the Renaissance, have made great cities the centres of intellectual progress.

Q23 Show how, in this paragraph, the writer creates a tone which conveys her disapproval of the 'solution'. **2 A**

Imagery questions

Writers use images to strengthen what they say by putting all sorts of pictures in the reader's mind. Imagery is not the same thing as description. A description tells us **what something is like**. An image shows that **one thing is somehow like another**. The comparison tells us more about the thing that is being compared. Similes, metaphors and personification are all different sorts of image, though most of the images you will be asked about will be metaphors.

To get us thinking about images, and how they add to our understanding, let's think about animal images. The writer of this book could describe herself as:

Ms Cooper, that educational hamster

Q21 extract: from "Impact! The Threat of Comets and Asteroids" by Verschur, Gerrit (1996). By permission of Oxford University Press, Inc.

How am I like a hamster? I'm very small, with chestnut hair. I move around the classroom constantly, and I hardly ever stop talking. So, if you were to analyse the image of me as a hamster, you could do it like this.

> Just as a hamster is small and brown, and scampers around squeaking, so Ms Cooper is a tiny woman with chestnut hair, who constantly scurries around her classroom talking all the time.

Now try this

Decide on an animal image that suits you. Try to think of one that applies to at least two aspects of your looks, behaviour or personality.

Then, get together with a partner who knows you quite well. Tell each other which animal images you have chosen for yourselves. Find all the ways in which your partner is like the animal image he or she chose.

There is a method for answering imagery questions. You begin with what the image **literally** is like, or **literally** means. Then you go on to the **metaphorical** meaning, showing how that image applies to and adds meaning to the subject under discussion.

Use this structure for your answer:

> Just as … (explain the literal meaning) … so … (explain the metaphorical meaning).

This is easier to understand if you look at some examples. Here's an extract from the passage about paranoid parents:

> Growing up devoid of freedom, decision-making, and the opportunity to learn from taking their own risks, our children are becoming trapped, neurotic, and as genetically weakened as battery hens.

How effective do you find the image of 'battery hens' in conveying the writer's view of how children are currently being brought up? 2 A

Just as a battery hen is kept cruelly shut up in a tiny cage, so modern children are restricted and denied freedom to take the risks the writer thinks they should be able to learn from.

The next example comes from the same Close Reading exam:

> It seems the childcare pendulum has swung: the principal threat to children is no longer neglectful parents, but excessively protective ones who are always worrying about germs.

Explain how the image supports the writer's point. 2 A

Just as a clock pendulum swings from one side to the other, so people's opinions on the dangers to children have gone from one extreme to the other.

Notice that although the first example above told you which image to look at – the image of the battery hens – in the second example you had first of all to work out that the image in the passage is the image of a pendulum. In answering most Higher questions, the first thing you'll have to do is to find the image. You won't get any marks for identifying it; you only begin to earn marks when you analyse how the image works.

Now try this

Now you are going to have a little help to examine some imagery. First, read the following extract. It comes from a passage in which the writer suggests that people are over-reacting when they protest against plans to build houses in rural areas.

The most cherished credo of the English middle classes is that the verdant hills and dales of the Home Counties should remain forever sacrosanct, and that the Government's 'Stalinist' decision to impose a million extra houses on southeast England is the most hideous threat to our way of life since the Luftwaffe made its energetic contribution to British town and country planning in 1940. Thousands of green acres will be choked by concrete, as rapacious housebuilders devour whole landscapes. England's cherished green belts – the fourteen great rings of protected fields that have stopped our major cities from sprawling outward for more than half a century – will be swept away.

Now answer the question. You'll be able to answer it eight times over, with less and less help each time. Each answer is worth two marks.

Show how the writer's use of imagery in these lines emphasises the extreme nature of the English middle classes' view of the threat to the countryside.

A24 Just as a 'cherished credo' is an important religious belief, so …

A25 Just as something that is sacrosanct is … , so …

A26 Just as Stalin was … , so …

A27 Base your answer on the image 'choked'

A28 Base your answer on the image 'devour whole landscapes'

A29 Base your answer on the image 'sprawling outward'

A30 Base your answer on the image 'will be swept away'

A31 There is one more image in the paragraph. Find and analyse it too.

Answer these imagery questions from Higher past papers. The first is from the passage about the threat of comet and asteroid impacts.

Many details referred to in our story are still controversial. Debate is particularly heated as regards the role of impacts in directing the course of human history. All of this is very exciting. The whole topic is in a state of ferment, a symptom that something significant is brewing.

Q32 Show how effective you find the writer's use of imagery in conveying the excitement of the 'debate'. **2 A**

The next extract is from the passage on obesity.

Thanks to rising agricultural productivity, lean years are rarer all over the globe. Pessimistic economists, who used to draw graphs proving that the world was shortly going to run out of food, have gone rather quiet lately. According to the UN, the number of people short of food fell from 920m in 1980 to 799m twenty years later, even though the world's population increased by 1.6 billion over the period. This is mostly a cause for celebration. Mankind had won what was, for most of his time on the planet, his biggest battle: to ensure that he and his offspring had enough to eat. But every silver lining has a cloud, and the consequence of prosperity is a new plague that brings with it a host of interesting policy dilemmas.

Q33 How effective do you find the imagery in these lines in illustrating the writer's line of thought? You should refer to two examples in your answer. **4 A**

This extract comes from the passage about libraries:

I have spent a substantial portion of my life in libraries, and I still enter them with a mixture of excitement and awe. I am not alone in this. Veneration for libraries is as old as writing itself, for a library is more to our culture than a collection of books: it is a temple, a symbol of power, the hushed core of civilisation, the citadel of memory, with its own mystique, social and sensual as well as intellectual.

Q32 extract: from "Impact! The Threat of Comets and Asteroids" by Verschur, Gerrit (1996). By permission of Oxford University Press, Inc.
Q33 extract: from "The Shape of Things to Come" © The Economist Newspaper Limited, London 2010.

Q34 By referring to one example, show how the writer's imagery in these lines conveys the importance of libraries. **2 A**

In the following extract, the writer is describing a meeting of people working in the aviation industry. Participants had complained that environmentalists put too much of the blame for global warming on flying.

> But even in this self-interested arena a representative from the US Federal Aviation Administration caused some sharp intakes of breath from the audience by showing an extraordinary map of current flightpaths etched over one another on the world's surface. The only places on Earth that are not scarred by routes are blocks of air space over the central Pacific, the southern Atlantic, and Antarctica.

Q35 How effective do you find the writer's use of imagery in conveying the impact that flying has on the environment? **2 A**

This next extract is from the passage about the growth of cities.

> London is different for all its people. They make the most of the elements in it that have meaning for them and ignore the rest. A city is an à la carte menu. That is what makes it different from a village, which has little room for tolerance and difference. And a great city is one in which as many people as possible can make the widest of choices from its menu.

Q36 Show how the image of the 'à la carte menu' illustrates the point the writer is making in these lines. **2 A**

Sentence structure questions

Sentence structure is how a sentence is made and built up. Very often, students get structure questions wrong because they don't actually answer the question. Many students end up rehashing the content of a sentence when they should be examining its structure.

Structure is not the same as content. The structure of a house might be bricks and mortar placed on a strong, deep foundation; its contents will include furniture and people. The structure of the bag you take to school might be leather, stitched together and attached with metal buckles; its content would probably include books, pens and your iPod.

A number of smaller techniques contribute to sentence structure:

- **length**: Look at whether a sentence is noticeably long, or noticeably short, or if its length contrasts with the length of other sentences nearby.

- **listing**: What is being listed and what does this list suggest?

- **repetition**: What is being repeated and what does this repetition suggest?

- **parenthesis**: What is the extra information inside the parenthesis about and what is the effect of this?

- **word order**: Have any words been put in a position in the sentence that particularly creates emphasis?

- **colons or semicolons**: What do these divide the sentence into? What do colons introduce?

- **minor sentence**: These ungrammatical (usually short) sentences are used to create some kind of impact, so what impact is it?

- **questions**: What is the effect of these on the reader?

Now try this

You are going to try some sentence structure questions, with some support at first. Let's start with an extract from the passage about comet and asteroid impacts:

A lot has been learned about the nature of cosmic collisions and this new knowledge has given a remarkable twist to the story of our origins. We now recognise that comet and asteroid impacts may be the most important driving force behind evolutionary change on the planet. Originally, such objects smashed into one another to build the Earth 4.5 billion years ago. After that, further comet impacts brought the waters of our oceans and the organic modules needed for life. Ever since then, impacts have continued to punctuate the story of evolution. On many occasions, comets slammed into Earth with such violence that they nearly precipitated the extinction of all life. In the aftermath of each catastrophe, new species emerged to take the place of those that had been wiped out.

Now try the question. The framework will help you get as much as possible out of it.

Q 37 How does the sentence structure of these lines highlight the writer's ideas?

By beginning a number of the sentences with references to time periods such as _____ and _____, the writer creates a sequence through time which suggests that comet impacts were part of the process of evolution. By ending the last two sentences with the phrases _____ and _____ the writer creates a climax that emphasises his point about the destructiveness of these impacts. The fact that he uses the word '_____' three times shows how important ...

The next two extracts again come from the passage on our obsession with all things rural.

One faction has cried constantly that the countryside is in mortal danger from greedy developers whose only motive is profit; another has kept roaring that farmers are killing every wild thing in sight and threatening the very soil on which we stand through overuse of machinery and chemicals; still another has been continually heard ululating over a decline in the bird population, or the loss of hedgerows, or the disappearance of marshland, or the appearance of coniferous forest.

Q 38 Show how the sentence structure here emphasises the strong feelings of those who feel the countryside is under threat.   **2 A**

The listing of ... emphasises ...
Repetition of ... emphasises ...

Then there is the proliferation of action groups dedicated to stopping construction of roads, airports, railway lines, factories, shopping centres and houses in rural areas, while multifarious organisations have become accustomed to expending their time and energies in monitoring and reporting on the state of grassland, water, trees, moorlands, uplands, lowlands, birds' eggs, wildflowers, badgers, historical sites and countless other aspects of the landscape and its inhabitants.

Q 39 Show how the writer's use of sentence structure in this paragraph conveys his disapproval of the 'action groups'.   **2 A**

The list of ... suggests ...
The list of ... suggests ...

Q37 extract: from "Impact! The Threat of Comets and Asteroids" by Verschur, Gerrit (1996). By permission of Oxford University Press, Inc.

Now read these extracts from a passage suggesting we shouldn't criticise plans to build houses in rural areas:

The green-belt protectionists claim to be saving unspoilt countryside from the rampant advance of bulldozers. Exactly what unspoilt countryside do they imagine they are saving? Primordial forest, unchanged since Boudicca thrashed the Romans? Hogwash. The English have been making and remaking their landscape for millennia to suit the needs of each passing generation.

How effective do you find the writer's use of sentence structure in conveying his attitude to this argument from the 'green-belt protectionists'?

A 40 (Look at the writer's use of repetition.) **2 A**

A 41 (Look at one other facet of sentence structure.) **2 A**

These protectionists are fond of deriding any housebuilding targets set by the Government as monstrous, Soviet-style diktats. Good grief, what on earth do they imagine that the planning laws protecting the green belts and agricultural land are, if not Government interventions that have had a huge, and often disastrous, impact not just on the property market, but on employment, on transport, on public services and on economic growth?

How effective do you find the writer's use of sentence structure in conveying his attitude to this argument from the 'green-belt protectionists'?

A 42 (Name one technique, quote, and explain the effect.) **2 A**

A 43 (Name another technique, quote, explain.) **2 A**

Now try this

Answer these sentence structure questions from Higher past papers. The first extract comes from the passage on paranoid parents.

Everywhere you turn there is an army of professionals – ably abetted by the media – hard at work encouraging parents to fear the worst. Don't let your children out in the sun – not unless they're wearing special UV-resistant T-shirts. Don't buy your children a Wendy house, they might crush their fingers in the hinges. Don't buy a baby walker, your toddlers might brain themselves. Don't buy plastic baby teethers, your baby might suck in harmful chemicals. Don't let them use mobile phones, they'll sizzle their brains. Don't buy a second-hand car seat, it will not protect them. And on and on it goes.

Q 44 How does the sentence structure of these lines emphasise the writer's feelings about the 'army of professionals'? **2 A**

The next two extracts come from the passage on obesity.

When the world was a simpler place the rich were fat, the poor were thin, and right-thinking people worried about how to feed the hungry. Now, in much of the world, the rich are thin, the poor are fat, and right-thinking people are worrying about obesity.

Q 45 Identify two ways in which the sentence structure in these lines emphasises the change in the concerns of 'right-thinking people'. **2 A**

There is no doubt that obesity is the world's biggest public-health issue today – the main cause of heart disease, which kills more people these days than AIDS, malaria, war; the principal risk factor in diabetes; heavily implicated in cancer and other diseases. Since the World Health Organization labelled obesity an epidemic in 2000, reports on its fearful consequences have come thick and fast.

Q45 and Q46 extracts: from "The Shape of Things to Come" © The Economist Newspaper Limited, London 2010.

Now try this *continued*

Q 46 How does the writer's sentence structure stress the seriousness of the health problem?

2 A

In the next extract, the writer is describing attending a meeting of people who work in the aviation industry.

> Speaker after speaker bemoaned how the public had somehow misunderstood the aviation industry and had come to believe that aviation is a huge and disproportionate polluter. Let's get this in perspective, said repeated speakers: this is small fry compared with cars, factories, even homes. Why are we being singled out, they cried? Why not, they said, chase after other industries that could easily make efficiency savings instead of picking on an industry that gives so much to the world, yet is currently so economically fragile?

Q 47 Show how the writer's use of sentence structure conveys his unsympathetic view of the speakers at the conference.

2 A

In this extract from the passage on cities, the writer explains how immigrants have had an effect on London over hundreds of years.

You see their traces in the Spitalfields district, where a French Huguenot chapel became, successively, a synagogue and a mosque, tracking the movement of waves of migrants from poverty to suburban comfort. London's a place without an apparent structure that has proved extraordinarily successful at growing and changing. Its old residential core, sheltering in the approaches to its Tower of London fortress, has made the transition into the world's busiest banking centre. Its market halls and power stations have become art galleries and piazzas. Its simple terraced streets, built for the clerks of the Great Western Railway in Southall, have become home to the largest Sikh community outside India.

Q 48 Show how the sentence structure of the paragraph as a whole emphasises the idea of change.

2 A

E for Evaluation questions

The number of marks available for these questions varies from year to year. In recent exams you could have earned as few as 5 marks or as many as 15 for answering **E** for Evaluation questions.

U for Understanding questions ask you about **what** the writer says; **A** for Analysis questions are about **how** the writer says it; **E** for Evaluation questions are about how well, how convincingly, how suitably or **how effectively** the writer says it.

However, many Evaluation questions will be marked with a mixture of key letters. For example, you might be asked how effective an image is. In this case the question would be labelled **A/E**, as you have to be able to analyse the image before you can show how effective it is. Or, you might be asked how effective an anecdote is in supporting the writer's point of view. This sort of question would be labelled **U/E**, as you need to understand the point of view before you can evaluate how well the anecdote supports it.

It isn't easy to look at examples of individual Evaluation questions as they often depend on your appreciation of an entire passage, or of an argument that has been developed over a number of paragraphs. This is certainly an area where working through the practice tasks at the end of this chapter, or doing whole past papers, will be hugely helpful to you. You can also use more specific textbooks such as *Higher English Close Reading* by Ann Bridges and Colin Eckford or *Higher English Close Reading Preparation* by Colin Eckford.

We will be able to tackle a few questions. First, look at this worked example. Read the extract from the passage on the threat posed by comets and asteroids.

> In comparison with the more immediate threats to the continued survival of our species (acid rain, destruction of stratospheric ozone, the greenhouse effect, overpopulation), the danger of comet or asteroid impacts may seem remote. The problem with impact events, however, is that their consequences are so awesome that we can barely imagine what it would be like to be struck by a large object from space. And there would be limited opportunity for reflection following such an event.

Here's the question students were asked:

> **In these lines, the writer deals with various threats to the survival of our species. Show how effective the last sentence is as a conclusion to this paragraph.**   2 E

The first thing you need to know is that this, like many Evaluation tasks, is a sort of trick question. When the examiners ask you 'how effective' something is, they don't expect you to say that you actually don't find it effective. They have really decided already that the final sentence **is** an effective conclusion to the paragraph; they want you to be able to show **why** it is, and **how** this effect is created. So, there is a lot of analysis hiding behind this Evaluation question.

To be able to answer this question, you first of all need to understand the main idea of the paragraph. You won't know if the last sentence is an effective conclusion unless you grasp the ideas it is trying to pull together or sum up. So, there

is also a lot of Understanding hiding behind this Evaluation question.

The main idea of the paragraph is that although we face other threats that are more likely, the consequences of a comet impact, while unlikely, are actually far more serious.

Read the passage extract and the question again. This time, look for all the techniques the writer uses to make that last sentence. You might see that the sentence intensifies and clarifies the main idea by doing the following things:

- It reinforces the idea of widespread devastation.
- It uses (perhaps rather ironic) understatement.
- It seems to be a sort of addition or afterthought.
- It is a relatively short sentence.
- It begins, unusually, with 'And'.

This is only a 2 mark question, so you aren't going to need to use all five of these ideas to answer it. What you do need to do to get the full 2 marks is to connect a specific aspect of the sentence with the main idea of the paragraph. Here's the question again, this time followed by one possible answer:

> **Q49 In these lines, the writer deals with various threats to the survival of our species. Show how effective the last sentence is as a conclusion to this paragraph.**   2 E

By beginning with the word 'And' the writer shows that he has reached a summing up. This summing up effect is added to by his use of a relatively short sentence. This sense of summing up or ending effectively shows that a comet could cause the end of everything.

Now try this

The specimen answer above only uses two of the five techniques listed. Now write an answer of your own to question 49, basing your answer on any other technique(s) not so far used.

Extract: from "Impact! The Threat of Comets and Asteroids" by Verschur, Gerrit (1996). By permission of Oxford University Press, Inc.

Now try this

Answer these Evaluation questions from Higher past papers. The first is from the passage on asteroids and comets:

Astrophysics expert, Dr Alan Fitzsimmons of Queen's University, Belfast, who advises the UK NEO (Near-Earth Objects) Information Centre in Leicester, is optimistic that Earth will come through the latest asteroid scare unscathed: 'In all probability, within the next month we will know its future orbit with an accuracy which will mean we will be able to rule out any impact.'

Take careful note of the words 'to what extent' in this question. You might decide that you have complete confidence in Dr Fitzsimmons. You might have no confidence in him at all. You might have some confidence, but also some doubts. You are allowed to have any amount of confidence in him, so long as you can justify this 'by commenting on specific words and phrases in these lines'.

Q50 By commenting on specific words or phrases in these lines, show to what extent you would have confidence in Dr Fitzsimmons.

2 A/E

This one comes from the passage on whether human behaviour is causing the destruction of the environment.

Warnings of catastrophe come and go. Whatever their validity, we cannot and should not ask people to go back to a more restricted way of life. The restrictions would not work anyway, because they are impracticable. If they were enforced, they would be grotesquely unfair and socially divisive. If we really are facing an environmental crisis, then we are going to have to innovate and engineer our way out of it.

Q51 How effective do you find the writer's language in emphasising her opposition to placing restrictions on people's way of life?

2 A/E

Questions on both passages

At the end of the Close Reading exam paper you will find the above heading. In fact there is usually just one question here. In this question, you will be asked to compare the two passages in some way. It's usually worth 5 marks and is always an **E** for Evaluation question, sometimes with an element of Understanding or Analysis mixed in.

As the heading makes clear, you can't answer this question until you know both passages well and in full, which makes it impossible to practise this type of question here. This is another area where working through the practice tasks at the end of this chapter, or doing whole past papers, will be hugely helpful to you. You can also use more specific

textbooks such as *Higher English Close Reading* by Ann Bridges and Colin Eckford or *Higher English Close Reading Preparation* by Colin Eckford.

What we can do here is look at some advice for tackling these questions.

Timing

There are 5 marks available here, 10 per cent of the total for this exam and almost certainly more marks than for any other single question. If you're going to do this question justice, you'll need at least ten minutes. Twelve to fifteen minutes would be even better. Past paper practice will give you a chance to learn to pace yourself, so that you do have time to get these valuable final marks.

The wording of the question

The questions usually invite you to state some sort of preference for one passage over the other. You might be asked which writer you are more inclined to agree with, or which you find more thought-provoking, or which captures your interest more, or whose argument you find more persuasive.

You will be asked to **justify** this preference by referring closely to both passages. This means that you must either use short, well-chosen quotations or refer specifically to details in the texts.

The small differences in the wording of these questions are crucial. If you don't answer the question you are asked, you won't earn the marks. Sometimes the examiners will tell you to justify your answer by looking at the **ideas** of the texts – **what** the writers say. For example:

> Which writer's response are you more inclined to agree with? You must refer closely to the ideas of both passages as evidence for your answer.

Sometimes they will want you to justify your answers by looking at the **style** of the texts – **how** the writers say what they say. For example:

> By comparing the style of these passages, show which you find more effective in capturing your interest.

Sometimes you will be asked to look at a combination of **ideas and style**, at both **what** the writers say and **how** they say it. For example:

> Which passage do you find more effective in making you think about the implications for the human race of comet and asteroid impact? Justify your choice by referring to the ideas and style of both passages.

It's vital that you check and recheck the wording of the question to make sure that you are not wasting time and effort writing something that examiners can't give you marks for.

The style of your answer

If you've been following the advice in this chapter you have been using bullet points, headings or numbers to organise your answers and break them down into smaller sections. However, it's better to tackle just this final question rather differently, and to approach it like a mini essay.

- Start by setting up a line of thought that gives your basic answer to the question.

> I am more inclined to agree with Tommy Atkins's response to the subject. **OR**
>
> I find the second passage, by Joe Bloggs, more effective in capturing my interest. **OR**
>
> I found the first passage, by Jane Doe, more effective in making me think.

- Carry on by writing a number of brief, clear paragraphs. Each should begin with a topic sentence. There are two ways you could tackle these paragraphs:

1 You could compare or contrast the two passages in every paragraph.

2 Or, you could have some paragraphs about why you find one passage effective, convincing, interesting or whatever, and a smaller number of paragraphs about why you feel the other passage has shortcomings or is less successful.

Whichever approach you take, you **must** refer to both passages, though you needn't do so equally. If you only refer to one passage, you'll never get more than 3 marks out of 5.

Don't be too scared by the idea of writing several paragraphs or creating a mini essay. The examiners are looking for a quality answer that tackles the question, not a vast or long one. To reassure you about this, and to let you see more about how to approach these questions, here's an extract from a marking scheme. It goes with this question, which you've seen already:

> Which passage do you find more effective in making you think about the implications for the human race of comet and asteroid impact? Justify your choice by referring to the ideas and style of both passages.

This is what the answer scheme told markers to look for:

5 marks clear and intelligent understanding of both passages; sensible comments on style; evaluative comment is thoughtful and convincing

4 marks clear understanding of both passages; sensible comments on style; evaluative comment is reasonably convincing

3 marks understanding of both passages; acceptable comment(s) on style; there is some evaluative comment

Obviously you might also get just 1 or 2 marks, or even none, but as the marking guidelines show, it's not that hard to get 3 or 4, and not impossible to get 5, bearing in mind that when you reach this question you will know both passages very well.

Now try this

It's time now, if you haven't had the chance already, to tackle some whole tests. The first one is an example of what the Close Reading NAB is like. It is based on a single passage, is worth 30 marks, and should take you an hour.

The most important advice of all is **answer the question**. In this task you will encounter a number of 'Show how the writer's use of language …' questions. Remember, you must look at any appropriate language feature, not just word choice. Notice also that the final question is a 'To what extent …' one. Part of your evaluation here is to decide if you agree totally, partly, or not at all, and you must be able to justify this level of agreement.

In this passage, Sam Taylor, a novelist, writes persuasively in *The Herald* newspaper about the threat to our privacy.

A DANGEROUS ASSUMPTION

'If you have something that you don't want anyone to know, maybe you shouldn't be doing it in the first place.' Who said this, do you think? Stalin? J. Edgar Hoover? Well, no: in fact, it was

5 the chief executive of Google, Eric Schmidt, who controls one of the biggest internet companies in the world. So we ought to take what he says seriously, even if – especially if – we disagree with it.

10 Why? Not simply because, in one blunt, bland phrase, this extremely powerful and completely unaccountable man has casually erased our right to privacy, but because 10 or 20 years from now his statement might not seem outrageous at all.

15 It might, indeed, be considered utterly normal and unobjectionable. If our children grow up in Schmidt's brave new world – a world of CCTV cameras in classrooms and intimate revelations posted on the internet – then how will they even

20 know what they are losing? The entire notion of privacy as a human right is being eroded, and at a speed which is frightening.

There is a growing assumption that what has for centuries seemed an essential division

25 between our private selves and the world at large is now vanishing – and that this is somehow a natural and irreversible process.

The assumption is false. We do not have to go down this dangerous road. But the fact that

30 so many changes have taken place without any great debate or protest is symptomatic of its insidiousness. We are sleepwalking into a version of Orwell's *Nineteen Eighty-Four*. If we do not wake up and open our eyes,

35 we will be living in the land of Big Brother before we know it. It is significant already that, to a whole generation, the phrase 'Big Brother' conjures not a nightmarish vision of totalitarianism, but a voyeuristic and relatively

40 harmless reality-TV show.

The very ubiquity and triviality of Big Brother, Facebook and Twitter is what blinds us to the dangers they pose. Not that I am suggesting there is anything specifically sinister about reality TV or social networking websites; rather, it is the underlying values of a society in which they are so popular that needs to be questioned.

The case of Facebook is worth examining in more detail. It has become a vast money-making machine with 400 million users worldwide, and recently overtook Google as the most-used website in the world. Last December, Facebook's founder Mark Zuckerberg announced new privacy settings for all its users: certain information such as profile photographs and lists of friends would now be visible to everyone, while text, photo and video updates – which had all previously been private by default (seen only by your list of friends) – now became public by default. And this is the crucial point. Everyone had the choice of changing their privacy settings, but as is usually the case, the majority of us didn't bother. By doing nothing, hundreds of millions of people suddenly went from sharing the intimate details of their lives with a circle of friends and acquaintances to sharing those details with anyone who wishes to see them.

Zuckerberg's justification for changing Facebook's privacy settings was that it was simply reflecting broader changes in society. 'People have really gotten comfortable not only sharing more information and different kinds, but more openly and with more people,' he said. Again, the phrasing is bland, but in a way what Zuckerberg is suggesting is every bit as sinister as Eric Schmidt's quote at the beginning of this piece. He is claiming that the popularity of blogs, Twitter, YouTube and reality TV shows indicates a new willingness among ordinary people to make their private lives public. There is perhaps some truth to this, but it is a moot point. Whether Facebook is a symptom or a cause, the fact remains that our 'default settings' for privacy in society have been changed. And most of us aren't even aware of it.

Did you know that the United Kingdom is surveyed, 24 hours a day, by more than five million CCTV cameras – the highest proportion of cameras per citizen in the world? That most British secondary schools have at least 20 such cameras? That Google Street View now provides panoramic images of 95% of the streets in the UK? That the proposed new Communications Data Bill will require internet service providers to hand their records, currently retained for commercial purposes, to the Home Office for 'the prevention and detection of crime and protection of national security'?

What's most worrying is that our children won't be as shocked and angry about all this as I am. They are growing up in a world where remote-controlled cameras are everywhere, where their friends post pictures of them drunk or naked on the internet, where nightly entertainment often consists of watching real people break down in tears or humiliate themselves on live television. It hardly requires much of a science-fictional leap to imagine *their* children's DNA, fingerprints, iris scans, hourly movements, home environments, bank details, their most intimate conversations, being monitored and recorded from cradle to grave. Our children are being desensitised to the idea of their private lives being public property. What will they answer when their son or daughter asks: 'Daddy, what does "privacy" mean?'

Think again about Eric Schmidt's words: 'If you have something that you don't want anyone to know, maybe you shouldn't be doing it in the first place.' Well, maybe you shouldn't be making that assumption, Eric. His statement is, when you think about it, a breathtaking inversion of long-held human values: the idea that the desire for privacy is somehow sinister and suspicious. Is it really inconceivable that people might not want anyone (or, rather, everyone) to know about some aspect of their lives without that aspect being criminal or shameful?

We are halfway down a road that will take us to a place most of us don't want to go: we should turn back before it is too late.

Single passage – 'privacy' – questions

1   Read lines 1–22.

   (a) Explain how lines 1–9 create an effective opening to the passage.   **2 A**

   (b) What are the writer's main objections to Schmidt's statement?   **2 U**

   (c) Show how the writer's use of language in lines 10–22 conveys his strong feelings   **4 A**
        on the subject. Refer in your answer to at least two language features such as word
        choice, sentence structure, imagery …

2   Read lines 23–40.

   (a) How effective do you find the imagery of 'sleepwalking' to convey what the writer   **2 A/E**
        is saying in these lines?

   (b) In what way, according to the writer, does the younger generation misunderstand   **2 U**
        the phrase 'Big Brother'?

3   What, according to the writer in lines 41–48, 'needs to be questioned'?   **1 U**

4   Read lines 49–87.

   (a) Summarise the main points the writer is making about privacy by using the   **3 U**
        example of Facebook.

   (b) Show how the writer's use of language in lines 70–87 makes clear his disapproval   **2 A**
        of Mark Zuckerberg.

5   Show how the writer's use of language in lines 88–101 increases the impact of what   **2 A**
    he is saying.

6   Read lines 102–120.

   (a) Why, according to the writer, are young people not as 'shocked and angry' as he is   **1 U**
        about the invasion of privacy?

   (b) What vision does he have of life for his grandchildren?   **1 U**

7   Read lines 121–133.

   (a) Explain why the writer thinks Schmidt's statement is 'a breathtaking inversion of   **2 U**
        long-held human values' (lines 126–128).

   (b) Referring to one language feature in these lines, discuss to what extent it provides   **2 A/E**
        an appropriate way to conclude the passage.

8   To what extent do you agree with the writer's concerns in the passage as a whole?   **4 E**

                                                                              Total marks   30

Now try this

The second test is an example of what the Close Reading exam is like. It is based on two passages,
is worth 50 marks, and should take you an hour and three quarters. Watch out for that Evaluation
question on both passages when you get to it!

Passage 1

Steve Connor, science editor of *The Independent* newspaper, outlines the history of Stonehenge and reports on some recent theories about its purpose.

BRITAIN'S MOST FAMOUS STONE AGE SITE

It is generally accepted that Stonehenge, Britain's most famous Stone Age site, was built in three stages by three different groups of people over a period of about 800 years. The first stage was a
5 circle of timbers surrounded by a ditch and bank and was constructed by what archaeologists have called the Windmill Hill people, named after their earthworks at the site of the same name. They used animal bones and antlers to dig the trench
10 and the circle of 56 holes to hold the wooden posts of the first structure. Radiocarbon dating of these utensils has recorded a date of 3100BC.

The next stage was built by the Beaker Folk, who came from Europe at the end of the
15 Neolithic Period, and began about 2500BC. They brought the bluestones from Prescelli Mountains in Pembroke, some 245 miles away. It was an impressive operation given that some of these stones weighed five tons and had to be hauled
20 over land and floated up rivers.

The final, third phase of the construction occurred about 2300BC by the Wessex People, who were Bronze Age pioneers. They dug up and re-arranged the bluestones and brought in even
25 bigger stones from Marlborough Downs some 20 miles away. These giant sandstones, called Sarsen stones, were hammered to size and shaped with carpenter's joints so that they could sit on top of each other to form the classic lintels that have
30 made Stonehenge so unique. The hauling and erection of the Sarsen stones is an engineering miracle – some of them weigh 45 tons.

Little can be said with certainty about the purpose of Stonehenge, but the site was almost
35 certainly a gathering place for many years for people from all over southern Britain and possibly Europe. Jane Evans of the British Geological Survey has found evidence for instance that people brought their own cattle to Stonehenge
40 from as far away as Wales, or even further afield. Isotope analysis on the cattle teeth found at Durrington Wells shows that the animals were reared in a different geological place to where they were slaughtered. Dr Evans suggests it shows
45 that there was a 'bring-your-own beef barbeque' at Stonehenge which was probably a centre for grand feasts long before the construction of the ancient stone circle.

There are many other speculations about
50 Stonehenge, some of them decidedly outlandish. It is widely claimed that Stonehenge was built to celebrate or mark the summer and winter solstices, when the Sun reaches its furthest point north and south of the equator, respectively,
55 which is denoted by the point at which the Sun rises or sets on the horizon. The alignment of the stones would appear to have been designed to mark the two solstices, and hence the points at which summer and winter reach their mid-
60 points.

Some scholars have gone further to suggest that Stonehenge was a far more sophisticated astronomical instrument that could, for instance, be used to predict lunar eclipses, when
65 the Earth passes in between the Sun and the Moon. They believe that the inner 'horseshoe' of 19 bluestones at the centre of the circle acted as a long-term calendar to calculate when the next lunar eclipse would occur – when, in other
70 words, the shadow of the Earth would fall upon the Moon.

Another theory is that Stonehenge was an elaborate burial site for important people. A Professor of archaeology at Sheffield University
75 believes that the stone structure was the 'domain of the dead', whereas the nearby 'wooden henge' structure at Durrington Wells a couple of miles away was the 'domain of the living'. Durrington Wells would have been one of the
80 biggest, if not the biggest, settlement in north-west Europe at that time. It would probably have been used as temporary accommodation for people attending Stonehenge in mid-winter and mid-summer, he said. No human burials
85 have been found at Durrington Wells, although 29 cremation burials have been found at Stonehenge during excavations that took place in the 1920s. The Professor believes there may

have been up to 240 people buried at Stonehenge during prehistoric times and that they may be the descendants of a single family – prehistoric chiefs, perhaps even ancient royalty – who over several generations were awarded the privilege of having their remains interred at the sacred site.

Most recently, archaeologists have excavated a small area within the site and found evidence to suggest that Stonehenge was once a centre of healing, where people would come from far and wide in the hope of being cured of their ills. The evidence for this claim is not very straightforward, but then again nothing ever is with this mysterious ancient monument. The two archaeologists, Professor Tim Darvill and Geoff Wainwright, first of all noted the abnormal number of corpses found in tombs near Stonehenge that display signs of serious physical injury or disease. One of the most famous of these is the 'Amesbury Archer' buried about two miles from Stonehenge. He is known to have originated from the Alps and had suffered a serious knee injury and a potentially fatal dental problem before he died.

His history seemed to match many of the other bodies found near the site. Analysis of the mineral isotopes found in human teeth show that about half of these people were not native to the Stonehenge area. Taken together, this could suggest that some people came to the site in order to benefit from some kind of healing powers that the bluestones were perhaps supposed to have.

Intriguingly, the two archaeologists also found that about three times as many stone chippings were taken from the bluestones compared to the Sarsen stones. Did people flake off pieces of the bluestones, in order to have a little bit to take away … as souvenirs … as lucky charms?

It is unlikely we will ever know the real truth behind Stonehenge – even why this particular part of southern England was deemed so important remains one of its most enduring mysteries. Although dating technology gets better all the time, and much of the site has still to be properly excavated, Stonehenge, because it represents what was in the minds of people long dead, will always be a mystery.

Passage 2

Robin McKie, science editor of *The Observer* newspaper, reflects on the same recent theories about Stonehenge.

THE THEORIES PILE UP

There was a familiar ring to last week's media fanfare surrounding the announcement that scientists had uncovered the true purpose of Stonehenge. According to the new theory's backer, archaeologist Geoffrey Wainwright, it was really the Lourdes of the Bronze Age, a place where the sick and wounded sought cures from the monument's great bluestones which had been dragged to Wiltshire from Wales specifically because of their magical healing properties. The evidence is, apparently, in all the ancient graves in the area filled with sick and deformed people. Thus Stonehenge was really an accident and emergency ward for the south west of England.

As a result, we were greeted with a cluster of headlines of the 'Revealed: the secret of Stonehenge' variety which, some readers might have noticed, had a close similarity to those that greeted the news earlier in the year that a different group of scientists had found the true purpose of the great Wiltshire stone circle: it was really a royal burial ground for an ancient dynasty of old Brits, said a group of researchers from Sheffield University. Radiocarbon dating of human remains found nearby suggested the place was used as a cemetery right from the start of construction work in 3000BC, it was argued. Not for the common folk, it must be stressed – strictly for prehistoric toffs.

And as we move back in time, the theories
30 about Stonehenge slowly pile up: we come across
news that researchers had shown the stone
circles had been used as a giant computer; that
others had found it was really an observatory for
studying stars and predicting the seasons; that a
35 couple of individuals had demonstrated beyond
doubt that its rings had acted as a docking pad for
alien spaceships; while one Canadian researcher
produced the jaw-dropping idea that the great
henge had been built as a giant fertility symbol,
40 constructed in the shape of the female sexual organ.
But that, of course, is the wonderful thing
about Stonehenge: there are more theories about its
meaning and purpose than there are stones inside
it. This is a trend that goes right back to the idea,
45 popular in the Middle Ages, that its monoliths
had been assembled on Salisbury Plain by King
Arthur's resident wizard, Merlin – though nobody
seems to have bothered to figure out why he did so.
In fact, Stonehenge took at least 1,000 years
50 to build, starting from rings of wooden poles
to its current complex status and its use clearly
changed over the millenniums. Recent studies
suggest it may have been 'Christianised' in the
first millennium AD and at one point was used as
55 a place of execution by the Anglo-Saxons to judge
from the 7th-century gallows found there.

This multiplicity of use increases
opportunities for archaeologists to pin their
pet theories to the great stone monument.
60 The crucial point is, as archaeologist Jacquetta
Hawkes once remarked, that every age gets
the Stonehenge it deserves. Hence in medieval
times, it was built by giants, while in the 1960s,
at the dawn of the computing era, researchers
65 said you could have used it as a giant calculating
machine, while in more mystical New Age times,
it was clearly a spaceport for aliens. In fact, you
can come up with just about any idea to explain
a structure like Stonehenge if you stare at it for
70 long enough.
Just what that the latest flurry of Stonehenge
theories says about the 21st century is less
clear. I would argue that it is probably best
viewed today as a monument to government
75 prevarication and deceit. Having promised a
decade ago that it would bury and realign the
roads that surround and disfigure Britain's most
important ancient monument, ministers now
seem to have abandoned any attempt to protect
80 the monument and restore the site to its ancient
glory, for the simple reason they are too mean-
spirited and short-sighted to see its value.

Questions on Passage 1

1 Read lines 1–32.

    (a) Outline very briefly the three stages in the construction of Stonehenge.   **3 U**

    (b) Show how the writer's word choice in lines 13–32 conveys his admiration for the work on Stonehenge.   **2 A**

2 To what extent would you have confidence in the theory of Dr Jane Evans? Justify your answer by close reference to lines 33–48.   **3 E**

3 Read lines 49–71.

    (a) Outline briefly the theories described in these lines.   **2 U**

    (b) Show how the writer's use of language in these lines makes clear that they are 'speculations' (line 49).   **2 A**

4 Read lines 72–94.

    (a) What, according to the Professor, was the function of Durrington Wells?   **2 U**

    (b) Show how the writer's word choice in these lines adds to the idea that Stonehenge is a very special place.   **2 A**

(c) How convincing do you find the Professor's theory about Stonehenge? Justify   **2 E**
your answer by close reference to the text.

5 Read lines 95–121.

  (a) Explain how the 'Amesbury Archer' supports the theory described in these lines.   **4 U**

  (b) Show how the writer's use of language in these lines makes clear that this is a   **2 A**
     mixture of fact and speculation.

6 Show how the writer makes effective use of sentence structure in lines 122–137 to   **3 A**
highlight the points he is making.

                                                                                 27

Questions on Passage 2

7 Show how the writer's use of language in lines 1–14 creates a tone which is less than   **4 A**
serious.

8 Show how the writer's use of language in lines 15–28 conveys his attitude to the   **2 A**
media coverage of the announcement.

9 Read lines 29–40.

  (a) Show how the structure of this paragraph helps the writer express his ideas clearly.   **2 A**

  (b) How does the writer convey his scepticism about any **two** of the theories in this   **2 A**
     paragraph?

10 Show how the style of lines 41–48 differs from that of lines 49–56.   **2 A**

11 What does the writer mean by 'every age gets the Stonehenge it deserves'? (lines 61–62)   **2 U**

12 Read lines 71–82.

  (a) What criticisms does the writer make of the Government?   **2 U**

  (b) Show how his use of language in these lines makes clear the strength of his   **2 A**
     feelings on the subject.

                                                                                 18

Question on both passages

13 Which passage is more effective in engaging your interest in the history and   **5 E**
interpretations of Stonehenge? Justify your choice by referring to the **ideas and/or
style** of **both passages**.

Total marks   **50**

You may have noticed that some of the types of questions you learned about in this chapter – for
example, link questions and meaning in context questions – did not appear in either of these longer
practice tasks. The examiners always ask the questions they feel passages deserve, and every sort of
question will not come up every time. However, you still need to know how to answer every question
type, because you don't know when they will come up.

CHAPTER 3 Poetry: 'Incident'

The three genres of literature you can write about in the exam are **Drama**, **Poetry** and **Prose**. Writing about **Drama** involves showing your knowledge and understanding of the script of a play. We can't cover that in this book, as there isn't space to include and study an entire drama text. You will find two pieces of **Prose** and work to go with them later in this book. First, though, we are going to study some **Poetry**.

 Getting in

You're about to read a poem. It's called 'Incident'. Before you read the poem, think about the word *incident* itself. It's often used in news reports, either on TV or in the papers.

Now try this

To get you thinking about how news reports often use that word *incident*, choose one of the following headlines and write the news story that goes with it. You can, if you want, try to make the story about quite a quirky or bizarre incident.

INCIDENT AT BUCKINGHAM PALACE

INCIDENT IN PARLIAMENT

INCIDENT AT
(use the name of a football ground)

INCIDENT AT
(use the name of your school)

INCIDENT AT
(use the name of your favourite shop)

When everyone has written their news stories, you may want to read them out in class.

 Meeting the text

You're about to see the poem for the first time, but it won't look quite the way the writer, Norman MacCaig, published it. He divided it into short lines and stanzas, which is after all what most poems look like. You're going to get it in one solid block.

Now try this

Look at the block version of the poem. Working with a partner, try to divide it into the lines and stanzas you think the writer used, and add any punctuation you think he used. You can have two clues to help you:

1 There are three stanzas in the poem.

2 The stanzas are all different lengths.

> Incident I look across the table and think fiery with love Ask me go on ask me to do something impossible something freakishly useless something unimaginable and inimitable like making a finger break into blossom or walking for half an hour in twenty minutes or remembering tomorrow I will you to ask it But all you say is Will you give me a cigarette And I smile and returning to the marvellous world of possibility I give you one with a hand that trembles with a human trembling

Once you've worked out how you think the poem should go, share your answers with the rest of the class. Make sure you can explain why you divided it up the way you did. What clues were you using to help you?

The final published poem is shown on page 74. You should only turn to that page when you've completed this task.

Norman MacCaig was born in Edinburgh in 1910 and died there in 1996. He went to Edinburgh University and then worked as a teacher and writer for the rest of his life. During the war he was imprisoned for being a conscientious objector, someone who refused to join the army.

Many of his poems were about Edinburgh, or about the area near Lochinver in the Highlands where he also spent a lot of time. Some of the techniques he used most often are ones that we will see in this poem: precise language, striking images, first person narration, wit and repetition.

Norman MacCaig

Thinking through

Now that you've spent some time thinking about the words of the poem, work out the answers to the following questions. Make sure you look at the correct text of the poem on page 74 to help you.

1   What is the incident in the poem?

2   At what point in the poem does this incident happen?

3   Think back to the short news stories you wrote before you read the poem. Do you think this incident is worth being called an incident? Explain your answer.

4   Why do you think the poet calls it an incident?

Share your answers with the rest of the class. Be ready to change your own answers, or add to them, in the light of what you hear other people say.

Let's get to work

This might seem like a very tiny, unimportant poem, about a very tiny, unimportant event. Actually, though, both the poem and the subject really do matter. The event in the poem, handing over a cigarette, is an incident in two ways. In the truest sense of the word, it is incidental; just a tiny happening that doesn't affect the rest of the world. But to the speaker in the poem, fired up with love, being able to hand over a cigarette is an incident in the other sense – it's worth writing about, newsworthy.

The poem itself matters, and is a good one to begin your Higher studies with, because it's such a good example of the way language works in poetry. Although it's only eighty-seven words and eighteen lines long, it demonstrates how poets make their language work incredibly hard. In this poem every mark on the page, even the one and only full stop, tells us something when we read it. As we study this poem we'll look at all the effects MacCaig gets from his chosen language.

Here's what the published version of the poem looks like:

> **INCIDENT**
>
> I look across the table and think
> (fiery with love)
> Ask me, go on, ask me
> to do something impossible
> 5 something freakishly useless
> something unimaginable and inimitable
>
> like making a finger break into blossom
> or walking for half an hour in twenty minutes
> or remembering tomorrow
>
> 10 I will you to ask it.
> But all you say is
> Will you give me a cigarette?
> And I smile and
> returning to the marvellous world
> 15 of possibility
> I give you one
> with a hand that trembles
> with a human trembling
>
> *Norman MacCaig*

Immediacy

This is a very immediate poem. In other words, it feels to us as if it is very alive and real. There are two main techniques MacCaig uses to create this effect.

1   He uses the first person, telling it by using the 'I' voice.

2   He writes the poem in present tense.

Now try this

You're going to rewrite the poem. Put it in third person, using **he** or **she** instead of **I** and **you**. As you rewrite the poem you should also change it from present to past tense. The first line has been done for you.

> He looked across the table and thought …

When you have finished your rewrite, answer these questions:

1   Which stanza changed most?

2   Which stanza changed least?

3   How do the changes affect the poem?

That immediacy helps us to work out something else about this relationship.

Now try this

Now answer these two questions:

1   Do you think this is a long-established relationship, or quite a new one?

2   How can you tell?

The narrator

This poem was written by Norman MacCaig. He made it up and all the language choices in it are of course his. However, the poem is told in first person, using the 'I' voice, so we have to read it pretending that all the language is coming from the mind of the narrator. When you write about the **language** of the poem in an essay it's better to say what MacCaig does, or to write about the techniques the poet uses. When you write about the **character** in the poem, or about what he thinks or does, make sure you are calling this person the **narrator** or the **speaker**.

Let's see what we can find out about that narrator from the poem. Most readers usually think the poem is spoken by a fairly young man. What evidence do we have to back up this feeling?

Now try this

Copy and complete the table to show how the poem gives evidence to suggest that the speaker is a young man. Part of the table has been filled in already to help you. The blank spaces at the end are there in case you need them – you might not.

Technique	Evidence/quotation	Explanation
conversational style	'Ask me, go on, ask me'	The informality of the conversation style suggests a younger speaker. So does the repetition – it's almost like a child begging for attention.
young person's attitude to time	'remembering tomorrow'	
	'trembling'	
lets slip that he may be blushing/ embarrassed		
desperation for a response		
optimism, not cynical about the world yet		

We said earlier that poets make their language work incredibly hard. For an example of that, let's just look at the word 'fiery' in line 2 when the speaker describes himself as '(fiery with love)'. It could suggest three equally possible things about the narrator:

1 He is blushing because he is nervous or embarrassed.

2 He is fired up, full of passion and energy because of the love he feels.

3 The table may be in a bar or pub (this poem was written long before the ban on smoking in public places) and he may be red in the face because he's been drinking – maybe he felt the need for a drink to get his courage up.

When writers create two or more possible meanings like this, without making one of those meanings seem more right or more likely than the other(s), this is known as **ambiguity**. It's a technique that we will see again when we study Philip Larkin's 'Afternoons'.

By the way, putting the words '(fiery with love)' in brackets like that is a technique called an **aside**. It means the speaker has broken away from his main line of thought.

Now try this

To help you work out why MacCaig uses an aside here, answer these questions:

1 Who is the narrator talking to in most of the poem?

2 Who do you think he is addressing in the aside?

3 Why do you think MacCaig chose to use an aside here?

Just before we leave the speaker alone for a bit, we should admit that we don't know for sure if the speaker is meant to be male, or if the 'you' in this poem is meant to be female. A writer can choose to use any kind of first person narrator at all. The speaker might be a young man in a bar, or he might be a bright green alien sitting at a table hovering a hundred miles above the surface of the planet Jupiter. However, since Norman MacCaig was male and married, it's easier for us to assume that the speaker is male and that his beloved is female.

The beloved

We know even less about her than we do about him. All we know for sure is that she smokes.

Now try this

Think about these two questions, and be ready to explain your answers to the rest of the class:

1 Does she love him?

2 In what sense does it actually not matter whether she does or not?

We'll think a little more about the question of whether she loves him when we look at how the writer uses the words 'will you' later in the poem.

Repetition

Your teachers probably tell you to vary your vocabulary in your own writing. When a professional writer doesn't do this, it doesn't mean he or she has a smaller vocabulary than you do; it means the repetition is there for a reason. That's certainly true in 'Incident'.

Now try this

Make a list of all the repetitions used in 'Incident'. You may need to copy out slightly longer quotations, then underline the repeated words. You should end up with five examples. The first one has been done for you.

1 <u>Ask me</u>, go on, <u>ask me</u>

2 _____

3 _____

4 _____

5 _____

Some of these repetitions deserve careful analysis, because they are an important part of how the poem works.

We've already seen that the repetition of 'ask me' is one sign that the speaker is probably quite a young man. Now let's look at the repeated use of 'something'.

> Ask me, go on, ask me
> to do **something** <u>impossible</u>
> **something** <u>freakishly useless</u>
> **something** <u>unimaginable</u> and <u>inimitable</u>

The more the speaker repeats the word 'something', the more we see that he's actually willing to do anything for his beloved. The repetition of 'something' suggests that other word 'anything'.

In fact, as well as repeating the specific word 'something' here, MacCaig is also repeating ideas in these lines. He does this with the words that come after each of the uses of 'something', and have been underlined in the quotation above. They all have pretty similar meanings to each other. They are all about unfeasible things. It's as if he wants to be a sort of superhero of love.

Interestingly, they are actually all negative words. The prefixes **im-**, **un-**, and **in-** are negative ones, and we wouldn't usually see any positive ideas in words like 'freakishly', or 'useless'. Yet MacCaig manages to make them part of a very positive poem, and make them seem like good things to do for someone we love.

Now try this

Have you ever had one of those odd moments with a friend, or a family member, when you both say the same thing at the same time? Have you ever been thinking about someone, just at the very minute that person phoned, or arrived at your door? Have you ever had your boyfriend or girlfriend say out loud what you were thinking at that precise moment?

If you've got a story about this happening to you, tell it to your partner or to the class. Then answer this question:

- When something like that happens to us, what do we believe it shows about our relationship with the other person?

That question leads us on to the next repetition that's worth looking at, which is this one:

> I **will you** to ask it.
> But all you say is
> **Will you** give me a cigarette?

Earlier on we looked at the question of whether the girl loves the young narrator. As far as the poem is concerned, it really doesn't matter if she does or not. The purpose of the poem is to show us how he is feeling, and how love affects him. To him, of course, it matters a great deal whether she loves him or not. That's why this repeated use of 'will you' matters. As soon as he thinks those words, she says them. That suggests that actually they are very well in tune with each other. It's almost as if she reads his mind, and that implies that maybe she does love him after all.

Now look at the last two lines of the poem:

> with a hand that trembles
> with a human trembling

They're nearly identical. They both begin with 'with a', the end words 'trembles' and 'trembling' are variations of each other, and there's even a sort of alliteration going on across the lines because after each 'with a' there's a word that starts with h, either 'hand' or 'human'.

MacCaig is doing this to emphasise the strength of the speaker's emotions. The young man is so moved by being in love, and so happy to be able to do a simple thing for his beloved, that his hand shakes as he hands the cigarette over. The repetition drives that home, and by calling his trembling 'human' he shows that he doesn't need to be the sort of superhero implied earlier to be successful.

There's one more repetition to look at now, one that you might not have noticed as the two words are so far apart in the poem. In fact it might be more correct to call it a sort of echo. In stanza 1 the young man wishes to do

> something **impossible**

while in stanza 3 he describes himself

> returning to the marvellous world of **possibility**

That contrast between impossible and possible is hugely important in helping us to understand what the poem is saying about love. The narrator loves the woman so much that he would do anything for her, and he'd love to do 'impossible' things to prove his love. Yet he loves her so much that even being able to fulfil one simple tiny request makes him happy. If the real 'world of possibility' is a place where he can do what she asks him to, then that world is 'marvellous' for him.

Imagery

One of the most striking things about this poem is the way that MacCaig uses three images, three word pictures, in the middle stanza. Each one is quite surreal and bizarre, which goes with the speaker's desire to do impossible things. We're going to look at the three images in turn.

> like making a finger break into blossom

This creates an immediate picture in our minds.

Women quite often get bunches of flowers from the men who love them, so we can see that MacCaig is using quite a common idea here. Yet he uses the idea in an uncommon way by having the narrator offer to do something magical or miraculous – he's not going to buy her a bunch of flowers, he's going to become flowers for her.

There's something else in that image too. Look at the picture above. For many people, love leads to marriage, and they start to wear a ring on a particular finger. This image might suggest that the narrator hopes to marry his beloved.

Here's the second image:

> or walking for half an hour in twenty minutes

This sounds like another part of the superhero idea we picked up on earlier, the idea that the narrator can somehow bend or defeat time to prove his love. It might suggest that whenever they are apart he wants to speed up either himself or time so that they can be together again.

The third image is

> or remembering tomorrow

This once again suggests impossible and superhuman power over time. It's very optimistic too, because it carries the idea that he thinks tomorrow will be

worth remembering, as if he is sure that they have a good future together ahead of them.

Both those images together

> or walking for half an hour in twenty minutes
> or remembering tomorrow

help us again to see that the speaker is meant to be a young man. He has a young view of time. The present (which is the tense he tells the poem in) and the future matter more to him than the past.

All three images together

> like making a finger break into blossom
> or walking for half an hour in twenty minutes
> or remembering tomorrow

show the great extent of the narrator's love.

Now try this

You have already seen a picture of the first image, the blossom one. Copy it into your notebook. Then draw a picture for each of the other two images. Label all three pictures with notes that will help you remember what the images suggest and how they work.

Turning point

A **turning point** is a point where things change. What comes after is very different to what went before. A turning point can go with a change in mood, or with a change in events (we'll see one of those later in the book in the poem 'Porphyria's Lover'), but in this poem the turning point marks a change between fantasy and reality.

The most fantastical point of the poem is the set of images in stanza 2, the ones we've just looked at. The turning point comes just after these images.

> I will you to ask it.
> But all you say is
> Will you give me a cigarette?

Turning point is a technique in itself. You can write in an essay, 'MacCaig uses a turning point in the poem.' But MacCaig actually creates that turning point by using two other, smaller techniques.

Now try this

Copy and complete the paragraph to explain how MacCaig creates the turning point.

MacCaig creates a _____ _____ in this poem by his use of two techniques. The first is his use of a _____ _____. This marks a clear end to the first stage of the poem, which is the part of the poem that is concerned with _____. The second technique is his use of the word _____. This is effective word choice because it suggests that _____ _____. It introduces the second stage of the poem, which is concerned with _____.

The fancy name for what MacCaig does with

> I will you to ask it.

is that he creates an **end-stopped line**, that is, a line of the poem that ends on a full stop at the end of a sentence. He doesn't do this by accident. If you look back at the whole poem, which was printed on page 74, you will see that the full stop here is the only one the writer uses in the whole poem. There were other places where he could have used a full stop but chose not to, so the fact that he does choose to use one here means that it's important. He needs it to help drive home the change between fantasy and reality that happens at the turning point.

Bathos

MacCaig's use of a turning point leads him on to his next technique: **bathos**. This word means a let-down created with words, usually created by a contrast between high and low. Bathos can be funny, even if that wasn't the effect the writer was after:

> The ballerina rose gracefully *en pointe* and extended one slender leg behind her, like a dog at a fire hydrant.

Earlier in the poem we saw the speaker offering to do the miraculous, heroic and impossible. Now we come down to earth with a bump as she asks him

> Will you give me a cigarette?

Because MacCaig is a skilled poet, his bathos isn't clumsy or ridiculous like the example of the ballerina above. Instead it draws us towards the end of the poem, where we can see how amazed and delighted the speaker is to give her what she asks for. He doesn't feel let down by only being given this task to do for her, so we don't feel let down in reading it.

Technique revision

Now that you've worked your way through the whole chapter about 'Incident' you should know the poem and its techniques very well. Before you prove this by writing an essay about it, here's a revision task.

In Chapter 8 you will learn how to use the **PEE** structure to build paragraphs in your essays. This stands for making a **Point** about something the writer is doing or a technique the writer uses; giving **Evidence** (preferably by quoting) from the text; and finally explaining the **Effect** on the reader.

Now try this

Take a large piece of paper. Mark it up into a grid like the one below. For every technique, fill in a quotation from the poem, and explain the effect it has on the reader. Some boxes have been filled in for you.

Point: a technique	Evidence: a quotation	Explanation of effect
title	Incident	Shows that what happens is incidental – just a very small event – but also is an incident in the newspaper sense of being worth recording
first person	I look across the table	Makes the poem seem immediate and engaging
present tense	I will you to ask it	
conversational style		

You can carry on the rest of the table yourself. You'll need a big bit of paper, maybe two, as you need to add the following techniques:

ambiguity   aside   negative prefixes

turning point   bathos   end-stopped line

images (several with different effects)

repetition (several quotations and different effects)

You'll find more of these revision exercises at the end of the other two poetry chapters in this book, and also at the end of each of the three prose chapters. The task won't be explained so fully again, you'll just get a list of the techniques to revise, but you can look back to this page to remind you what to do.

Essay writing

Later in this book there is a chapter about how to write a Critical Essay (Chapter 8). Although the advice in that chapter is general, and will help you to write all your Critical Essays, most of the examples in that chapter are based on 'Incident' and on the work we've done on this poem.

You may want to go to that chapter now and work through it to write your first literature essay.

By the way, one reason why this particular poem is brilliant to write essays about is because it's very easy to get to know the whole poem. By the time you've studied it in this chapter, and revised it again before an exam, you'll probably find that you actually know it by heart. That means you'll easily be able to pick out suitable quotations. You can then go on and use these to prove points in your essay, or you can analyse them to show the writer's style and technique.

Possible essay choices

Once you have studied the chapter on essay writing, you might like to try one of the following essays, which are also suitable for 'Incident'.

Above the poetry essay choices on the exam paper you'll see the following words:

> Answers to questions on poetry should address relevantly the central concern(s)/theme(s) of the text(s) and be supported by reference to appropriate poetic techniques such as: imagery, verse form, structure, mood, tone, sound, rhythm, rhyme, characterisation, contrast, setting, symbolism, word choice …

Now look at the essay choices:

> Choose a poem in which a chance encounter or a seemingly unimportant incident acquires increased significance by the end of the poem.

> Show how the poet's development of the encounter or incident leads you to a deeper understanding of the poem's theme.

OR

Choose a poem whose main feature is the striking use of imagery.

Show how the writer has made use of imagery to add significantly to your appreciation of the poem as a whole.

OR

Choose a poem in which contrast is important in developing a theme.

Explore the poet's use of contrast and show why it is important in developing a key theme of the poem.

OR

Choose a poem in which the central concern(s) is/are clarified for you in the closing lines.

Show how these closing lines provide an effective clarification of the central concerns of the poem.

Comparing and contrasting

One of the other poems in this book, 'Porphyria's Lover' by Robert Browning, is also told in the first person, and is also narrated by a young man in love. Once you have studied that poem too, you could compare and contrast it with 'Incident'.

Now try this

Work with a partner or a small group. Get a large sheet of paper and divide it in two. Mark one side **Similarities** and the other side **Differences**. Compare and contrast the two poems and use the sheet to create a record or poster of your discoveries. The first few lines have been done for you.

Similarities	Differences
both use first person narration	'Incident' in present tense, 'PL' in past
both narrated by young man in love	

CHAPTER 4
Poetry: 'Porphyria's Lover'

 Getting in

You need to prepare for this task a few days before starting work on this chapter of the book. Everyone in the class needs to try to find a news story about a bizarre crime. You could bring in a newspaper clipping, or a printout of a web page. Here are two to get you started.

> A Hungarian bank lost more than $28,000 in cash after a security van was rammed – by a prison van carrying convicted bank robbers.
>
> While rescue personnel saved the prisoners from their burning van, a small fortune disappeared from the security van as bags of money spilled out onto the streets of Budapest.
>
> Civilians were seen driving up and grabbing the cash before speeding off again.
>
> By the time law enforcement arrived the money was gone and there was no trace of those that had taken it.
>
> Police suspected the robbery may have been organised from jail by crime bosses and carried out by gang members still on the outside.
>
> But after interviews with the inmates – who were being transported from court back to jail – those suspicions were quickly refuted. The prisoners claimed they had nothing to do with the crash.
>
> 'The bank remains very suspicious. Of all the vehicles that could have hit their van, it had to be one full of bank robbers,' said a police spokesman.

> Italian police have issued video footage of a man who has been hypnotising supermarket checkout staff and getting them to hand over the cash.
>
> In every case, according to reports, the last thing staff remember is a man leaning over and saying 'Look into my eyes' before suddenly finding the till is empty.
>
> In the latest incident, captured on CCTV, the man walked into a bank in Ancona in northern Italy. He waited until he got to a female bank clerk and, according to the video footage, appears to hypnotise her into handing over more than £600. He then calmly walked out.
>
> The cashier, who was shown the film, reportedly has no memory of the incident. She only realised what had happened when she saw the money missing. Checks of CCTV cameras in the bank showed her being hypnotised by the man.
>
> Italian police are now looking for the suspect – who bears an uncanny resemblance to Saddam Hussein – who they believe is of either Indian or North African extraction.

Read your clipping to the rest of the class, or to your group. Explain why you chose it.

 Meeting the text

You are about to read a poem in which the narrator confesses to a crime. As you read it for the first time, see if you can work out the answers to these questions:

1 What is the **crime**?
2 Who is the **criminal**?
3 Who is the **victim**?
4 **Where** and **when** does the crime take place?
5 What is the **motive**?
6 What unusual **weapon** is used to commit this crime?

Madhouse Cell
PORPHYRIA'S LOVER

The rain set early in tonight,
The sullen wind was soon awake,
It tore the elm-tops down for spite,
And did its worst to vex the lake:
5   I listened with heart fit to break,
When glided in Porphyria; straight
She shut the cold out and the storm,
And kneeled and made the cheerless grate
Blaze up, and all the cottage warm;
10 Which done, she rose, and from her form
Withdrew the dripping cloak and shawl,
And laid her soiled gloves by, untied
Her hat and let her damp hair fall,
And, last, she sat down by my side
15 And called me. When no voice replied,
She put my arm around her waist,
And made her smooth white shoulder bare,
And all her yellow hair displaced,
And, stooping, made my cheek lie there,
20 And spread, o'er all, her yellow hair,
Murmuring how she loved me – she
Too weak for all her heart's endeavour,
To set its struggling passion free
From pride, and vainer ties dissever,
25 And give herself to me forever.
But passion sometimes would prevail,
Nor could tonight's gay feast restrain
A sudden thought for one so pale
For love of her, and all in vain:
30 So, she was come through wind and rain.
Be sure I looked up at her eyes

Happy and proud; at last I knew
Porphyria worshipped me; surprise
Made my heart swell, and still it grew
35 While I debated what to do.
That moment she was mine, mine, fair,
Perfectly pure and good: I found
A thing to do, and all her hair
In one long yellow string I wound
40 Three times her little throat around,
And strangled her. No pain felt she;
I am quite sure she felt no pain.
As a shut bud that holds a bee,
I warily oped her lids: again
45 Laughed the blue eyes without a stain.
And I untightened next the tress
About her neck; her cheek once more
Blushed bright beneath my burning kiss:
I propped her head up as before,
50 Only, this time my shoulder bore
Her head, which droops upon it still:
The smiling rosy little head,
So glad it has its utmost will,
That all it scorned at once is fled,
55 And I, its love, am gained instead!
Porphyria's love, she guessed not how
Her darling one wish would be heard.
And thus we sit together now,
And all night long we have not stirred,
60 And yet God has not said a word!

Robert Browning, 1836

Thinking through

First, share your answers to the 'Meeting the text' questions you were given at the start of the poem. Then think carefully about the **supertitle** (the words above the main title), 'Madhouse Cell' as you answer these questions:

1 **Where** does the narrator think he is as he makes his confession?

2 **Where** is he actually?

3 **Who** might he think he is talking to?

4 **Who** do you think he is actually talking to?

5 **When** does he think it is at the end of the poem?

6 **When** might it be really?

Share your answers with the class. We'll return to these ideas in a bit more detail later when we look at the idea of the **unreliable narrator**. For now, though, it's important that you get the difference between the real situation, and the one the speaker perceives.

Now try this

As you can see from the date at the end, this poem was written quite some time ago. Read it over again and jot down any words or phrases whose meanings you are not sure of. Then either find someone in the class who can explain these to you, or ask your teacher.

Let's get to work

As we study this poem we will look at how Browning uses a number of techniques together to build a full picture of the narrator, and of his mental state. First, we need to find out a bit about the poetic form this poem is written in.

Dramatic monologue

This type of poem is called a **dramatic monologue**. The word **monologue** tells us that someone is speaking uninterrupted, rather than taking part in a conversation. The word **dramatic** means that the speaker is not on his own and talking to himself, but that someone else is supposed to be there listening.

You should have worked out already that this speaker is really talking to a doctor or a guard in the 'madhouse' he's been locked up in, but that he thinks he is talking to the person who found him with Porphyria's body the morning after the murder.

Incidentally, Robert Browning was famous for writing in this genre, and he created some

memorable nasty characters. In one of his other dramatic monologues, 'My Last Duchess', a duke unintentionally gives away that he had his first wife killed because he was jealous of the attention she paid to others.

In another, called 'The Bishop Orders His Tomb at Saint Praxed's', a dying Catholic bishop, a man who should be having highly spiritual thoughts after a life of giving up sex and money for the sake of the church, turns out to have a lot of illegitimate sons and to be obsessed with the number of jewels that will be used on his tomb.

One feature of dramatic monologues is that their speakers often let slip some of their nastier or more unpleasant thoughts, habits or actions. In this poem, the man who calls himself Porphyria's 'lover' quite openly tells us that he strangled her. He thinks his actions are reasonable and understandable, so what comes out accidentally is quite how controlling, and how mad, he is. Also, we should doubt whether 'lover' is really the right word to describe him.

We are never meant to think that the speaker in a dramatic monologue is the voice of the poet. The speaker is a distinct character that the author has invented. This kind of character is sometimes called a **persona**. The difference between an author and his persona is like the difference between an actor and his character. One brings the other to life, but that doesn't mean that we think one is the other. We'll spend much of this chapter looking at how Browning creates the persona in this poem.

The opening of the poem – pathetic fallacy

Here are the first few lines of the poem, with some key words highlighted for you.

> The rain set early in tonight,
> The **sullen** wind was soon awake,
> It tore the elm-tops down for **spite**,
> And **did its worst** to **vex** the lake:
> I listened with heart fit to break,
> When glided in Porphyria; straight
> She shut the cold out and the storm,
> And kneeled and made the cheerless grate
> Blaze up, and all the cottage warm;

This is a very striking way to start. Browning seems to be personifying the weather, bringing it to life to show us how terrible the storm is. But he's also using a technique called the **pathetic fallacy**. (The word pathetic here doesn't mean weak, or rubbishy, it means connected to the emotions.) The **pathetic fallacy** is when a writer uses weather to suggest a character's emotions, or the mood of a story.

Now try this

Look at the highlighted words. What do they all have in common? What is being suggested about the narrator by the fact that he uses words like these to describe the weather?

Now look at how Browning immediately creates a **contrast**. Right after this imagery of wild weather we get the very serene word, 'glided' to show how Porphyria came in. She immediately transforms the cottage, making it warm and cheerful. Her effect seems entirely positive, but sadly she can't change the narrator as easily as she cheers up his house. He's deeply damaged and his terrible anger cannot be calmed down.

How structure reveals character

Nothing in this poem is accidental. Browning makes every little detail work together to give us a full picture of the speaker. One way he does this is by giving the poem a very particular structure.

Now try this

It will really help you at this stage if you have a paper copy of the poem in front of you so that you can mark the text. It's widely available on the internet. Once everyone in your class has a copy of the poem, go round the class giving everyone a letter A, B, C, D, A, B, C, D … and so on. Spend ten minutes working on these tasks, marking the text as you do so. All the A people should start at task A, the B people at Task B and so on. If you finish your first task before the ten minutes are up, you can move on to the next.

A
Count the number of syllables in each line, and write the number at the end of each line. Is there a pattern?

B
Re-read the poem, paying particular attention to the rhyming words at the ends of the lines. By drawing lines across the page in between the lines of the poem, divide the poem into verses. How many verses do you get? How many lines are in each verse? Can you describe the rhyming pattern within each verse?

C
Re-read the poem, this time thinking about the plot of it and the story it tells. Mark an asterisk in the text where you think the turning point is. Remember this might not necessarily be at the end of a verse or line.

D
Re-read the poem, looking for the word 'and' and circling it every time you find it.

Now try this

Once the ten minutes are up, share your answers as a class. There will probably be at least two tasks you didn't have time to do, so pay careful attention. Then copy and complete the following paragraph:

'Porphyria's Lover' is _____ lines long and though it is printed in one unbroken block, actually divides into _____ verses of _____ lines each. Within each verse, the rhyming pattern is as follows: the first line rhymes with the _____ line, and the _____, _____ and _____ lines rhyme with each other. This is known as an a, b, a, b, b rhyme scheme. The line lengths in this poem are also highly regular. Of the 60 lines, _____ are _____ syllables in length, with just a few having _____ syllables.

So why has Browning done all this? It's quite a long poem, and it must have been very difficult to stick to such a tight pattern for sixty lines. Was he just showing off his skill? No. The structure of the poem tells us two things about the mind of the speaker:

1 The structure is incredibly tightly **controlled** because the speaker is incredibly **controlling**. He wants to control Porphyria. This is mirrored by the way his mind takes control of and shapes the words that come out of his mouth.

2 The structure is initially **hidden** from us because there are no verse breaks in the poem. This mirrors the fact that the speaker's insanity is somehow **hidden** from those around him until it is too late. We can tell that his insanity is **hidden** because Porphyria behaves so trustingly when she is in his house.

In fact the structure is even cleverer than that. Though the poem sticks absolutely to a rhyme scheme, the rhymes themselves aren't too obvious. This is because Browning uses a technique called **enjambment**. This means that the end of the line in the poem is not the end of the sentence, or the end of the idea. Sentences in the poem run on from one line to the next, and sometimes from one verse to the next. So as you read it, imagining the speaker's voice in your head, the rhyming words don't get too much weight or stress.

To show you what we mean, look at this extract. The verse breaks have been put in this time, and the last word of each sentence or idea has been printed in bold. You can see that these are not the same as the rhyming words.

I found
A thing to **do**, and all her hair
In one long yellow string I wound
Three times her little throat around,

And strangled **her**. No pain felt **she**;
I am quite sure she felt no **pain**.
As a shut bud that holds a bee,
I warily oped her **lids**: again
Laughed the blue eyes without a **stain**.

The rhymes, like his mental state, are hidden at first because we read past the rhyme to the end of the idea or sentence.

Ambiguity

Ambiguity is when a word or phrase has two possible meanings. We can't tell for sure which is meant to apply so they both stay in our mind and work together as we read. (We'll see this technique again in Chapter 5 on the Philip Larkin poem, 'Afternoons'.)

In line 36, just after the speaker decides that Porphyria worships him, he tells us very ambiguously:

> That moment she was mine, mine, fair,
> Perfectly pure and good

He could be saying that she was fair – fair-haired, beautiful – and that she was a perfectly pure and good person.

He could be saying that she was his, so whatever he did to her was absolutely fair. She was his, so his actions were pure and good.

Both meanings are true as far as we can tell, and he never makes clear which he means, so we have to hold on to both.

Turning point

When you were marking up the poem earlier you were asked to find the **turning point**, the moment when everything changes. You should have decided that it comes immediately after the above quotation, when the speaker tells us that he 'found a thing to do.'

Now try this

Copy the following table into your notebook and complete it to show how things are different before and after the turning point. Each box should include a quotation from the poem, along with some explanation in your own words. One has been done for you as an example.

	Before TP	After TP
Who controls the situation?	Porphyria does. She 'shut' out the cold, and 'made the cheerless grate blaze up and all the cottage warm'. She 'called' him and 'made' his cheek lie on her shoulder. Anything that changes does so because of her.	
What is the narrator's mood?		
How are Porphyria and the narrator sitting?		

Now try this

Draw pictures of the two different positions that Porphyria and the speaker sit together in. The first picture should depict lines 14 to 19; the second should show lines 49 to 51.

It's worth noticing that 'I found a thing to do,' is a terrifyingly matter-of-fact way to talk about deciding to commit a murder. It might be the right phrase for working out how to spend a wet day at the seaside, but it's hardly suitable for this situation. He must be insane if he sees this act in such simple terms.

Repetition

Repetition of 'and'

When you were text-marking the poem, you were also asked to look for uses of the word 'and'.

- How many did you find?
- How many times was 'and' the first word of the line?

You've probably been told by teachers never to start a sentence with this word, and a poetry teacher might give the same advice about lines of poems. So why does Browning do it? Once again it's not an accident as it tells us something about the mind of the speaker. It shows that he is in some ways very immature (children use 'and' more than we do to connect ideas in what they say or write) and it ties in with his selfish and immature desire to control another human being.

We can see another aspect of him being selfish and childish in the way he behaves when Porphyria comes in. The first thing she does is make his fire blaze up to heat the cottage (something he could easily have done for himself). She doesn't think about her own needs, keeping on a 'dripping' wet cloak, and getting her gloves 'soiled' and dirty as she tends his fire. Yet he complains that she sits beside him 'last' and when she says his name he doesn't answer. In fact he sits there completely passively until she arranges his arm around her waist. He's ignoring her as a punishment for not giving him the kind of immediate attention he wanted, and he doesn't see that by warming up his cottage she is actually giving him her attention.

We can see yet another use of repetition to indicate his selfishness in line 36 when he calls Porphyria, 'mine, mine'. In fact there's a lot of significant repetition in the poem.

Repetition of 'her' and 'she'

Time for some more counting, and a quick question:

- Count how many times the word 'her' is used in the poem.
- Count how many times the word 'she' is used in the poem.
- What do you think the overuse of these two words is meant to tell you about the narrator?

Repetition of 'hair'

This word comes up three times in just a few lines – you'll find it in lines 13, 18 and 20. Then it reappears again in line 38 when Porphyria's long thick 'hair' is used against her as the murder weapon. The same idea, though not the same word, comes up in line 46 when the killer loosens the 'tress' around her neck.

That earlier cluster of repetitions lets Browning do two things:

1 It tells us that her hair is important, so we accept it as a weapon when it's used that way later.

2 We've already seen that repetition of 'her' and 'she' shows that the narrator is obsessed with Porphyria. Now the repetition of 'hair' shows us which part of her body he is most obsessed with.

In fact this may give us a clue as to why the speaker snaps, and kills Porphyria on this particular night. It's not just because he has the opportunity to do so when she arrives alone at his cottage.

Something triggers this off. Nineteenth-century young ladies kept themselves quite well covered up, and their hair tended to be very formally done, tied up or tied back. We know from the use of pathetic fallacy at the start of the poem that his mental state is already stormy and disordered before poor Porphyria arrives. All he needs to tip him over the edge is for her to innocently undo that hair that he finds so fascinating. She must feel safe with him, both physically and sexually, or she wouldn't do it at all. Ironically, it's this act that puts her in most danger.

Now try this

Everyone in your class needs to get up on their feet. Get someone to write PORPHYRIA on one piece of paper and stick it to the wall at one end of the room. Get someone to write SPEAKER on another piece of paper and stick it to the wall at the other end of the room.

Decide to what extent you think each of the characters is to blame for Porphyria's death. If you blame him entirely, you'll end up standing beside the SPEAKER sign; if you think it's all her fault you'll end up by the PORPHYRIA wall, but

Now try this *continued*

you'll probably be somewhere in between. Once everyone has lined up, be ready to explain why you are standing in the spot you've chosen.

It's her fault. She totally led him on.

It's his fault. We can never blame the victim for such a hideous crime.

It's his fault she's dead, but she should never have gone to his house alone without telling anyone.

Now try this

As we've just seen, Porphyria must know and trust him to behave the way she does in his house. But she seems to be much richer than he is. He lives in a 'cheerless' cottage; she has slipped away from a 'feast' to see him. Read the poem for clues and write a paragraph in your notebook to explain what you think the connection is between them. How and why do they know each other? Get everyone to read out their paragraphs. How many different explanations does your class come up with? Which seems most likely? Do any of these explanations help you understand where his obsession came from?

Repetition of 'passion'

In lines 22 to 30 the speaker describes Porphyria like this:

> Too weak for all her heart's endeavour,
> To set its struggling **passion** free
> From pride, and vainer ties dissever,
> And give herself to me forever.
> But **passion** sometimes would prevail,
> Nor could tonight's gay feast restrain
> A sudden thought for one so pale
> For love of her, and all in vain:
> So, she was come through wind and rain.

He wants us to believe that she was as passionate about him as he was about her, and that on the night of the murder she gave in to these passions at last and came to see him. Is he telling the truth?

Now try this

List all the things Porphyria does after coming into the cottage but before line 22.

- Do any of these actions suggest passion?
- Why is it significant that the first thing she does is not go to him but get the fire blazing?
- What do you think is the main emotion Porphyria felt towards the speaker?

His belief that Porphyria felt passionate about him is echoed in line 34 when he claims that

> Porphyria worshipped me

We shouldn't believe him then either. Just a couple of lines earlier he tells us that

> I looked up at her eyes

We often say we 'look up' to someone to mean that we admire or respect them. If we worship someone or something, we think of it, or of that person, as being somehow above us. So, when the speaker tells us he 'looked up' at Porphyria, it's clear that if there is any worshipping going on in this poem, he worships her and not the other way round.

The unreliable narrator

This misuse of the words 'passion' and 'worshipped' are just two examples of the speaker in this poem being what we call an **unreliable narrator**. This means that we can't always believe what he tells us. Many of the details in the poem are quite suspect. He may be deliberately lying to us, so that we'll accept that his actions were justified. Or, he may not even be aware that he is unreliable – he may be so mad that he is unaware that his perceptions are wrong.

Let's look at some more examples of his unreliability.

Now try this

Here's another section of the poem, from near the end. Some sections have been printed in bold, and numbered. Read the extracts, and answer the questions below. You need to think a bit like a police pathologist in one of those programmes like *CSI*.

> **(1) No pain felt she;**
> **I am quite sure she felt no pain.**
> As a shut bud that holds a bee,
> I warily oped her lids: **(2) again**
> **Laughed the blue eyes without a stain.**
> And I untightened next the tress
> About her neck; **(3) her cheek once more**
> **Blushed bright beneath my burning kiss:**
> I propped her head up as before,
> Only, this time my shoulder bore
> Her head, which droops upon it still:
> The smiling **(4) rosy** little head,
> **(5) So glad it has its utmost will,**
> **That all it scorned at once is fled,**
> **And I, its love, am gained instead!**

1 How does his repetition of the claim that Porphyria felt 'no pain' actually make it less believable? Why must his claim be untrue?

2 He tells us her blue eyes laughed 'without a stain'. Bearing in mind that she's been strangled, what are her eyes much more likely to look like?

3 He tells us that she 'blushed'. Why is it impossible for her to do so at this point? Why does he want us to think that she is blushing?

4 Why is it impossible for her head to be 'rosy' at this moment?

5 What does he think Porphyria's 'utmost will' was? What evidence is there in the poem to prove that this can't be what she wanted?

Taken together, all of these untruths show that he wants us (and maybe also wants himself) to accept that what he did to Porphyria wasn't a crime, but an act of mercy, that he didn't take life from her but that he gave her the life she really wanted, a life loving him.

Did you notice his use of the word 'bud' as well as 'rosy' in these lines? Just as we saw in the earlier chapter on 'Incident', this speaker is calling upon the language of love, and the idea that men in love often give their beloved roses. He thinks he's gone one stage further. He hasn't given her flowers, he's transformed her into a flower. Not a nasty corpse, a flower.

The ending

There is of course one more proof of his unreliability, and it's one that you discovered at the very start of your studies in this poem when you thought about the **supertitle**. The speaker thinks he is still sitting in his own cottage on the morning after the night of the murder, holding Porphyria's dead body in his arms. Yet we know that he is in the madhouse, and that the crime might have happened weeks, months or even years ago.

After the murder, the speaker arranges Porphyria's body, telling us:

> I propped her head up as before,
> Only, this time my shoulder bore
> Her head, which droops upon it still

This, as we've seen, is a mirror image of the way she held him earlier in the poem.

He ends the poem by telling us:

> And all night long we have not stirred,
> And yet God has not said a word!

All of this gives us more information about the narrator's mental state. Firstly, he does seem to have made himself believe that she is somehow not really dead. He uses the word 'we' as if she is still alive and manipulates her body into an affectionate posture. Secondly, lines 49 to 51 show that he now controls her as he always wanted to. Thirdly, that phrase 'all night long we have not stirred' is what proves that the trauma of committing the crime has robbed him of his last shreds of sanity and he cannot move on beyond that night. Finally, and chillingly, that **final line** tells us that he believes he has done nothing wrong. He feels no moral judgement.

Now try this

Throughout this chapter we've gathered a huge amount of evidence about this speaker's very complex mental state. **Read back over** this chapter and your own notes and answers. **Now imagine** you are a psychiatrist who has heard him say all of the things he says in the poem. **Write a medical report** about your patient:

- Make each feature of his insanity clear and back each up with evidence.
- Suggest a suitable treatment regime.
- Make clear recommendations about how others are to be protected from him.

Write your report in clear formal English. Here's an opening paragraph to get you started:

BADDESLEY ASYLUM

It is clear that the subject was suffering from overwhelming anger even before these tragic events. His tendency to describe even weather as sullen and spiteful merely indicates his own fury …

Technique revision

Now that you've worked your way through the whole chapter about 'Porphyria's Lover', you should know the poem very well. Before you prove this by writing an essay about it, revise your knowledge of Browning's techniques.

You're going to carry out the same exercise that you did at the end of Chapter 3, the 'Incident' chapter. (Look back to pp. 79–80 now if you need to be more fully reminded of the instructions.) Take a large piece of paper and mark it up into a **PEE** grid. For every technique, fill in a quotation from the poem, and explain the effect it has on the reader. For a grid about 'Porphyria's Lover', you need to work with the following techniques:

supertitle   dramatic monologue   persona
pathetic fallacy   contrast   rhythm   rhyme
verse structure   enjambment   ambiguity
turning point   repetition of 'and'
repetition of 'her/she'   repetition of 'mine'
repetition of 'hair'   repetition of 'passion'
unreliable narrator   flower word choice
final line

Possible essay choices

Once you have studied Chapter 8 on essay writing, you might like to try one of the following essays, which are all suitable for 'Porphyria's Lover'.

Above the poetry essay choices on the exam paper you'll see the following words:

Answers to questions on poetry should address relevantly the central concern(s)/theme(s) of the text(s) and be supported by reference to appropriate poetic techniques such as: imagery, verse form, structure, mood, tone, sound, rhythm, rhyme, characterisation, contrast, setting, symbolism, word choice …

Now look at the essay choices:

Choose a poem in which the poet has created a perfect blend of form and content.

Show how the poet does this and discuss how it adds to your appreciation of the poem.

OR

Choose a poem in which the poet creates a picture of a heroic or a corrupt figure.

Discuss the means by which the personality is clearly depicted.

OR

Choose a poem in which there is effective use of one or more of the following: verse form, rhythm, repetition, sound.

Show how the poet effectively uses the feature(s) to enhance your appreciation of the poem as a whole.

OR

Choose a poem in which the speaker's personality is gradually revealed.

Show how, through the content and language of the poem, aspects of the character gradually emerge.

CHAPTER 5 Poetry: 'Afternoons'

Getting in

Have a look at the wedding photos below. For each picture, try to work out:

- How old the bride and groom were when it was taken.
- Which year they got married.

Now think about the following questions. You might share your answers with the class, but they're quite personal questions, so it's all right if you don't.

- If your parents are, or have been, married, have you ever seen their wedding photographs?
- Can you describe their outfits? How do their clothes, or hairstyles, give clues about when they got married?
- What changes can you see when you compare how they looked then with what they look like now?

Now try this

Work with a partner or a small group. Half the groups in the class should do task A; the other groups should do task B.

A Come up with two lists. In one, list all the reasons why people **do** have children. In the other list, give as many reasons as you can for **not** having children.

B Come up with two lists. In one, list all the reasons why people **do** get married. In the other list, give as many reasons as you can for **not** getting married.

Share your group's answers with the class, and keep the lists. You'll need them later.

Meeting the text

As you read through the poem for the first time, see if you can work out the answers to these questions:

1 **Where** is the poem mostly set?

2 **Where** else do we 'go' in the poem?

3 **Who** is the speaker mostly looking at and thinking about in the poem?

4 **Which** other characters are mentioned?

5 **When** in the year is the poem set?

6 **When** during the day is it set?

7 **What** are the main characters in the poem doing?

8 **Why** have they chosen this particular time of day to do this?

AFTERNOONS

Summer is fading:
The leaves fall in ones and twos
From trees bordering
The new recreation ground.
5 In the hollows of afternoons
Young mothers assemble
At swing and sandpit
Setting free their children.

Behind them, at intervals,
10 Stand husbands in skilled trades,
An estateful of washing,
And the albums, lettered
Our Wedding, lying
Near the television:
15 Before them, the wind
Is ruining their courting places

That are still courting places
(But the lovers are all in school),
And their children, so intent on
20 Finding more unripe acorns,
Expect to be taken home.
Their beauty has thickened.
Something is pushing them
To the side of their own lives.

Philip Larkin, 1959

Thinking through

First, share your answers to the 'Meeting the text' questions you were given at the start of the poem.

Before we start to look at Larkin's ideas in this poem, and the techniques he uses to put them across, it's useful to think a little bit about the writer himself.

Philip Larkin was born in 1922 and died in 1985. He lived all his life in England, hardly ever travelled abroad, and never married. He spent his career working as a librarian, mostly at the University of Hull. Though he was also a highly successful and well-known poet during his lifetime, he didn't like to give readings from or interviews about his work. When he was offered the post of Poet Laureate (Britain's official poet and a very great honour) he turned it down.

This might all make him seem rather quiet and dull. He starts to sound even sadder when you read some of the things he was recorded as saying.

He called marriage a 'revolting institution … imagine sharing a bedroom with a withered old woman'.

He realised that 'It was not people I disliked, but children.'

He said family life was 'an enormous absurdity'.

'I think writing about unhappiness is probably the source of my popularity, if I have any. After all, most people are unhappy, don't you think?'

You might also want to look up his most famous poem, 'This Be the Verse'. The opening lines contain some language that's a bit strong for a textbook, but it gives another example of what Larkin said about family life.

Now try this

Go back to your lists of reasons for and against having children or getting married. **Highlight** the points you think Larkin would most strongly agree with. **Underline** the ones you think he would most strongly disagree with. How well does the poem seem to fit Larkin's statements?

All of this sounds very negative, but there is another side to Larkin. Despite the things he said or wrote about family life, he showed genuine grief when his father died and was a great support to his mother through her long widowhood. He never married but had a number of long relationships, and at one stage had three partners simultaneously, which suggests that women found him quite attractive.

In fact, there's a lot of evidence to suggest that Larkin deliberately presented himself as a grumpy recluse, creating a **persona** for himself. For example, in a poem called 'Church Going' he describes a visit to a church and then says that he left some Irish money in the collection plate. This sounds as if he was being mean and difficult. But he wrote the poem after visiting an Irish church, so his donation was a genuine one. He wants us to think that he is nastier than he really is. Keep this idea in mind as you study 'Afternoons' – it might not be as negative as it first appears.

 Let's get to work

As we study this poem we'll look especially at how Larkin explores the theme of passing time, and how he suggests people and their relationships change over time.

How word choice creates mood

The mood of this poem can seem decidedly sad and regretful. Larkin creates this impression by his word choice. He's an expert at playing on all the connotations of words.

Fading

You should feel that the word 'fading' in line 1 suggests a sad or regretful mood. Larkin isn't just applying that word to the season of the year. It has a **metaphorical** application too – it says something about the lives of the young mothers.

- What stage of their lives might be represented by the word 'summer'?
- What is Larkin suggesting about their lives if he says that 'summer is fading'?

The first two lines of the poem, where we find 'fading' being used, tell us autumn is on its way.

- Find and quote the other two lines in the poem that suggest autumn.

Larkin is using a technique here that we already met in Chapter 4 on 'Porphyria's Lover', the **pathetic fallacy**. He is using weather and the season to suggest a mood.

Now try this

You're going to draw three pictures, one for line 1, one for line 2 and one for lines 15 and 16. Beside each picture, quote the relevant line(s), and underneath write yourself a note about how Larkin's words create a certain mood.

Hollows

Larkin has the young mothers taking their children to the recreation ground

In the hollows of afternoons

If something is hollow it has a hole or an empty space inside. More metaphorically, hollow can mean insignificant, as in the expression 'a hollow victory'. When Larkin writes about 'the hollows of afternoons', he's writing about that slack part of the day when there's nothing particularly important that has to be done, an empty bit of time that the mothers can fill with whatever they want. However, his word choice also suggests it's a time that doesn't matter, as if what the mothers are doing is meaningless and empty. His description of the time becomes a judgement on their lives.

- Stop and think. Do you agree with what Larkin is suggesting here? Why/why not?

The last few lines

This is how the poem ends, as Larkin returns to examining the young mothers:

> Their beauty has thickened.
> Something is pushing them
> To the side of their own lives.

- What does the first of these lines mean? What has caused their beauty to thicken?
- Whom do the second and third lines refer to? What is 'pushing' them?

This ending is striking, memorable, and in some ways quite chilling.

- What does Larkin seem to be saying here about how becoming a mother can affect a woman's life?

But these lines also give us an opportunity to see something more positive. Look at the pictures below.

Larkin doesn't say the women have lost their beauty. He doesn't say they're plain or ugly. He only says 'their beauty' – which is still there – 'has thickened'. He doesn't say that motherhood brings destruction, just change.

There's a clever piece of language going on here. The word 'beauty' is what we call an **abstract**. These words, words like **truth**, **love**, **anger**, **care**, are the names of ideas, feelings and qualities. Abstracts aren't something we can touch, or physically hold. What Larkin does is take an **abstract** word like beauty and make it **concrete**. When he says that 'beauty' can become 'thickened', it becomes real, and physical. It's much more interesting than writing, 'They've put on weight', which is, after all, what the line means.

Ambiguity

We've already seen how Larkin creates mood by playing on all the suggestions and connotations of his chosen words. He's also wonderful at giving us two ideas at once by using ambiguity.

Ambiguity is when a word or phrase has two possible meanings. We can't tell for sure which is meant to apply so they both stay in our mind and work together as we read. (We also met this technique in the chapter on 'Porphyria's Lover'.) There are four clear examples of this technique in 'Afternoons'.

Setting free their children

The mothers at the recreation ground are said to be

> Setting free their children.

If you think Larkin is presenting a rather dismal picture of family life, then this line makes the mothers sound controlling. They dominate their children's lives and only give them limited freedom at certain times in certain places.

On the other hand, if you have a more positive view, you could say that the mothers are doing something wonderful for their children by setting them free in a place where they are safe to play and explore (including getting happily dirty as they hunt for acorns). The mothers are being good parents because their very young children feel free even while their mothers are keeping a safe eye on them from nearby.

Behind them

Larkin says in line 9 that the women's husbands are 'behind them'. If you think he is presenting a rather dismal picture of family life, then he's saying that these marriages have changed for the worse. The women's husbands are 'behind them' in the sense of being unimportant, something from the past. Their romance is over, that part of life is 'behind them', and their life now is all about their children.

On the other hand, if you have a more positive view, you could say that the husbands are 'behind' their wives in the sense of being supportive, such as in, 'When I asked the boss for a pay rise my team leader was completely behind me.' This more optimistic interpretation is backed up by the detail that the husbands are 'in skilled trades'. They are plasterers, mechanics, builders and so on, doing jobs that took them years to learn and need some expertise. They are 'behind' their wives, supporting the family financially by their efforts and income.

Expect

Line 21 tells us that the children

> Expect to be taken home.

This example of ambiguity, like 'setting free' before, looks at the mothers' relationship with their children. Larkin might be saying that the children are making demands on their mothers, that they have an expectation of being taken home, fed, read to, tucked up in bed. Or he might be saying that the children are resigned to the fact

that their mothers will soon drag them off home and spoil their nice time playing in the sandpit. In this case, both interpretations paint a fairly gloomy picture of family life.

Lying

In lines 12 to 14 Larkin pictures

> the albums, lettered
> Our Wedding, lying
> Near the television

This word 'lying' is actually the most important example of ambiguity in the poem, but it's also the easiest to analyse.

Now try this

Work out and explain in your own words what the two meanings of this word could be. One is pretty harmless, one very negative. Then answer this question as fully as possible:

- If we believe the negative interpretation, what is Larkin saying about these marriages?

Now try this

In your notebook, create a rib and spine diagram to show your understanding of all the ambiguities in the poem. The first one has been done for you.

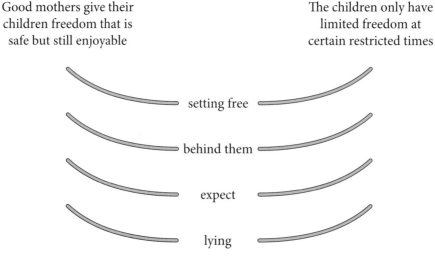

Good mothers give their children freedom that is safe but still enjoyable

The children only have limited freedom at certain restricted times

setting free

behind them

expect

lying

Symbolism

A **symbol** is an object, something real, which stands for a more abstract idea. Look at lines 19 and 20:

> And their children, so intent on
> Finding more unripe acorns

An acorn is a tiny little seed, but it eventually becomes an oak, a tree so huge and powerful that for centuries its timber was used to build ships for the British navy.

Have you ever heard the saying, 'Great oaks from little acorns grow'? It's not just a piece of gardening knowledge, it's a metaphor that tells us that great things can come from very small beginnings.

By placing the children and the unripe acorns together here in the poem, Larkin is telling us that the acorns symbolise the children. The children are young and small now, but, like the acorns, they are full of potential. They could grow up to do something amazing. Once again, the poem isn't entirely negative.

Something else is used symbolically in this poem.

> And the albums, lettered
> Our Wedding, lying
> Near the television

You've already thought about the ambiguity of 'lying' in these lines. Now think about how the albums symbolise the marriages. Look at where the albums are. Not on a shelf. Not in pride of place. Larkin is suggesting that what happened on their wedding day is now no more important than what they watch on television, or maybe even that the happiness of that day is now just as unreal as what they might watch on television.

Now try this

It's time for another drawing task. Draw one picture to convey lines 19 and 20, and another for lines 12 to 14. Beside or around each picture, add notes to help you understand Larkin's use of these symbols.

Groups of characters

Nobody in this poem has a name. In fact nobody is an individual at all. Instead this poem has groups of characters: young mothers, children, husbands, and teenage lovers who are all in school. Larkin makes assumptions about what all of their lives are like.

Now try this

Discuss these questions with a partner or group:

- What does Larkin gain by dealing with groups of characters rather than distinct individuals?

- What does he lose by doing this?

- Does this approach make his view of family life seem more convincing, or less?

Share your answers with the rest of the class.

You might think that his view of these people is quite stereotypical, perhaps because he wasn't really able to write from experience, as he never married or had children himself.

On the other hand, you might think it's quite unusual for an unmarried and childless man in the 1950s to take such an interest in how motherhood affects women's lives – even if most of the conclusions he comes to are pretty bleak.

In the second stanza we find these expressions:

> behind them … before them …

The two **prepositions**, 'behind' and 'before', are very important. (A preposition is a word like *in*, *on*, *after*, *above* etc. These words usually come before a noun or a pronoun and are used to show how one word relates to another such as 'My homework is in the dog' or 'The cat is on the dinner table again'.) Larkin's chosen prepositions make the women sound trapped. There is something 'behind' them, and something else 'before' or in front of them. They can't get away.

In the same stanza he describes:

> An estateful of washing

That **suffix**, '-ful' (a suffix is a group of letters commonly used to make a word ending), suggests that the women's work will never end – there is always washing to do. In 1959 most of this would still have been done by hand as very few people owned any kind of washing machine.

Again, Larkin makes the mothers sound trapped by their work and responsibilities. The other characters in this poem also have restrictions on them. Yet all the characters in this poem are free in some way too.

Now try this

Copy and complete the table.

Characters	Restricted by	Free to
		meet friends during the day
small children		
		work outside the home
	school timetable and school work	

So once again we can see that this poem isn't entirely miserable. We can see this idea even more clearly if we look at two deeper ideas that run through it.

Cycles and circles

The poem begins by telling us that 'summer is fading'. This is clearly quite gradual, as Larkin tells us that the leaves 'fall in ones and twos'. Although the end of summer might seem sad, we also accept it is necessary and natural. Seasons must follow each other, and even in winter we know that spring will return and will be followed again by summer.

This idea of seasons in the poem leads us on to the idea of generations. The small children in this poem will grow up to be the next generation of teenage lovers, who in turn become parents to children of their own. This too is natural.

And their young mothers, trapped at the moment by their home and family responsibilities, will get their freedom back. Have you ever heard the expression 'Life begins at forty'? It applies perfectly to women like those in the poem. In 1950, the average age at which women got married was twenty and most women got pregnant within seven months of being married. (At the time this book is being written, the average age at which women get married is twenty-nine and the average age for having a first child is also twenty-nine.)

When these mothers in the poem are forty, their children will be ready for independence. The mothers will get their freedom back and life will begin again at forty, an age when most women in our own generation are still juggling work and family life.

This poem, then, doesn't just show us a natural cycle of seasons, but of generations, something we might call the circle of life. And, though Larkin himself seems very bleak about the effect that motherhood is having on these women, there's nothing in the poem to say that they resent their children or the time they spend with them.

Making your own decision

At the start of this chapter you found out about some quite bitter and gloomy things Larkin said about marriage and family life, but you were also told that he quite liked people to think he was grumpier and more difficult than he might really have been.

In the same way this poem, especially the last two lines, might seem to present a rather gloomy view of family life, but we've seen by looking at the ideas of a cycle of seasons and of generations that there are more hopeful elements too.

Now try this

It's time for you to make up your own mind about this poem. What do you think is the poem's view of marriage and family life? Is it:

1 mostly pessimistic, OR

2 mostly optimistic, OR

3 realistically mixed?

First write a mini essay to explain your position. Spend twenty minutes writing, and give at least three pieces of evidence from the poem to back up your point of view.

Then try to find two people in your class who have taken up the other two positions. Read your essays to each other, and try to persuade the other two members of your trio to agree with you.

Now try this

Two more questions to help you think about the poem as a whole. In each answer, use at least three quotations to support what you say.

1 How does 'Afternoons' deal with the theme of time? (This includes how passing time changes things.)

2 How does 'Afternoons' show that Larkin is a poet who is interested in ordinary things?

Technique revision

Now that you've worked your way through the whole chapter about 'Afternoons', you should know the poem very well. Before you prove

this by writing an essay about it, revise your knowledge of Larkin's techniques.

You're going to carry out the same exercise that you did at the end of Chapter 3 on 'Incident'. (Look back to pp. 79–80 now if you need to be more fully reminded of the instructions.) Take a large piece of paper and mark it up into a **PEE** grid. For every technique, fill in a quotation from the poem, and explain the effect it has on the reader. For a grid about 'Afternoons', you need to work with the following techniques:

> word choice: fading   word choice: hollows
> word choice: pushing   word choice: thickened
> symbolism: unripe acorns   symbolism:
> wedding albums   ambiguity: setting free
> ambiguity: behind them   ambiguity: expect
> ambiguity: lying   idea of seasons
> idea of generations   suffix   pathetic fallacy
> use of groups, not individuals   abstract
> prepositions

Possible essay choices

Once you have studied Chapter 8 on essay writing, you might like to try one of the following essays, which are all suitable for 'Afternoons'.

Above the poetry essay choices on the exam paper you'll see the following words:

> **Answers to questions on poetry should address relevantly the central concern(s)/theme(s) of the text(s) and be supported by reference to appropriate poetic techniques such as: imagery, verse form, structure, mood, tone, sound, rhythm, rhyme, characterisation, contrast, setting, symbolism, word choice …**

Now look at the essay choices:

> **Choose a poem which explores either the significance of the past or the importance of family relationships.**

> **Show how the poet treats the subject, and explain to what extent you find the treatment convincing.**

OR

Choose a poem in which the poet explores the significance of the passage of time.

Explain why the passage of time is significant in this poem and discuss the means by which the poet explores its significance.

OR

Choose a poem which depicts a particular stage of life, such as childhood, adolescence, middle age, old age.

Discuss how effectively the poet evokes the essence of this stage of life.

OR

Choose a poem in which there is an element of ambiguity.

Show how the poet's use of ambiguity enriches your appreciation of the poem as a whole.

OR

Choose a poem in which the central concern(s) is/are clarified for you in the closing lines.

Show how these closing lines provide an effective clarification of the central concern(s) of the poem.

CHAPTER 6
Prose: 'All the Little Loved Ones'

 Getting in

You're probably about sixteen or seventeen years old now. Think ahead, twice a lifetime away, and imagine yourself at the age of thirty-five. Be realistic – you most likely aren't going to be an Oscar winner or a millionaire sports star – but do think about what you plan to do with your life, and what you want from it.

- Where do you think you'll be living? City, town, village or countryside? What sort of house or flat?
- Who do you think you'll be living with, or will you be on your own?
- What will your family circumstances be?
- What will take up your time and energy in life?

These are quite personal questions, so you might not want to share the answers with others in your class, but you can if you feel comfortable doing so.

You've been asked to imagine yourself at age thirty-five because that's probably how old the narrator of this story is. She is living a life that her friends seem to think is ideal, but that's not how it feels to her.

 Meeting the text

As you read through the story for the first time do these things:

- Make a note of how many times the writer uses the adjective 'little', and who or what is being described each time the adjective is used.
- Note down the wording of the two questions the narrator's husband repeatedly asks her.
- Count how many times each of these questions is asked.

ALL THE LITTLE LOVED ONES

1 I love my kids. My husband too, though sometimes he asks me whether I do, asks the question, Do you still love me? He asks it while I am in the middle of rinsing spinach or loading washing into the machine, or chasing a trail of toys across the kitchen floor. When he asks the question at a time like that it's like he's speaking an ancient, forgotten language. I can remember a few isolated words but can't connect them, can't get the gist, don't know how to answer. Of course I could say, Yes I love you, still love you, of course I still love you. If I didn't still love you I wouldn't be here, would I, wouldn't have hung around just to go through the motions of companionship and sex. Being alone never bothered me. It was something I chose. Before I chose you. But of

course, that is not accurate. Once you become a parent there is no longer a simple equation.

2 We have three children. All our own. Blood of our blood, flesh of our flesh etc, delivered into our hands in the usual way, a slithering mess of blood and slime and wonder, another tiny miracle.

3 In reply to his question my husband really doesn't want to hear any of my irritating justifications for sticking around, my caustic logic. He doesn't really want to hear anything at all. The response he wants is a visual and tactile one. He wants me to drop the spinach, the laundry, the toys, sweep my hair out of my eyes, turn round, look away from what I'm doing and look at him, look lovingly into his dark, demanding eyes, walk across the kitchen floor – which needs to be swept again – stand over him as he sits at the table fingering a daffodil, still bright in its fluted centre but crisp and brown at the edges, as if it's been singed. My husband wants me to cuddle up close.

4 Sometimes I can do it, the right thing, what's needed. Other times, when I hear those words it's like I've been turned to marble or ice, to something cold and hard and unyielding. I can't even turn my head away from the sink, far less walk those few steps across the floor. I can't even think about it. And when he asks, What are you thinking? Again I'm stuck. Does it count as thinking to be considering whether there is time to bring down the laundry from the pulley to make room for the next load before I shake off the rinsing water, pat the leaves dry, chop off the stalks and spin the green stuff around the magimix? That's usually what my mind is doing, that is its activity and if it can be called thinking, then that is what I'm doing. Thinking about something not worth relating.

5 What are you thinking?

6 Nothing, I'm not thinking about anything.

7 Which isn't the same thing. Thinking about nothing means mental activity, a focusing of the mind on the fact or idea of nothing and that's not what I'm doing. I've no interest in that kind of activity, no time for it, no time to ponder the true meaning of life, the essential nature of the universe and so on. Such speculation is beyond me. Usually when I'm asked what I'm thinking my mind is simply vacant and so my reply is made with a clear, vacant conscience.

8 I'm approaching a precipice. Each day I'm drawn nearer to the edge. I look only at the view.

I avoid looking at the drop but I know what's there. At least, I can imagine it. I don't want to be asked either question, the conversation must be kept moving, hopping across the surface of our lives like a smooth, flat stone.

9 . . . Thought is not the point. I am feeling it, the flush, the rush of blood, the sensation of, yes, swooning. It comes in waves. Does it show? I'm sure it must show on my face, the way pain might, the way pain would show on my husband's face.

10 Do you still love me? What are you thinking?

11 Tonight I couldn't even manage my usual, Nothing. It wouldn't come out right, I try it out in my head, practise it, imagine the word as it would come out. It would sound unnatural, false, a strangled, evasive mumble or else a spat denial. Either way it wouldn't pass. It would lead to probing. A strained, suspicious little duet would begin in the midst of preparing the dinner and I know where this edgy, halting tune leads. I know the notes by heart.

12 (Practice makes perfect. Up and down the same old scales until you can do them without tripping up, without twisting fingers or breaking resolutions, without swearing, yelling, failing or resentment at the necessity of repetition. Without scales the fingers are insufficiently developed to be capable of … until you can do it in your sleep, until you do do it in your sleep, up and down as fast as dexterity permits. Without practice, life skills also atrophy.)

13 For years we've shared everything we had to share, which wasn't much at first and now is way too much. In the way of possessions at least. We started simply: one room, a bed we nailed together from pine planks and lasted a decade; a few lingering relics from previous couplings (and still I long to ditch that nasty little bronze figurine made by the woman before me. A troll face, with gouged-out eyes. Scary at night, glowering from a corner of the bedroom.) Money was scarce but new love has no need of money. Somewhere to go, to be together is all and we were lucky. We had that. Hell is love with no place to go.

14 While around us couples were splitting at the seams, we remained intact. In the midst of break-ups and breakouts, we tootled on, sympathetic listeners, providers of impromptu pasta, a pull-out bed for the night, the

occasional alibi. We listened to the personal disasters of our friends but wondered in private, in bed, alone together at the end of another too-late night, what all the fuss was about. Beyond our ken, all that heartbreak, all that angst. What did it have to do with us, our lives, our kids? We had no room for it. Nor, for that matter, a great deal of space for passion.

15   An example to us all, we've been told, You two are an example to us all. Of course it was meant to be taken with a pinch of salt, a knowing smile but said frequently enough for the phrase to stick, as if our friends in their cracked, snapped, torn-to-shreds state, our friends who had just said goodbye to someone they loved, or someone they didn't love after all or any more, as if all of them were suddenly united in a wilderness of unrequited love. While we, in our dusty, cluttered home, had achieved something other than an accumulation of consecutive time together.

16   This is true, of course, and we can be relied upon to provide some display of the example that we are. My husband is likely to take advantage of the opportunity and engage in a bit of public necking. Me, I sling mud, with affection. Either way, between us we manage to steer the chat away from our domestic compatibility, top up our friends' drinks, turn up the volume on the stereo, stir up a bit of jollity until it's time to say Goodnight. See you soon. Look after yourself, until it's time to be left alone together again with our example. Our differences remain.

17   Do you still love me? What are you thinking?

18   Saturday night. The children are asleep. Three little dark heads are thrown back on pillows printed with characters from Lewis Carroll, Disney and Masters of the Universe. Three little mouths blow snores into the intimate, bedroom air. Upstairs, the neighbours hammer tacks into a carpet, their dogs romp and bark, their antique plumbing gurgles down the wall but the children sleep on, their sweet breath rising and falling in unison.

19   We are able to eat in peace, take time to taste the food which my husband has gone to impossible lengths to prepare. The dinner turns out to be an unqualified success: the curry is smooth, spicy, aromatic, the rice dry, each firm little ellipse brushing against the tongue. The dinner is a joy and a relief. My husband is touchy about his cooking and requires almost as much in the way of reassurance and compliments in this as he does about whether I still love him or not. A bad meal dampens the spirits, is distressing both for the cook and the cooked-for. A bad meal can be passed over, unmentioned but not ignored. The stomach too has longings for more than simply to be filled. A bad meal can be worse than no meal at all.

20   But it was an extremely good meal and I was wholehearted and voluble in my appreciation. Everything was going well. We drank more wine, turned off the overhead light, lit a candle, fetched the cassette recorder from the kids' room and put on some old favourites; smoochy, lyrical, emotive stuff, tunes we knew so well we didn't have to listen, just let them fill the gaps in our conversation. So far so good.

21   Saturdays have to be good. It's pretty much all we have. Of us, the two of us just. One night a week, tiptoeing through the hall so as not to disturb the kids, lingering in the kitchen because it's further away from their bedroom than the sitting room, we can speak more freely, don't need to keep the talk turned down to a whisper. We drink wine and catch up. It is necessary to catch up, to keep track of each other.

22   Across the country, while all the little loved ones are asleep, wives and husbands, single parents and surrogates are sitting down together or alone, working out what has to be done. There are always things to be done, to make tomorrow pass smoothly, to make tomorrow work. I look through the glasses and bottles and the shivering candle flame at my husband. The sleeves of his favourite shirt – washed-out blue with pearly buttons, last year's Christmas present from me – are rolled up. His elbows rest on the table which he recently sanded and polished by hand. It took forever. We camped out in the living room while coat after coat of asphyxiating varnish was applied. It looks good now, better than before. But was the effort worth the effect?

23   My husband's fine pale fingers are pushed deep into his hair. I look past him out of the kitchen window, up the dark sloping street at parked cars and sodium lights, lit windows and smoking chimneys, the blinking red eye of a plane crossing a small trough of blue-black sky. My house is where my life happens. In it there is love, work, a roof, a floor, solidity, houseplants, toys, pots and pans, achievements and failures,

inspirations and mistakes, recipes and instruction booklets, guarantees and spare parts, plans, dreams, memories. And there is no need, nothing here pushing me. It is nobody's fault.

24   I go to playparks a lot, for air, for less mess in the house and of course because the kids like to get out. Pushing a swing, watching a little one arcing away and rushing back into your hands, it's natural to talk to another parent. It passes the time. You don't get so bored pushing, the little one is kept lulled and amenable. There's no way of reckoning up fault or blame or responsibility, nothing is stable enough, specific enough to be held to account and that's not the point. The swing swung back, I tossed my hair out of my eyes and glance up at a complete stranger, a father. The father smiled back.

25   We know each other's names, the names of children and spouses. That's about all. We ask few questions. No need for questions. We meet and push our children on swings and sometimes we stand just close enough for our shoulders to touch, just close enough to feel that fluttering hollowness, like hunger. We visit the park – even in the rain, to watch the wind shaking the trees and tossing cherry blossoms on to the grass, the joggers and dog walkers lapping the flat green park – to be near each other.

26   Millions have stood on this very same ledge, in the privacy of their own homes, the unweeded gardens of their minds. Millions have stood on the edge and tested their balance, their common sense, strength of will, they have reckoned up the cost, in mess and misery, have wondered whether below the netless drop a large tree with spread branches awaits to cushion their fall. So simple, so easy. All I have to do is rock on my heels, rock just a shade too far and we will all fall down. Two husbands, two wives, and all the little loved ones.

Dilys Rose

 Thinking through

First, share the answers to the 'Meeting the text' questions you were given at the start of the story. Then work with a partner or a small group to work out the answers to these questions.

You know **which** questions the husband keeps asking, and **how often** he asks them.

- **Why** do you think he asks these questions?
- **What** does it say about him, or about the state of their marriage?

 Let's get to work

As we study this story we are going to look at the state of the narrator's marriage, and at how Rose uses language to bring the narrator and her situation to life. There are many techniques in the story, including a rich and varied use of all sorts of imagery. However, we're going to start by looking at two things that **aren't** in the story, names and speech punctuation, because it matters that Rose has chosen not to use them.

Names

There are six significant characters in the story: the narrator, her husband, their three children and the father she meets at the park. Did you notice as you read the story that none of them seem to have names? It's quite unusual for a writer to behave this way. If you were writing a story for your Higher Folio, your teacher would advise you to give your characters names as part of your attempt to bring them to life and make them seem real.

Now try this

What do you think the characters in this story should be called? What names would you give to the narrator, her husband, her children and the father she meets at the park? Think carefully. Don't just pick names you like; choose ones that fit what these characters seem to be like, names that fit their ages, their family life and their social situations.

Now try this

Now that you have chosen names for the characters, rewrite paragraphs 17 to 19, and then paragraph 24, using these names when you think it's appropriate to do so. Read your version over when you finish. How does it stand up in comparison to the original?

Now try this

Discuss these questions with a partner or a group. Try to find as many answers as possible for each question:

- What does Rose gain by not giving her characters names? How does it help the story have an impact?
- What does Rose lose by not giving her characters names? How does it weaken the story?
- Why do you think Rose chose not to give her characters names?

Share your answers with the rest of the class, and add to your own list any answers other groups mention that yours did not think of.

Speech

The usual rules for using speech in a story would say:

- Put speech marks round the words characters say.
- The words that let us know who is speaking go in the same paragraph as the words that character says.
- In a conversation, change to a new paragraph when you are about to change who is speaking.

Though there is some speech in 'All the Little Loved Ones', we don't spot it at first because Rose doesn't use the above rules to make it stand out.

Now try this

Look at paragraph 1 of the story. Rewrite it in your notebook, following the rules of speech as outlined above. Remember, you don't need to use speech marks for the narrator's words to us, only for those anyone says or could say out loud in the story.

Once you've punctuated the speech, and remembering that all the dialogue in the story is equally hidden from us, answer these questions:

- Why do you think Dilys Rose chose to 'hide' the speech from readers in this way? What is she trying to say about communication within the narrator's marriage?
- Not only is the speech unpunctuated, but not all of the characters get to speak. In fact, only the narrator and her husband do. We never hear any words from any of her three children, nor from the father she meets at the park. Why do you think Rose keeps the other characters silent?

Having looked now at the techniques Rose chooses deliberately to avoid, let's look at those she does use.

Tenses

This story is told mostly in present tense. Although it is more usual for writers to write fiction in the past tense, present tense is not that odd a choice, especially in a piece like this when the narrator is speaking directly to us, the readers. It creates **immediacy**, a sense that the narrator is real and that events are happening as we watch them unfold.

What makes Rose's story a little unusual is that she sometimes deliberately moves into past tense. This happens four times.

Now try this

Copy and complete the table to show where and why Rose sometimes uses past tense. The examples go through the story in order.

Paragraph	Sample quotation	Why in past tense?
14	'While around us couples were splitting at the seams, we remained intact.'	Perhaps to show that the best and strongest phase of their marriage is now behind them, and they may now be as much in danger of splitting as the friends they supported in the past.
		It shows this happy evening is like something that they would have done in the past, but is actually very unusual nowadays.
24		
	'Millions have stood on this very same ledge.'	

Listing

Rose puts lists in the story again and again. This isn't because she's a boring or repetitive writer, but because the narrator's constant use of lists tells

us that she feels her life at the moment is boring and repetitive – which may be why she is feeling tempted to have an affair.

Now try this

You will see a list of the narrator's lists below. Copy this into your notebook as you work through the task. Beside the subject of each list, write down the number of the paragraph where we find that list, and quote the words of the list. Note that these are deliberately not in the same order in which they come up in the story, so you'll have to read carefully to find them. The first one has been done for you.

- A list of what the neighbours are up to: paragraph 18.
  'Upstairs, the neighbours hammer tacks into a carpet, their dogs romp and bark, their antique plumbing gurgles down the wall.'
- A list of the things in her house.
- A list of what her husband would like her to do to show she loves him.
- A list of what happens after their successful Saturday night meal.
- A list of kinds of support they gave their friends.
- Two lists of her domestic tasks.
- A list of the things she and the other man see often in the park.

As we've seen already, Rose takes the risk of boring us with repeated lists to show that it's a risky thing to go through life feeling tired and bored. However, some of these lists also give us particular insight.

Now try this

Answer the following questions:

1 You should have found **two** occasions when the narrator lists small and perhaps rather meaningless domestic tasks she has to do. Why do you think Rose particularly repeated this sort of list? What is she saying about the woman's life and about the demands upon her?

→

Now try this continued

2 Look again at the list you found of the things the narrator has in her house. Some of the things on the list are genuine, actual, physical things and objects, some of them are more abstract feelings and qualities.

   a Circle the feelings and qualities in your quotation of that list to make them stand out.

   b Now look at the physical things on that list. How many of them would you judge to be highly valuable or important? What is Rose saying about the narrator's life by getting her to mix together objects and abstracts in this way?

There's one more list that's worth thinking about, the one from near the end of paragraph 25, when the narrator tells us this:

> We visit the park – even in the rain, to watch the wind shaking the trees and tossing cherry blossoms on to the grass, the joggers and dog walkers lapping the flat green park – to be near each other.

She lists three things she and the father go to the park to see, before admitting that they really go 'to be near each other'. By putting this admission at the end of her list she's trying to make it seem as if seeing each other is nothing significant, no big deal. It's about as subtle as all the times you ever tried to casually drop the name of someone you fancy into a conversation. We still see immediately how much they want to be with each other. It's time to find out more about that father now.

The father at the playpark

It is not until paragraph 24 that we find out that the narrator has met 'a complete stranger, a father' at the playpark. The first time you read it, it's easy to think that she does not meet him until the end of the story, because we are shown this meeting at the end. However, that's not true.

Now try this

You're going to find the clues scattered throughout the story that show she has known this other man since before she began talking to us, the readers. Look in the following paragraphs:

   8, 9, 11

For each paragraph, find and quote the language that suggests she is already thinking about and tempted by this other man. Then explain how the language you have quoted shows this.

The fact that she seems to know this man already before she begins speaking to us affects our sympathy for the narrator. Think about these questions:

- If she only met him at the end of the story, after we have learnt all about her daily life and her relationships with her husband and children, how would we feel about her?
- How do we feel about her once we realise that she has known this other man for some time, and that she has probably only begun telling us her story because he is already on her mind?

Now look at this extract from paragraph 25. Pay particular attention to the sections in bold:

> We know each other's names, the names of children and spouses. That's about all. **We ask few questions.** No need for questions. **We meet** and push our children on swings and **sometimes we stand** just close enough for our shoulders to touch, just close enough to feel that fluttering hollowness, like hunger. **We visit** the park – even in the rain, to watch the wind shaking the trees and tossing cherry blossoms on to the grass, the joggers and dog walkers lapping the flat green park – to be near each other.

Almost the whole story, as we've seen, is in the present tense, but the particular present tense expressions that have been printed in bold above are not here to tell us what she is doing right now. They are more **habitual** – that is, they tell us about things she and the father do again and again as their relationship is developing. The expression 'even in the rain' is another clue as to how much they both want to see each other. Bad weather doesn't stop them visiting the park because they want 'to be near each other'.

At the moment the narrator's actions are still actually quite innocent. All she and the father have done is met, always in public and always with their children nearby, and talked a little. Yet she's clearly very tempted, which we can tell from her use of the image of standing on the edge of the precipice in paragraphs 8 and 26. (We will explore this image in more detail later.)

Now try this

First, decide which of the following two options is, in your opinion, more likely:

> **Option A** The narrator's relationship with this father will become more serious and they will have an affair.
>
> **Option B** The narrator will resist temptation and stay faithful to her own husband.

Next, spend fifteen minutes finding evidence from the story to back up your opinion. You should try to find at least five points. Arrange them in order with your strongest and most convincing point first.

> Now find someone who holds the opposite opinion to you. Sit down together and try to change each other's minds.

The narrator's marriage

The narrator wouldn't be interested in this other man if there weren't issues in her marriage. She and her husband were certainly happy in the past, as paragraph 13 tells us:

> For years we've shared everything we had to share, which wasn't much at first … We started simply: one room, a bed we nailed together from pine planks and lasted a decade … Money was scarce but new love has no need of money. Somewhere to go, to be together is all and we were lucky.

Their friends seem to think she and her husband have a perfect relationship, as we see in paragraph 15:

> An example to us all, we've been told, You two are an example to us all.

However, if we look more closely, even the rest of that paragraph doesn't make their marriage seem quite so good. Firstly, the phrase 'we've been told' tells us their marriage was praised in the past rather than recently, and it's clear from the use of expressions like 'it was meant' elsewhere in the paragraph that the relationship was more exemplary in the past than it is now.

Secondly, there's an expression at the end of paragraph 15 that casts a bleaker light on what their relationship is like now:

> an accumulation of consecutive time together.

It seems that while their marriage has, so far, lasted, it is significant only because it has lasted, because they have accumulated time together, not necessarily because they are actually still happy. The word '**accumulation**' makes it sound quite accidental too, not as if they have worked at it.

In fact it's clear to us from the start of the story that the marriage is not perfect at the moment, so when we find out in the middle, in paragraph 15, that their relationship used to be the envy of all their friends, it just makes the problems the narrator and her husband are experiencing at the moment seem sadder and more poignant.

What's not clear is whether the narrator's husband is aware of the difficulties.

Now try this

Work with a partner or a small group. Make two lists:

1 In the first, list all the evidence you can think of from the story that suggests he does know, or suspect, that his wife is unhappy with the way things are just now.

2 In the second, list all the evidence you can think of from the story that suggests he has no idea of her feelings.

Whether he is aware of these issues or not, it seems clear that she is certainly not discussing them with him, but just letting them go round and round inside her head.

Now try this

Read paragraph 14 again, and answer these two questions:

1 Rose uses some interesting word choice in this paragraph when she has the narrator say that she and her husband 'tootled' along. What does this suggest about what their marriage was like even in the good days?

2 What does the final sentence of that paragraph imply about their marriage?

Paragraph 16 also sheds a lot of light on their marriage, and about the difference between how their friends see the relationship and how the narrator herself sees it. She tells us that: 'we can be relied upon to provide some **display** of the example that we are.'

- What is significant about her choice of the word 'display'?

She goes on to tell us what form this display takes for each of them: 'My husband is likely to take advantage of **the opportunity** and engage in a bit of public **necking**. Me, I **sling mud**, with affection.'

- What is significant about her choice of the word 'opportunity'?

- Her husband displays how good their relationship is by 'necking'. What does that tell us about what matters to him in the relationship? How does it relate to what she thinks he wants her to do in paragraph 3?

- Now look at what she does to display the good example of their marriage. It's very different to what her husband does. First of all, check that everyone in the class agrees on what she means by the expression 'sling mud'. Why is it significant that this is what she does?

Next she admits that: 'Either way, between us we manage **to steer the chat away from** our domestic compatibility.'

- Why do you think they both seem not to want to have people talking about their 'compatibility'?

The narrator ends paragraph 16 by saying: 'Our differences remain.' She doesn't mean the differences between them and their friends, she means the differences between her and her husband.

There may be some evidence to suggest that one of those differences is that he cares about her more than she now cares about him.

- How does the contrast between what they both do to display their compatibility suggest this?

- How do the two questions he keeps asking her suggest this? Do the questions suggest any other, less positive, feelings he might have?

- Read paragraph 22, where we are told about his favourite shirt. How does it provide a clue that he cares about her, and perhaps more than she does about him?

So, if their marriage is that complex, what keeps our narrator there? The answer might be at the very start of the story. 'I love my kids.' She may be staying in her marriage, as people often do, for the sake of her children. As she tells us at the end of that same paragraph, 'Once you become a parent there is no longer a simple equation.'

- How does the story's title support the idea that she may be staying because of her children?

Just one more detail for now. We've spent quite a bit of time looking at the narrator's marriage, which seems to have been better in the past than it is now. There is one worrying little detail in paragraph 14, where she tells us that she and her husband used to provide their friends with 'the occasional alibi'. In other words, both of them seem to have been prepared to cover up the fact that other people were being unfaithful to their partners, even to help them to do so. Now it is their own marriage that is at risk from infidelity.

Much of Rose's picture of that marriage is created by two particular aspects of her style.

Imagery and symbolism

These are two techniques that Rose deploys throughout the story. Sometimes she uses an image to tell us more about the narrator, her life, or her relationship with her husband. Sometimes she turns an object that is actually in the story into a symbol, making it stand for an important idea.

If you have been practising Close Reading, either by working through the relevant chapter of this book or by using other textbooks or past papers, you should know how to examine an image. You begin with what the image **literally** is like, or **literally** means. Then you go on to the **metaphorical** meaning, showing how that image applies to and adds meaning to the subject under discussion.

Again, if you are used to examining images already, you should be used to using this formula:

> Just as … (explain the literal meaning) … so … (explain the metaphorical meaning).

We're going to use this formula to examine some of the images in the story. The first two will be done for you, then you'll have a chance to pick some of them apart yourself.

The first comes from paragraph 1:

> I love my kids. My husband too, though sometimes he asks me whether I do, asks the question, Do you still love me? He asks it while I am in the middle of rinsing spinach or loading washing into the machine, or chasing a trail of toys across the kitchen floor. When he asks the question at a time like that **it's like he's speaking an ancient, forgotten language**.

You could analyse the image of the forgotten language like this:

Just as an ancient language is something that was once familiar, but now has no speakers who are fluent in it, so the idea of loving her husband was once recognisable to the narrator, but is now something she can barely understand.

In fact the narrator admits that herself, and more or less analyses her own image in the very next sentence of the story:

> I can remember a few isolated words but can't connect them, can't get the gist, don't know how to answer.

Now look at this image from paragraph 3, in which the narrator tells us what her husband is doing:

> he sits at the table fingering a daffodil, still bright in its fluted centre but crisp and brown at the edges, as if it's been singed.

You could analyse the image of the daffodil like this:

> Just as the daffodil is still bright in the centre but damaged around the edges, so their marriage may still have some love at its heart, but is past its best.

Now try this

You are going to examine some of the other images and symbols that Rose uses in the story. You may wish to work with a partner to do this. As there are so many images, you may want to have some pairs look at some images while other pairs look at others.

You ought to be able to use the *Just as ... , so ...* method to look at each image, and sometimes you will be given a further hint, prompt or question to help you get the most out of an image. Remember, they all tell us something about the narrator, her life or her relationships.

Examine the following images:

A The image of the **precipice** which comes up in paragraphs 8 and 26. Once you have done your *Just as ... , so ...* analysis, go deeper into the image as it is used in paragraph 8. What does the 'view' mean? What is the 'drop'?

B The image of the narrator being turned to **marble or ice** in paragraph 4.

C The image in paragraph 8 of their conversation being like a smooth, flat **stone**.

D The images in paragraph 11 of their conversation as a **duet**. Once you have done your *Just as ... , so ...* analysis, go deeper into the musical image as it is continued in paragraph 12. What does she mean by the idea of practising scales?

E The image of a **wilderness** in paragraph 15.

F The **tree** image in the final paragraph of the story. Once you have done your *Just as ... , so ...* analysis, go deeper into the image. If the tree stands for a person, who would that person be: her husband, the father from the playpark, or somebody else?

Some of the other images and symbols in the story are a little more subtle, and not quite so straightforward to analyse. They are full of ideas and connotations that again shed more light on the narrator and her relationships.

The meal

Look again at paragraph 19:

> We are able to eat in peace, take time to taste the food which my husband has gone to impossible lengths to prepare. The dinner turns out to be an unqualified success: the curry is smooth, spicy, aromatic, the rice dry, each firm little ellipse brushing against the tongue. The dinner is a joy and a relief. My husband is touchy about his cooking and requires almost as much in the way of reassurance and compliments in this as he does about whether I still love him or not. A bad meal dampens

the spirits, is distressing both for the cook and the cooked-for. A bad meal can be passed over, unmentioned but not ignored. The stomach too has longings for more than simply to be filled. A bad meal can be worse than no meal at all.

This whole description of the meal is a kind of **extended metaphor** for their marriage:

- The effort her husband puts into cooking for them both (after all, most people who fancy a curry on a Saturday night probably get a takeaway) may show how important the relationship is to him.
- The fact that he is touchy about his cooking is, as his wife tells us, somehow connected to his need for reassurance and compliments in their relationship.
- Her statement that 'The stomach too has longings for more than simply to be filled' may have a sexual connotation. We can see in paragraphs 3 and 16 that the physical side of their partnership is very important to him, but her words here suggest she wants more. If we compare this to her words in paragraph 25 about a 'fluttering hollowness, like hunger' when she is with the playpark father, that might suggest that her feelings towards him are more than simply sexual.
- The closing idea that a bad one is worse than none at all applies to marriage even more than it does to curries.

So we can see that the extended metaphor of a meal standing for their marriage is made up of four quite complex ideas. It's important to notice that the curry is a big success.

Now try this

Answer these two questions:

1 If the meal somehow symbolises their marriage, how does its success act as a small optimistic note in the story?

2 Read the whole paragraph about the meal again carefully. Does it sound as if their meals together are usually so successful? What does this tell us about their marriage?

Music

In paragraph 20 the narrator tells us:

We drank more wine, turned off the overhead light, lit a candle, fetched the cassette recorder from the kids' room and put on some old favourites; smoochy, lyrical, emotive stuff, **tunes we knew so well we didn't have to listen**, just let them fill the gaps in our conversation. So far so good.

Look at the words in bold. This tells us something metaphorical about the intimacy and familiarity in their relationship.

- How could this familiarity be a **good** thing?
- How could this familiarity be a **bad** thing?

The table

In paragraph 22, the narrator tells us that her husband's

elbows rest on the table which he recently sanded and polished by hand. It took forever. We camped out in the living room while coat after coat of asphyxiating varnish was applied. It looks good now, better than before. But was the effort worth the effect?

There are two things we can get out of this image:

- How does the effort he put into restoring the table add to the picture we already have of the husband, and his feelings about their family life?
- Look at the question the narrator asks at the end of the paragraph. How could we apply it to more than just the actual table in front of her?

The shirt

In paragraph 22 the narrator describes her husband sitting at the table:

> The sleeves of his favourite shirt – washed-out blue with pearly buttons, last year's Christmas present from me – are rolled up.

- What ideas are suggested by the phrases 'washed out' and 'last year's'?

Things to do

Again in paragraph 22, the speaker tells us:

> There are always things to be done, to make tomorrow pass smoothly, to make tomorrow work.

She's not just talking about household chores and domestic duties.

- Explain how what she is saying could be a lesson or message about good marriages.

Word choice and repetition

As you know from your work on Close Reading, writers choose some words especially carefully because they have certain shades of meaning, or because their connotations set off certain ideas in the reader's mind. You also know that we should pay attention when writers decide to repeat certain words. Rose uses both these techniques, often combining them.

Little

When you first read the story, you were asked to count how many times this word is used. You should have found it nine times in the main text, and once in the title.

Now try this

Read the story again. As you read, note down the paragraph number each time the word 'little' is used. Beside the number, note down what is being described this way. Then answer the questions:

- Of the nine uses of this word, how many of them are somehow connected to children?
- What is Rose trying to make us feel towards the children by repeatedly using this word?

Blood

Look at paragraph 2:

> We have three children. All our own. Blood of our blood, flesh of our flesh etc, delivered into our hands in the usual way, a slithering mess of blood and slime and wonder, another tiny miracle.

Rose's word choice here is very clever and subtle. Having the narrator describe her children as a 'miracle' makes them sound special, treasured. However, this impression is entirely undermined by three other examples of word choice in the same paragraph: 'etc', 'in the usual way' and 'another'.

- Explain how the writer's use of these words makes the children seem less special.

Now look at Rose's use of repetition here. She has the narrator say 'blood' three times. The first two uses are in the expression 'blood of our blood', which sounds very positive as it seems to reinforce how strongly both she and her husband are connected to the children.

- Which three much more negative words does Rose have the narrator use in the same sentence?
- What overall effect does she create by using 'blood' three times?

Now considering all the word choice examples you have examined in the paragraph, discuss this question with a partner, a group, or the class:

- How do you think the narrator feels about her children?

Word choice for self-justification

Perhaps because the speaker feels very guilty about the temptation she is facing, she tries to justify her actions and thoughts to herself and to us. In paragraph 24 she tells us that 'it's natural to talk to another parent' and gives us three reasons why this is so.

● What are these reasons?

She also tells us that 'There's no way of reckoning up **fault** or **blame** or **responsibility**'. The very fact that she uses those three very emotive nouns, which all reinforce the same idea, tells us she feels guilty and doesn't want us to make her feel more so.

Now read the final paragraph of the story.

● Explain how the speaker uses a number to make herself sound less personally responsible.

● How does the expression 'All I have to do …' in that paragraph also make her sound less responsible?

Allusion

Now try this

Re-read the final paragraph of the story, noticing the following words in particular:

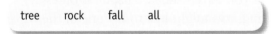

tree   rock   fall   all

An **allusion** is an indirect reference made by a writer to something he or she thinks we will recognise.

Rose is alluding to a nursery rhyme that she thinks her readers will recognise. Working with a group, or as a class, search your memories until you can reconstruct the text of that nursery rhyme.

Now that you know **what** she is alluding to, think about **why** she is making that allusion. Decide together what Rose is saying about what will happen if the speaker gives in to the temptation she is facing.

Dramatic monologue

If you have worked through the chapter on the poem 'Porphyria's Lover', you'll know about the genre of **dramatic monologue**. In dramatic monologues, a speaker tells a story that reveals something about himself or herself. One key feature of this genre is that speakers often let slip some of their nastier or more unpleasant thoughts, habits or actions without realising it. You're getting to the end of your studies on this story, and should know it very well by now.

Now try this

Here are four possible ideas about the narrator:

1 She is so exhausted and unhappy that she mentions the playpark father by accident as she tells us about her life.

2 She is using the monologue to justify her actions to us because she feels they are justifiable.

3 She is using the monologue to justify her actions to herself because she actually feels very guilty.

4 She is speaking as a way of thinking over her options because she doesn't know what to do.

First, decide which of these statements you agree with, maybe just one, perhaps more. **Next** find a partner who agrees with one statement you also agree with. Work together to find evidence in the story to support your position. After five minutes, **swap** partners and find someone who agrees with another statement that you also thought was correct. Work together again to gather evidence to support your position.

Your own response

Some people read this story and feel sympathy for the narrator because she feels worn down in her marriage and guilty about the temptation she's experiencing. Some people feel sympathy for the husband because he seems to have no idea what's on his wife's mind. Some people feel sympathy for the nameless children whose lives would be so affected if their parents' marriage breaks up. Now that you have studied the story in depth, you should be ready to come to your own response.

Now try this

Answer these questions, justifying your response by making references to, or quoting from, the story.

- Who do you feel most sympathy for, and why?
- Is anyone to blame, or are these sad events nobody's personal fault?
- Is there any evidence in the story that this situation could improve?

A comparison

You won't ever get a Higher essay question which allows you to compare texts from two different genres, so this particular task isn't going to help you with your exams. However, it's always good to be able to see connections between different parts of your learning. So, if you've also worked on the Philip Larkin poem 'Afternoons' earlier in this book, you should be able to make some links now.

Now try this

Work with a partner. Make a list or mind map to show all the ways in which the narrator in this story is similar to the young mothers in 'Afternoons'.

Technique revision

Now that you've worked your way through the whole chapter about 'All the Little Loved Ones' you should know the story very well. Before you prove this by writing an essay about it, revise your knowledge of Rose's techniques.

You're going to carry out the same exercise that you did at the end of Chapter 3 on 'Incident'. (Look back to pp. 79–80 now if you need to be more fully reminded of the instructions.) Take a large piece of paper and mark it up into a **PEE** grid. For every technique, fill in a quotation from the story, and explain the effect it has on the reader. For a grid about 'All the Little Loved Ones', you need to work with the following techniques:

> lack of names   lack of speech punctuation
> present tense   past tense   listing   the title
> word choice of little; tootled; display; blood
> repetition of little; blood   allusion
> symbols: the table; the daffodil; her husband's shirt; the music they dance to; things to do
> imagery: the precipice; marble or ice; stone; duet; wilderness; tree
> the extended metaphor of the curry

Possible essay choices

Once you have studied Chapter 8 on essay writing, you might like to try one of the following essays, which are all suitable for 'All the Little Loved Ones'.

Above the prose fiction essay choices on the exam paper you'll see the following words:

> **Answers to questions on prose fiction should address relevantly the central concern(s)/ theme(s) of the text(s) and be supported by reference to appropriate techniques of prose fiction such as: characterisation, setting, key incident(s), narrative technique, symbolism, structure, climax, plot, atmosphere, dialogue, imagery …**

Now look at the essay choices:

> Choose a novel or a short story in which a technique (such as symbolism) is used by the author and is, in your opinion, vital to the success of the text.
>
> Explain how the writer employs this technique and why, in your opinion, it is so important to your appreciation of the text.

OR

> Choose a novel or short story which features a relationship between two characters which is confrontational or corrosive.
>
> Describe how the relationship is portrayed and discuss to what extent the nature of the relationship influences your understanding of the text as a whole.

OR

> Choose a novel or short story which deals with true love, unrequited love or love betrayed.
>
> Discuss the writer's exploration of the theme and show to what extent it conveys a powerful message about the nature of love.

CHAPTER 7
Prose: 'Shooting an Elephant'

 ## Getting in

You're about to read a piece of non-fiction. The writer, George Orwell, tells us about a time when he did something he didn't at first want to do. Before you read the essay, think about the following questions. You might feel able to share your answers with a partner, a small group, or your class. However, some of these questions are quite personal and it's fine if you want to keep your answers to yourself.

- Have you ever done something you initially didn't want to do, simply because other people made you feel that you had to do it?
- How did you feel about this at the time?
- Looking back on this experience, how do you feel about it now?

 ## Meeting the text

The piece you are going to read is an **essay**. This doesn't mean that Orwell had to write it because a teacher told him to, or that he wrote it in an exam. An essay is short piece of writing on a single subject, usually presenting the personal view of the author.

One of your options for Higher Writing, either for your NAB or for your Folio, is to write a Personal Reflective Essay. The skills for this are covered in depth in the Writing chapter of this book (Chapter 1). As you read and work on this essay by Orwell, notice how he uses the skills of Personal Reflective Writing. He brings an incident to life in detail; tells us about his own thoughts and feelings at the time; reflects on his own behaviour and that of others around him; and reflects more widely on the nature of empires. All of this makes 'Shooting an Elephant' an excellent example of the Personal Reflective Essay.

Now try this

In this essay, Orwell tells us how he ended up shooting an elephant that he did not want to shoot.

As you read, make two lists, one of the reasons not to shoot the animal, one of reasons in favour of shooting it. Note down where you find each reason. The first item of each list has been done for you.

Reasons against shooting	Reasons for shooting
Shooting a working elephant is like destroying a valuable piece of machinery (para 6)	It's done lots of damage and killed a cow (para 3)

SHOOTING AN ELEPHANT

1   In Moulmein, in Lower Burma,[1] I was hated by large numbers of people – the only time in my life that I have been important enough for this to happen to me. I was sub-divisional police officer of the town, and in an aimless, petty kind of way anti-European feeling was very bitter. No one had the guts to raise a riot, but if a European woman went through the bazaars alone somebody would probably spit betel[2] juice over her dress. As a police officer I was an obvious target and was baited whenever it seemed safe to do so. When a nimble Burman tripped me up on the football field and the referee (another Burman) looked the other way, the crowd yelled with

---

[1] Burma was part of British India in the 1920s, and is now an independent country.
[2] Betel is a kind of nut.

hideous laughter. This happened more than once. In the end the sneering yellow faces of young men that met me everywhere, the insults hooted after me when I was at a safe distance, got badly on my nerves. The young Buddhist priests were the worst of all. There were several thousands of them in the town and none of them seemed to have anything to do except stand on street corners and jeer at Europeans.

2   All this was perplexing and upsetting. For at that time I had already made up my mind that imperialism was an evil thing and the sooner I chucked up my job and got out of it the better. Theoretically – and secretly, of course – I was all for the Burmese and all against their oppressors, the British. As for the job I was doing, I hated it more bitterly than I can perhaps make clear. In a job like that you see the dirty work of Empire at close quarters. The wretched prisoners huddling in the stinking cages of the lock-ups, the grey, cowed faces of the long-term convicts, the scarred buttocks of the men who had been flogged with bamboos — all these oppressed me with an intolerable sense of guilt. But I could get nothing into perspective. I was young and ill-educated and I had had to think out my problems in the utter silence that is imposed on every Englishman in the East. I did not even know that the British Empire is dying, still less did I know that it is a great deal better than the younger empires that are going to supplant it. All I knew was that I was stuck between my hatred of the empire I served and my rage against the evil-spirited little beasts who tried to make my job impossible. With one part of my mind I thought of the British Raj[3] as an unbreakable tyranny, as something clamped down, *in saecula saeculorum*,[4] upon the will of prostrate peoples; with another part I thought that the greatest joy in the world would be to drive a bayonet into a Buddhist priest's guts. Feelings like these are the normal by-products of imperialism; ask any Anglo-Indian official, if you can catch him off duty.

3   One day something happened which in a roundabout way was enlightening. It was a tiny incident in itself, but it gave me a better glimpse than I had had before of the real nature of imperialism – the real motives for which despotic governments act. Early one morning the sub-inspector at a police station the other end of the town rang me up on the phone and said that an elephant was ravaging the bazaar. Would I please come and do something about it? I did not know what I could do, but I wanted to see what was happening and I got on to a pony and started out. I took my rifle, an old .44 Winchester and much too small to kill an elephant, but I thought the noise might be useful *in terrorem*.[5] Various Burmans stopped me on the way and told me about the elephant's doings. It was not, of course, a wild elephant, but a tame one which had gone 'must'.[6] It had been chained up, as tame elephants always are when their attack of 'must' is due, but on the previous night it had broken its chain and escaped. Its mahout,[7] the only person who could manage it when it was in that state, had set out in pursuit, but had taken the wrong direction and was now twelve hours' journey away, and in the morning the elephant had suddenly reappeared in the town. The Burmese population had no weapons and were quite helpless against it. It had already destroyed somebody's bamboo hut, killed a cow and raided some fruit-stalls and devoured the stock; also it had met the municipal rubbish van and, when the driver jumped out and took to his heels, had turned the van over and inflicted violences upon it.

4   The Burmese sub-inspector and some Indian constables were waiting for me in the quarter where the elephant had been seen. It was a very poor quarter, a labyrinth of squalid bamboo huts, thatched with palmleaf, winding all over a steep hillside. I remember that it was a cloudy, stuffy morning at the beginning of the rains. We began questioning the people as to where the elephant had gone and, as usual, failed to get any definite information. That is invariably the case in the East; a story always

---

[3]The Raj was the system through which Britain owned and controlled India until 1948.

[4]*In saecula saeculorum* is Latin for 'for ever and ever', 'for eternity'.

[5]*In terrorem* is Latin for 'as a warning'.

[6]Must is a time when male elephants become very aggressive because of a surge in testosterone, and during which a usually placid elephant may try to kill humans.

[7]A mahout is a person who drives, and works with, an elephant.

sounds clear enough at a distance, but the nearer you get to the scene of events the vaguer it becomes. Some of the people said that the elephant had gone in one direction, some said that he had gone in another, some professed not even to have heard of any elephant. I had almost made up my mind that the whole story was a pack of lies, when we heard yells a little distance away. There was a loud, scandalised cry of 'Go away, child! Go away this instant!' and an old woman with a switch in her hand came round the corner of a hut, violently shooing away a crowd of naked children. Some more women followed, clicking their tongues and exclaiming; evidently there was something that the children ought not to have seen. I rounded the hut and saw a man's dead body sprawling in the mud. He was an Indian, a black Dravidian coolie,[8] almost naked, and he could not have been dead many minutes. The people said that the elephant had come suddenly upon him round the corner of the hut, caught him with its trunk, put its foot on his back and ground him into the earth. This was the rainy season and the ground was soft, and his face had scored a trench a foot deep and a couple of yards long. He was lying on his belly with arms crucified and head sharply twisted to one side. His face was coated with mud, the eyes wide open, the teeth bared and grinning with an expression of unendurable agony. (Never tell me, by the way, that the dead look peaceful. Most of the corpses I have seen looked devilish.) The friction of the great beast's foot had stripped the skin from his back as neatly as one skins a rabbit. As soon as I saw the dead man I sent an orderly to a friend's house nearby to borrow an elephant rifle. I had already sent back the pony, not wanting it to go mad with fright and throw me if it smelt the elephant.

5   The orderly came back in a few minutes with a rifle and five cartridges, and meanwhile some Burmans had arrived and told us that the elephant was in the paddy fields below, only a few hundred yards away. As I started forward practically the whole population of the quarter flocked out of the houses and followed me. They had seen the rifle and were all shouting excitedly that I was going to shoot the elephant. They had not shown much interest in the

elephant when he was merely ravaging their homes, but it was different now that he was going to be shot. It was a bit of fun to them, as it would be to an English crowd; besides they wanted the meat. It made me vaguely uneasy. I had no intention of shooting the elephant – I had merely sent for the rifle to defend myself if necessary – and it is always unnerving to have a crowd following you. I marched down the hill, looking and feeling a fool, with the rifle over my shoulder and an ever-growing army of people jostling at my heels. At the bottom, when you got away from the huts, there was a metalled road and beyond that a miry waste of paddy fields a thousand yards across, not yet ploughed but soggy from the first rains and dotted with coarse grass. The elephant was standing eight yards from the road, his left side towards us. He took not the slightest notice of the crowd's approach. He was tearing up bunches of grass, beating them against his knees to clean them and stuffing them into his mouth.

6   I had halted on the road. As soon as I saw the elephant I knew with perfect certainty that I ought not to shoot him. It is a serious matter to shoot a working elephant – it is comparable to destroying a huge and costly piece of machinery – and obviously one ought not to do it if it can possibly be avoided. And at that distance, peacefully eating, the elephant looked no more dangerous than a cow. I thought then and I think now that his attack of 'must' was already passing off; in which case he would merely wander harmlessly about until the

[8]A coolie is a labourer, and the word Dravidian tells us he comes from a lower caste, a lower group in society.

mahout came back and caught him. Moreover, I did not in the least want to shoot him. I decided that I would watch him for a little while to make sure that he did not turn savage again, and then go home.

7   But at that moment I glanced round at the crowd that had followed me. It was an immense crowd, two thousand at the least and growing every minute. It blocked the road for a long distance on either side. I looked at the sea of yellow faces above the garish clothes – faces all happy and excited over this bit of fun, all certain that the elephant was going to be shot. They were watching me as they would watch a conjurer about to perform a trick. They did not like me, but with the magical rifle in my hands I was momentarily worth watching. And suddenly I realised that I should have to shoot the elephant after all. The people expected it of me and I had got to do it; I could feel their two thousand wills pressing me forward, irresistibly. And it was at this moment, as I stood there with the rifle in my hands, that I first grasped the hollowness, the futility of the white man's dominion in the East. Here was I, the white man with his gun, standing in front of the unarmed native crowd – seemingly the leading actor of the piece; but in reality I was only an absurd puppet pushed to and fro by the will of those yellow faces behind. I perceived in this moment that when the white man turns tyrant it is his own freedom that he destroys. He becomes a sort of hollow, posing dummy, the conventionalized figure of a sahib.[9] For it is the condition of his rule that he shall spend his life in trying to impress the 'natives', and so in every crisis he has got to do what the 'natives' expect of him. He wears a mask, and his face grows to fit it. I had got to shoot the elephant. I had committed myself to doing it when I sent for the rifle. A sahib has got to act like a sahib; he has got to appear resolute, to know his own mind and do definite things. To come all that way, rifle in hand, with two thousand people marching at my heels, and then to trail feebly away, having done nothing – no, that was impossible. The crowd would laugh at me. And my whole life, every white man's life in the East, was one long struggle not to be laughed at.

8   But I did not want to shoot the elephant. I watched him beating his bunch of grass against his knees, with that preoccupied grandmotherly air that elephants have. It seemed to me that it would be murder to shoot him. At that age I was not squeamish about killing animals, but I had never shot an elephant and never wanted to. (Somehow it always seems worse to kill a large animal.) Besides, there was the beast's owner to be considered. Alive, the elephant was worth at least a hundred pounds; dead, he would only be worth the value of his tusks, five pounds, possibly.[10] But I had got to act quickly. I turned to some experienced-looking Burmans who had been there when we arrived, and asked them how the elephant had been behaving. They all said the same thing: he took no notice of you if you left him alone, but he might charge if you went too close to him.

9   It was perfectly clear to me what I ought to do. I ought to walk up to within, say, twenty-five yards of the elephant and test his behaviour. If he charged, I could shoot; if he took no notice of me, it would be safe to leave him until the mahout came back. But also I knew that I was going to do no such thing. I was a poor shot with a rifle and the ground was soft mud into which one would sink at every step. If the elephant charged and I missed him, I should have about as much chance as a toad under a steam-roller. But even then I was not thinking particularly of my own skin, only of the watchful yellow faces behind. For at that moment, with the crowd watching me, I was not afraid in the ordinary sense, as I would have been if I had been alone. A white man mustn't be frightened in front of 'natives'; and so, in general, he isn't frightened. The sole thought in my mind was that if anything went wrong those two thousand Burmans would see me pursued, caught, trampled on and reduced to a grinning corpse like that Indian up the hill. And if that happened it was quite probable that some of them would

[9]A sahib was the name given to a male European in India, usually a term of respect used of or to such a person by native Indians.
[10]These sums of money from the mid-1920s are worth about £4,467 and £223, respectively, at the time of writing of this book.

laugh. That would never do. There was only one alternative. I shoved the cartridges into the magazine and lay down on the road to get a better aim.

10   The crowd grew very still, and a deep, low, happy sigh, as of people who see the theatre curtain go up at last, breathed from innumerable throats. They were going to have their bit of fun after all. The rifle was a beautiful German thing with cross-hair sights. I did not then know that in shooting an elephant one would shoot to cut an imaginary bar running from ear-hole to ear-hole. I ought, therefore, as the elephant was sideways on, to have aimed straight at his ear-hole, actually I aimed several inches in front of this, thinking the brain would be further forward.

11   When I pulled the trigger I did not hear the bang or feel the kick – one never does when a shot goes home – but I heard the devilish roar of glee that went up from the crowd. In that instant, in too short a time, one would have thought, even for the bullet to get there, a mysterious, terrible change had come over the elephant. He neither stirred nor fell, but every line of his body had altered. He looked suddenly stricken, shrunken, immensely old, as though the frightful impact of the bullet had paralysed him without knocking him down. At last, after what seemed a long time – it might have been five seconds, I dare say – he sagged flabbily to his knees. His mouth slobbered. An enormous senility seemed to have settled upon him. One could have imagined him thousands of years old. I fired again into the same spot. At the second shot he did not collapse but climbed with desperate slowness to his feet and stood weakly upright, with legs sagging and head drooping. I fired a third time. That was the shot that did for him. You could see the agony of it jolt his whole body and knock the last remnant of strength from his legs. But in falling he seemed for a moment to rise, for as his hind legs collapsed beneath him he seemed to tower upward like a huge rock toppling, his trunk reaching skyward like a tree. He trumpeted, for the first and only time. And then down he came, his belly towards me, with a crash that seemed to shake the ground even where I lay.

12   I got up. The Burmans were already racing past me across the mud. It was obvious that the elephant would never rise again, but he was not dead. He was breathing very rhythmically with long rattling gasps, his great mound of a side painfully rising and falling. His mouth was wide open – I could see far down into caverns of pale pink throat. I waited a long time for him to die, but his breathing did not weaken. Finally I fired my two remaining shots into the spot where I thought his heart must be. The thick blood welled out of him like red velvet, but still he did not die. His body did not even jerk when the shots hit him, the tortured breathing continued without a pause. He was dying, very slowly and in great agony, but in some world remote from me where not even a bullet could damage him further. I felt that I had got to put an end to that dreadful noise. It seemed dreadful to see the great beast lying there, powerless to move and yet powerless to die, and not even to be able to finish him. I sent back for my small rifle and poured shot after shot into his heart and down his throat. They seemed to make no impression. The tortured gasps continued as steadily as the ticking of a clock.

13   In the end I could not stand it any longer and went away. I heard later that it took him half an hour to die. Burmans were bringing dash and baskets even before I left, and I was told they had stripped his body almost to the bones by the afternoon.

14   Afterwards, of course, there were endless discussions about the shooting of the elephant. The owner was furious, but he was only an Indian and could do nothing. Besides, legally I had done the right thing, for a mad elephant has to be killed, like a mad dog, if its owner fails to control it. Among the Europeans opinion was divided. The older men said I was right, the younger men said it was a damn shame to shoot an elephant for killing a coolie, because an elephant was worth more than any damn Coringhee coolie. And afterwards I was very glad that the coolie had been killed; it put me legally in the right and it gave me a sufficient pretext for shooting the elephant. I often wondered whether any of the others grasped that I had done it solely to avoid looking a fool.

George Orwell, 1936

Thinking through

First, share your answers to the 'Meeting the text' task you were given at the start of the story. Then discuss this question with your class and come to an agreement about the answer:

- Of all the reasons why Orwell **could** or **should** have shot the elephant, what is the key reason why he **did** do this?

Now try this

Work with a partner or a small group to work out the answers to these questions.

Like any well-structured essay, this one has an introduction, a main body and a conclusion.

- Which paragraph(s) make up the introduction?
- Which paragraph(s) make up the main body?
- Which word at the start of a paragraph marks a turning point?
- Which paragraph(s) make up the conclusion?

Let's get to work

Before we look closely at 'Shooting an Elephant', it's useful to know a bit about Orwell and his own life and background, as he tells us in the essay that he is writing from experience.

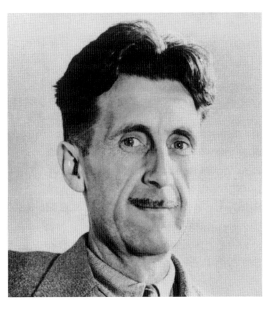

His real name was Eric Arthur Blair and he was born in Bengal (which was then part of India, but is now the independent nation of Bangladesh) in 1903. Bengal was part of the British Empire and under British rule, and his father worked there as a customs officer. Orwell called his background, 'lower-upper-middle-class'. His father retired and the family returned to England when Orwell was three. After that they were often short of money.

He was sent to boarding school aged eight on a scholarship, and later went to Eton, also on a scholarship – facts which demonstrate both how clever he was, and how little money his family had. Eton is an exclusive and prestigious private school and nineteen British Prime Ministers have been pupils there. You might think that being at Eton would have turned Orwell into an insider, part of the powerful establishment. However, he always felt like an outsider, unworthy and very aware of how little money his family had.

After school, rather than going to university he joined the Indian Imperial Police and served in Burma from 1922 to 1927. He spent much of his time there feeling disillusioned and frustrated, saying later, 'Not only were we hanging people and putting them into jail and so forth, we were doing it in the capacity of unwanted foreign invaders.' He returned to Britain, 'conscious of an immense weight of guilt that I had got to expiate.' (To expiate means to apologise or make up for.)

After leaving Burma he lived for a while among poor and marginalised people in Britain and France, taking low-paid and dirty jobs. He wrote about this later in a book called *Down and Out in Paris and London*. He had wanted to be a writer from a very early age and spent most of the rest of his life writing, not only essays but also journalism, longer non-fiction books and novels. Two of his most famous books are *Animal Farm* and *Nineteen Eighty-Four*, and in the latter he created two ideas which have become part of our culture: the notion that Big Brother is watching us, and the idea of a Room 101 where the things that upset each of us most can be found.

One critic said that Orwell had 'the mind of an intellectual but the feelings of a common man'. Much of his writing supported the needs and rights of ordinary working people. He didn't believe in Russian Stalinist communism (in fact *Animal Farm* was written to point out the dangers of this kind of system) but did believe in socialism based on freedom, justice and common decency.

His pseudonym (the name he chose for his writing work) also tells us something about him and his love for England. He chose Orwell as it is the name of a river in Suffolk, and George after the English patron saint. He was a patriot who loved his country, without being a nationalist or a bigot who wanted his country to dominate others. We can see in this essay how deeply he is thinking about the role Britain should play in the world, and about how British people should react to those from other countries.

This is an essay, not a story. Orwell has spent years thinking over this incident, which he now has clear ideas about. He wants us to understand these ideas clearly, so he spells them out to us. One key moment when he does this is at the start of paragraph 3, just before he begins to describe the actual incident:

> One day something happened which in a roundabout way was enlightening. It was a tiny incident in itself, but it gave me a better glimpse than I had had before of **the real nature of imperialism** – the real motives for which despotic governments act.

If you are learning quotations from this text to use in your own essays, this would be a very

helpful one to know. We could say that this idea about imperialism is his **wider**, **societal theme**. He also has a **personal theme** about peer pressure, which he spells out at the very end:

> I often wondered whether any of the others grasped that I had done it solely **to avoid looking a fool**.

We'll keep returning to these two themes as we work through this essay and through Orwell's ideas and techniques.

The pathetic fallacy

If you have worked on Chapter 4 about the poem 'Porphyria's Lover', you will be familiar with the technique of the **pathetic fallacy**. This is when a writer uses weather to suggest a character's emotions, or the mood of a text.

In paragraph 4, as he sets off to look for the rampaging elephant, Orwell tells us:

> I remember that it was a cloudy, stuffy morning at the beginning of the rains.

This is one of the many precise details used to tell the story credibly. However, it is also an example of the pathetic fallacy. The writer's mention of a 'cloudy, stuffy' atmosphere tells us that the weather feels calm at the moment but also oppressive and overwhelming. The mention of 'the beginning of the rains' tells us that there will soon be a huge, perhaps even violent, storm.

Now try this

Think about those two ideas: calm but oppressive now; violence later. Answer these questions:

- How do these ideas apply to what we read in paragraph 4?
- How do they apply to the whole incident with the elephant?
- How do they apply to the wider situation of the British Empire controlling India?

Paragraph length

Orwell writes very long paragraphs. This is partly because he wrote this essay almost eighty years ago when writers did tend to write like this.

- Which paragraph is shortest? How many words does it contain?
- Which paragraph is longest? How many words does it contain?

One effect of this style is to make his essay seem more considered, and reflective, whereas if Orwell had wanted a more immediate piece of journalism he would probably have used shorter paragraphs.

Now try this

Using your understanding of the rules of paragraphing, decide how you would break paragraph 4 down into shorter paragraphs. You could do this by rewriting the whole thing, or by making a photocopy of the page and marking **NP** in coloured ink every time you think you could begin a new paragraph. Then answer these questions:

1 How many new paragraphs did you divide paragraph 4 into?

2 In what ways is your version better than Orwell's?

3 What have you lost by altering his writing in this way?

4 Why do you think Orwell chose to use long paragraphs as he did in this essay?

5 What does his use of long paragraphs tell you about the way he thinks?

Share your answers with the rest of the class and note down any responses you didn't think of by yourself.

Explanations and tenses

Orwell tells us in paragraph 2, 'I was young and ill-educated'. We can see that there are many times in the incident with the elephant when he feels uncomfortable or ignorant, or is unsure about what he should do. This is not surprising as he

must have been between nineteen and twenty-four years old when this happened – very young, and very far from home. However, he wrote 'Shooting an Elephant' in 1936 when he was thirty-three, and the older Orwell, the writer, is far more confident. Having had time to consider the event, he often tells us exactly what he knows or believes.

Sometimes he gives us information, such as how to shoot an elephant to kill it quickly, or how the shooter experiences the firing of a shot. Sometimes he gives us his firmly held opinions, such as how any Anglo-Indian official might feel about the people he is supposed to be governing. These examples are all quite easy to spot because Orwell changes from past to **present tense** whenever he writes about them.

Now try this

First **divide** your class into ten small groups. You will need a group each for paragraphs 1, 2, 3, 4, 7 and 12. You will also need groups to look at paragraphs 5 and 6 together; 8 and 9; 10 and 11; and paragraphs 13 and 14.

Next work with your small group to look at the paragraph(s) you have been given. **Skim read** your paragraph(s) looking for present tense verbs, especially *is* and *are*, as these will lead you to Orwell's explanations and opinions.

As you find them, **note down** the things Orwell tells the reader. At the end of each note, mark whether you think this is a piece of **factual information**, or whether he is giving us his **opinion**. Spend about five minutes on this. If you finish looking at the paragraph you were first given, keep moving forward through the essay, looking for present tenses and noting what Orwell tells us as you go.

Once the five minutes are up, **share** your answers with the rest of the class.

You should be able to see that the essay is full of moments when Orwell quite clearly tells us things. Remember, though, that these are the realisations and thoughts of an older man writing about events with hindsight. The young Orwell, to whom this actually happened, is much less knowledgeable and feels quite powerless, despite his apparent authority as an Englishman in Burma.

Sympathy

It sometimes seems as if Orwell has more sympathy for the killer elephant than the vulnerable people. Read this extract from paragraph 8:

> But I did not want to shoot the elephant. I watched him beating his bunch of grass against his knees, with that preoccupied grandmotherly air that elephants have. It seemed to me that it would be murder to shoot him.

- Which two different words in this paragraph create sympathy for the elephant? How do they do this?

Now read this extract from paragraph 11:

> When I pulled the trigger I did not hear the bang or feel the kick – one never does when a shot goes home – but I heard the devilish roar of glee that went up from the crowd.

- Which word in this paragraph shows a lack of sympathy or empathy between Orwell and the Burmans?

We should not perhaps judge Orwell too harshly for this. He was a product of his own culture and society. This isn't an excuse – there are no excuses for racism – but it is a reason for what he was like as a young man. It's important to remember that he grew up to question and re-evaluate the attitudes he'd been brought up with. This very essay shows him doing this.

Also it is clear that, even as a young man, Orwell had a rather more enlightened attitude to the Burmese people than many others of his age and class, as we can see from the final paragraph:

> the younger men said it was a damn shame to shoot an elephant for killing a coolie, because an elephant was worth more than any damn Coringhee coolie.

This leads us on to how he feels about the British Empire and his position in it.

Orwell and the Empire

It used to be said that the sun never set on the British Empire. Right up to the late 1940s, Britain controlled much of Africa, all of what is now India, Pakistan, Bangladesh and Burma, and many other modern nations.

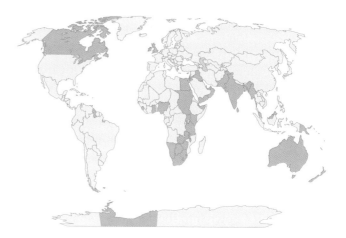

It's hard for us now to grasp how powerful Britain was, but Orwell expects his 1936 readers to understand this completely. He jumps right in with, 'In Moulmein, in Lower Burma', expecting them to know where this is and why he would have been there.

Orwell sounds rather xenophobic at first. He talks about the 'sneering yellow faces of the young men' and complains about how the Burmans behaved. He almost seems to have a grudge against them.

- How many examples does he give in paragraph 1 of unpleasant things they did?

It might seem that he carries on like this in the rest of the essay. For example, he uses the word 'yellow' three more times to describe Burmans, but tells us nothing else about their looks, and tends to describe them as a 'crowd' or group rather than individuals. (We will explore this idea of the crowd elsewhere.) However, most of the essay shows that Orwell is not an unquestioning supporter of the Empire, nor did he simply hate the Burmese.

Now try this

Re-read paragraph 2. Make a note of everything that either shows Orwell questioning the British Empire, or sympathising with the Burmese.

Nor does Orwell think the problem lies solely with the British Empire. Writing in 1936, he says in paragraph 2 that it is 'a great deal better than the younger empires that are going to supplant it'. He later wrote *Animal Farm* as a criticism of Stalin's Russia, which controlled most of Eastern Europe after the Second World War, and this comment here shows that he was already aware of the Soviet threat.

His feelings about the British Empire, and about empires in general, are thoughtful and complex. As mentioned already, we could say the **wider societal theme** of this essay is an exploration of empires and imperialism.

As we have seen, Orwell expects his 1936 readers to know what the Empire is, but there are many ideas in this essay which would surprise them. Paragraph 2 shows him hating both his job in the Raj and the Buddhist priests who jeer at him. When he writes that 'Feelings like these are the normal by-products of imperialism', he is telling the readers something they might not expect.

They might also be very surprised to read his explanation in paragraph 7 of 'the futility of the white man's dominion in the East'. If you're going to learn just one quotation from this entire essay, learn that one. It sums up what he has to say about his **wider theme** of empire. It also connects to his more **personal theme** about pressure, as he was unable to resist the pressure from the crowd to shoot the elephant, even though he was meant to be an authority figure.

The elephant and the Empire

Some critics believe that the elephant is a metaphor for the power of empire.

Now try this

Re-read paragraphs 3 and 4. Make a list of all the harm the elephant causes before Orwell catches up with it.

If you agree with these critics you would say that, just as the rampaging animal destroys homes, food, businesses and people, so empires destroy the homes, lives and livelihoods of the people whose countries they dominate.

Other critics say that the elephant isn't a metaphor for the British Empire, but for Burma.

Re-read paragraph 11. Orwell fires three shots, and even then only manages to wound the beast. There were three Anglo-Burmese wars, in 1824, 1852 and 1885, before Britain finally took control. If you agree with these critics, the animal symbolises Burma and its struggle to survive. It still lives after the third shot, just as the Burmese people still survive and resist in all the small ways Orwell describes at the start of the text.

Orwell's realisation

Read this extract from paragraph 7. It comes from almost the very middle of the essay, and it is here that Orwell begins to explore what we might call the moral of his story.

And it was at this moment, as I stood there with the rifle in my hands, that I first grasped the hollowness, the futility of the white man's dominion in the East … I was only an absurd puppet pushed to and fro by the will of those yellow faces behind. I perceived in this moment that when the white man turns tyrant it is his own freedom that he destroys … For it is the condition of his rule that he shall spend his life in trying to impress the 'natives', and so in every crisis he has got to do what the 'natives' expect of him … A sahib has got to act like a sahib; he has got to appear resolute, to know his own mind and do definite things. To come all that way, rifle in hand, with two thousand people marching at my heels, and then to trail feebly away, having done nothing – no, that was impossible. The crowd would laugh at me. And my whole life, every white man's life in the East, was one long struggle not to be laughed at.

Having outlined these ideas here, he keeps returning to them later in the essay.

> ### Now try this
>
> Read paragraph 9. How does he return to and expand on the ideas from paragraph 7 which have been printed on the previous page?

Earlier in this chapter we said that one key idea in 'Shooting an Elephant' is at the start of paragraph 3 when he tells us that the incident showed him:

> **the real nature of imperialism** – the real motives for which despotic governments act

and that this idea about imperialism is the wider, societal theme of the essay.

> ### Now try this
>
> You should understand Orwell's ideas about empires and imperialism quite well now, so it's time to draw these ideas together. Work with a small group to create a spider plan poster. Write the word IMPERIALISM in the middle of a large sheet of paper. Give your spider at least three legs, though not more than five. At the end of each leg, write one thing Orwell is trying to say about imperialism. Add evidence from the text to show how he explores each of his ideas about imperialism.

By the way, his ideas about the wider theme of empire are very much tied in with his more **personal theme** about pressure. He tells us in paragraph 9 that 'A white man mustn't be frightened in front of "natives".' He is far more afraid of them laughing at him if the elephant kills him than he is of the elephant actually killing him. He spells this out again at the very end:

> I often wondered whether any of the others grasped that I had done it solely **to avoid looking a fool.**

Orwell knows he's not important in the British administration. He's just 'a sub-divisional police officer', ironically just important enough, as he tells us at the start, to be hated. Being a white British man doesn't make him feel powerful compared to the Burmese; it makes him a target for their loathing and for the ridicule he fears.

- Does this opening idea make us feel more sympathetic towards him?
- Does admitting this make him seem more engaging?

The crowd

We have already noted that Orwell tends to describe the Burmese as a 'crowd' or group rather than as individuals. We could argue that the crowd is actually a character in the story.

> ### Now try this
>
> Divide the story up around your class so that everyone has one or two paragraphs to look at.
> - Count how many times the word 'crowd' is used in the essay.
> - How many people does he say were in the crowd?
> - How many times does he tell us about the size of the crowd?

Writing about them like this denies the Burmese people their individuality. This in itself is a clever technique of Orwell's – it lets him show us that empires view their subjects as groups of nameless people, not as individuals. By taking away their individuality, the writer also shows us the power of the crowd, and how impossible it was for him as a young man to resist what they wanted. He ends up, in paragraph 7 'pushed to and fro by the will of those yellow faces behind'.

> ### Now try this
>
> Skim read the story to find the point where Orwell compares the Burmese crowd to an English one.
> - How does he say the two sorts of crowd are similar?
> - How does pointing out these similarities show again that Orwell is not xenophobic or racist?

Imagery used by Orwell to depict himself

This essay is full of imagery. Orwell uses similes, metaphors and symbolism to bring the incident to life and to make his ideas clear.

If you have been practising Close Reading, either by working through Chapter 2 of this book, or by using other textbooks or past papers, you should know how to examine an image. You begin with what the image **literally** is like, or **literally** means. Then you go on to the **metaphorical** meaning, showing how that image applies to and adds meaning to the subject under discussion.

Again, if you are used to examining images already, you should be used to using this formula:

> Just as … (explain the literal meaning) … so … (explain the metaphorical meaning).

We're going to use this formula to examine some of the images in the essay. The first two will be done for you, then you'll have a chance to pick some of them apart yourself. Let's start with a simple one from paragraph 9:

> If the elephant charged and I missed him, I should have about as much chance as a toad under a steam-roller.

You could analyse the image like this:

Just as a toad is a small animal which would be utterly crushed if run over by a steamroller, so Orwell is much smaller than the heavy elephant and would be flattened if it rushed at him.

Now look at this image from paragraph 7, in which Orwell tells us about the crowd's expectations, and read the analysis:

> They were watching me as they would watch a conjurer about to perform a trick.

Just as an audience expects a conjurer to do something clever and entertaining, so the crowd expects Orwell to amuse them by dealing skilfully with the elephant.

Now try this

You are going to examine some of the other images and symbols that Orwell uses. You may wish to work with a partner to do this and you may want to have some pairs look at some images while other pairs look at others. You ought to be able to use the *Just as … , so …* method to look at each image.

1 The image of the actor in paragraph 7.

2 The image of the puppet in paragraph 7.

3 The image of a posing dummy in paragraph 7.

4 The image of a man in a mask in paragraph 7.

You should have noticed that all of these images rest somehow on ideas of acting, falseness, or pretence. Orwell feels he cannot be himself or follow his own conscience and judgement. This leads us on to the next area of imagery.

Imagery used to depict other people

In paragraph 10, Orwell describes the crowd:

> The crowd grew very still, and a deep, low, happy sigh, as of people who see the theatre curtain go up at last, breathed from innumerable throats.

Now try this

Using *Just as ..., so ...* analyse these images:
- The image of the crowd as an audience quoted above.
- The image of the crowd as an army in paragraph 5.

There's an image worth noticing in paragraph 4, in the description of the dead man:

> The friction of the great beast's foot had stripped the skin from his back as neatly as one skins a rabbit.

As we have noticed, Orwell rarely writes about individuals. This man, though individual, is not only diminished by being dead, but has his humanity taken away when he is compared to a rabbit.

Imagery used to depict the elephant

Now try this

Analyse these images from paragraph 11:
- The image of the elephant as a rock.
- The image of its trunk being like a tree.

It's worth noticing other images that affect our idea of the elephant in contrasting ways. In paragraph 12 we read that 'The thick blood welled out of him like red velvet.' As we think of velvet as a luxurious and special fabric, this comparison gives the dying animal some beauty and dignity.

However, a later image is used to diminish the elephant. Just as comparing the dead man to a skinned rabbit reduced his value, so the comparison with 'a mad dog' in paragraph 14 downgrades the elephant, as a mad dog is a much smaller and less noble creature.

Authenticity

So far we have discussed this essay as if Orwell were telling us a true story. You should know, however, that Orwell experts are not sure if it did really happen. There's no independent record of Orwell shooting an elephant while he was in Burma, which is unusual considering that he destroyed a valuable piece of property. This suggests the essay may be fiction.

On the other hand, a man called George Stuart, who served in Burma at the same time as the writer, said that Orwell was transferred to a different town, as punishment for shooting an elephant. This suggests the essay may be factual.

A newspaper item in the *Rangoon Gazette*, published on 22 March 1926, describes a Major E. C. Kenny shooting an elephant in similar circumstances to those outlined in the text. This suggests that Orwell was at least basing his essay on a real event, if not on a personal experience.

This might leave us a little confused, but how much does it actually matter if the elephant incident itself is true? Isn't the story really there as a vehicle to let him express his opinions about the Empire, about Britain's role in 1920s India, and about why we do the things we do?

Now try this

Divide your class into two halves. Then divide each half into smaller groups with about three people in each group. Work in these groups for about fifteen minutes.
- All the groups in the first half of the class should look for details in the 'story' part of the essay that suggest that the events are true. You may wish to particularly concentrate on paragraphs 4, 5 and 11, though you will find many helpful details in other parts too. Different groups should look at different paragraphs.

Now try this continued

- All the groups in the second half of the class should list ways in which the essay would still be 'true' even if the story itself did not happen to Orwell.

Share your group's answers with the rest of the class, taking careful note of any answers your own group did not come up with.

Orwell comes across as a reliable narrator because he is so detailed, and because he doesn't paint a very glowing picture of himself or his actions. He seems honest simply because he does not seem to be trying to present himself in a good light. Also remember that even if the incident did not happen exactly as he describes it, his discoveries about himself, about other people, and about empire, are all still valid.

Evaluating the essay

Now try this

You should know 'Shooting an Elephant' very well by now. Here's a comment about it from a critic called George Bott. He called this essay:

> clear, unaffected, strong, economical and capable of being adapted to a variety of uses – exposition, description, argument, criticism.

Bott uses four different adjectives to describe the piece, and then suggests four uses Orwell gets from it.

First make sure that you know what each of those eight key words means. You may need some help from your teacher here.

Next in your notebook, write down the four adjectives that describe the piece. Beside each, quote a section of the essay where Orwell's language fits that description.

Then in your notebook, write down the four 'uses' to which Bott says the piece can be adapted. Beside each, write an explanation of how 'Shooting an Elephant' can be used for this purpose, and add a quotation that would help someone to use the essay in this way.

Technique revision

Now that you've worked your way through the whole chapter about 'Shooting an Elephant' you should know the essay very well. Before you prove this by writing an essay about it, revise your knowledge of Orwell's techniques.

You're going to carry out the same exercise that you did at the end of Chapter 3 on 'Incident'. (Look back to pp. 79–80 now if you need to be more fully reminded of the instructions.) Take a large piece of paper and mark it up into a **PEE** grid. For every technique, fill in a quotation from the essay, and explain the effect it has on the reader. For a grid about 'Shooting an Elephant', you need to work with the following techniques:

> essay structure   pathetic fallacy
> long paragraphs   present tense
> word choice to show sympathy or lack of it
> wider societal theme of empire
> personal theme of pressure
> the elephant as a metaphor for the Empire or for Burma   use of the crowd as a character
> imagery about Orwell: toad, conjurer, actor, puppet, dummy, masked man
> imagery about other people: audience, army, rabbit   imagery about the elephant: rock, tree, velvet, mad dog
> use of vivid detail to create a sense of authenticity

Possible essay choices

Once you have studied Chapter 8 on essay writing, you might like to try one of the following essays, which are all suitable for 'Shooting an Elephant'.

Above the prose non–fiction essay choices on the exam paper you'll see the following words:

> Answers to questions on prose non-fiction should address relevantly the central concern(s)/theme(s) of the text(s) and be supported by reference to appropriate techniques of prose non-fiction such as: ideas, use of evidence, selection of detail, point of view, stance, setting, anecdote, narrative voice, style, language, structure, organisation of material …

Now look at the essay choices:

Choose a non-fiction text which is set in a society which is different from your own.

Explain what is significantly different and discuss how effectively the writer makes you aware of this.

OR

Choose an essay or a piece of journalism which has made an impact on you because of its effective style.

Discuss how the writer's style adds to the impact of its content.

OR

Choose a non-fiction text in which you consider the writer's stance on a particular issue to be ambiguous.

Show how the writer's presentation of this issue illustrates the ambiguity of his/her stance.

OR

Choose a non-fiction text in which vivid description is an important feature.

Discuss in detail how the vivid description is created and go on to explain how it contributes to your appreciation of the text as a whole.

CHAPTER 8 The Critical Essay

At the end of the Higher course there are two exams, which you will sit in May.

The first of these is the **Close Reading** exam, which is dealt with in Chapter 2 of this book. The second exam paper is called the **Critical Essay**.

In a Critical Essay you have to show your knowledge and understanding of a text you have studied. You should also be able to explain some of the ways in which the author achieved what he or she wanted to with that text. You'll have written essays like this in English before, even if your teacher did not call them this.

To be able to write a Higher Critical Essay you need to know everything there is to know about your literature texts, and pick the right details from that knowledge to use in the exam. You must be able to work very quickly, as in the exam you have to write two essays in 90 minutes. That's just 45 minutes each! If you've done Intermediate 2 on your way to Higher, this won't be too much of a shock, but it's a big change for students who come straight from Standard Grade.

Why do the examiners want you to write an essay? What do they want you to prove about your skills? They actually tell you this on the exam paper every year, but rather than make you wait until May to find out what they want you to do, let's look at their criteria now. On the second page of the Higher Critical Essay exam paper you'll find these words:

The following will be assessed:

- the relevance of your essays to the questions you have chosen, and the extent to which you sustain an appropriate line of thought

- your knowledge and understanding of key elements, central concerns and significant details of the chosen texts, supported by detailed and relevant evidence

- your understanding, as appropriate to the questions chosen, of how relevant aspects of structure/style/language contribute to the meaning/effect/impact of the chosen texts, supported by detailed and relevant evidence

- your evaluation, as appropriate to the questions chosen, of the effectiveness of the chosen texts, supported by detailed and relevant evidence

- the quality of your written expression and the technical accuracy of your writing.

Now try this

It's obviously very important that you understand the markers' demands. So, to prove that you understand what you've just read, work with a partner to 'translate' those words from the exam paper into your own words.

As you work through this chapter you will learn to produce essays that display all these skills.

Let's start by looking at how the Critical Essay exam paper is organised. It comes in the form of a booklet. If your teacher can give you a past paper to look at just now, that would be very helpful.

- The front page has the name and date of the exam, and tells you the start and finish times. It also reminds you to 'Answer **two** questions', and tells you that each is worth up to 25 marks. It's very important that these two questions come from different sections of the exam paper.

- At the top of the next page you will see that explanation you've just seen of the skills the examiners are assessing.

- The next few pages contain all the possible essays. They are organised into five sections like this:

> SECTION A – DRAMA
> SECTION B – PROSE (divided into Fiction and
>   Non-fiction)
> SECTION C – POETRY
> SECTION D – FILM AND TV DRAMA
> SECTION E – LANGUAGE

There are four essays in each section, except in the Prose category where you will find four Fiction choices and three Non-fiction choices. At the start of each section you will see specific advice for that type of essay. We will find out more about that later in this chapter. Remember that the two essays you choose must come from different sections of the exam paper.

Not many schools prepare their students to write about Film and TV Drama and even fewer encourage their students to study for the Language option. Most students sitting Higher study a mixture of poetry, plays, short prose and novels. All the texts in this book are suitable for essays from the Poetry and Prose sections of the exam papers, but the techniques you will learn in this chapter will help you to write about any kind of text you study.

To learn how to choose suitable essay questions, we need to look at the way the individual questions are worded.

All the essay tasks follow the same pattern and are set out in two paragraphs. For example:

Choose a poem on the subject of love.

Show how the poet treats the subject, and explain to what extent you find the treatment convincing.

To choose which essay to write you're going to start by looking at just the **first paragraph** of each essay question.

As soon as you see these words, you need to run through a quick mental checklist. Let's assume you go into the exam knowing all the texts in this book. You can ask yourself:

> Have I studied any poems?

To which the answer would be:

> Yes, three of them: 'Incident', 'Afternoons' and 'Porphyria's Lover'.

So, you **might** be able to write this essay. Now it's time to focus in even tighter on that first paragraph and look at **what kind of poem** the examiners want you to write about.

So now you need to ask yourself:

> Have I studied any poems on the subject of love?

This essay question turns out to be quite a good one, because you get two quite positive answers:

> 'Incident' is about the new and exciting love the narrator feels for his beloved.
> 'Porphyria's Lover' is about the obsessive love the narrator feels for Porphyria.

It's time to narrow down your choice. To help you do this, take another look at the words in the **second paragraph** of the task. This paragraph is where the examiners tell you how they actually want you to tackle the essay. The words of the second paragraph give you instructions that you must follow. If you don't obey these instructions, you aren't answering the essay question and you will certainly not pass.

For this essay, the words in paragraph 2 are:

Now you can narrow down your options by asking yourself:

> Does one of these poems treat love in a more convincing way than the other?

Let's assume (and hope!) that it's actually unusual to show how much you love someone by killing them. This means that 'Incident' is probably going to be a more convincing and therefore useful poem for this question than 'Porphyria's Lover'.

At this stage you should just double-check:

> Do I know this poem well?
> Have I revised my notes about it carefully?

The answers should both be 'Yes', of course, making this an essay you could write.

Now try this

Below you will see just the first paragraph from a number of essay questions taken from old exam papers. All of them could be used to get you to write about at least one of poems in this book. Some of them might fit more than one poem.

For each one, decide which poem or poems you could base the essay on.

1 Choose a poem in which a chance encounter or a seemingly unimportant incident acquires increased significance by the end of the poem.

2 Choose a poem in which you feel there is a significant moment which reveals the central idea of the poem.

3 Choose a poet who reflects on the idea of change.

4 Choose a poem in which the poet creates a picture of a heroic or a corrupt figure.

5 Choose a poem written in the form of a dramatic monologue.

6 Choose a poem in which the poet explores the significance of the passage of time.

7 Choose a poem which explores either the significance of the past or the importance of family relationships.

8 Choose a poem whose main feature is the striking use of imagery.

9 Choose a poem in which the poet has created a perfect blend of form and content.

Now try this

Get your teacher to give you some past papers. Looking at the other sections apart from the Poetry one, see if you can find suitable essays that you could write about any other texts that you've studied for Higher.

Writing your introduction

The first paragraph you write in the essay will be your introduction. Whenever you write a literature essay, the same three things should appear early in the introduction:

1 the title of the text you read

2 the name of the author

3 a clear indication of what you will be writing about.

As we've already seen, the first paragraph of the essay task helps you to choose which task you are going to do. Once you have chosen an essay to tackle, that same first paragraph of the task instructions is also useful for something else. It helps you to write the introduction to your essay. To do this, you are going to **recycle** many of the words from that paragraph.

Let's assume that you have chosen to do the essay task we looked at in detail earlier, and that you are going to write about 'Incident'. Here's the first paragraph from that essay question. Look at the key words.

You can recycle all of those words in the opening sentence of your essay. Those words help you to give a clear indication of what you will be writing about. You still need to add the title and author to these to have a complete introduction, which could end up looking like this:

One poem on the subject of love is 'Incident' by Norman MacCaig.

Can you see the words that have been recycled from the task instructions?

Now go back and look at the long list of opening paragraphs of essay tasks printed in this book on page 135. As it happens, the first paragraph on that list can also lead you into writing an essay about 'Incident'. That paragraph said this:

Choose a poem in which a chance encounter or a seemingly unimportant incident acquires increased significance by the end of the poem.

So your introduction this time would look like this:

A poem in which a seemingly unimportant incident acquires increased significance by the end is 'Incident' by Norman MacCaig. The incident in question consists of the speaker giving a cigarette to a woman.

Again, look for the words that have been recycled from the task instructions.

You should have noticed too that this time the student has had to add a little more information to the introduction, and has said what the incident is.

Line of thought

Another important part of your introduction is establishing what the examiners call a **line of thought**. It's mentioned in that list of skills the examiners are assessing. The first thing they look for in fact is:

● the relevance of your essays to the questions you have chosen, and the extent to which you sustain an appropriate line of thought.

As you can see, line of thought is closely tied in with making your answer relevant to the question. Your line of thought should be a clear idea that you stick to throughout your essay. It does not have to be a hugely complex or fancy idea, and you don't need to try to come up with an original idea that nobody in the world has ever had before.

Look again at this essay task from the list:

Choose a poet who reflects on the idea of change.

This is an ideal question for examining Philip Larkin's poem 'Afternoons'. Your line of thought might be that Larkin shows that change is an inevitable part of life. So, your introduction to this essay could sound something like this.

> In his poem 'Afternoons', Philip Larkin reflects on the idea of change. He shows that change, whether good or bad, is an inevitable part of the cycle of life.

An introduction like that lets you go on and look at both the good and bad changes in the poem. If you were writing that essay you would keep using words like *inevitable*, *unavoidable*, *predictable* or *expected* to show that you are sticking to that line of thought. Notice again that in writing your introduction and setting up your line of thought, you have used some of the key words from the question. This is a crucial part of making sure that you answer the question, and of showing that you are doing so.

Now try this

Go back again to that list of first paragraphs from essay questions. Remember that each one fits at least one of the poems in this book. Working with a partner or small group, decide on a line of thought for each essay.

Now try this

Look back one more time at that whole list of opening paragraphs from essay instructions. Can you turn each one into a complete introduction to an essay?

The summary paragraph

As part of the introduction, it's a good idea to write a **short** summary of your text. There's no set list of Higher texts that teachers have to choose from. This means that you may end up writing your Critical Essay about a text that the exam marker has never read, and doesn't know about. Writing a **short** summary will give the marker a little bit of context and background, making it easier for him or her to understand comments you make about that text in your essay.

 **Warning**

You'll have noticed two bold type reminders that you should be writing a **short** summary. The summary itself does not earn you any marks. It just helps you and the exam marker to get your heads clear. You must not waste precious exam time by waffling.

To let you see what I mean by a **short** summary, here's one for 'Incident':

> In this poem the speaker longs to demonstrate his love by doing something amazing for his beloved, but is happy in the end just to be able to fulfil her simple request for a cigarette.

That summary is just thirty-five words long. It should be easily possible to summarise most texts in fewer than fifty words.

Now try this

Read the following summary of a text you can read and study in this book. Which text is being summarised?

> The speaker describes a group of women, doing so in a way that shows what he imagines their lives as wives and mothers to be like.

Now try this

There are three more texts in this book that have not been summarised. Can you write summaries of those texts in fifty words or less? And, if you have studied other literature texts in class, can you summarise them too?

The main body of your essay

Once you've written the introduction and summary, it's time for the main body of your essay. This will be made up of about four or five paragraphs.

We've already looked very carefully at the fact that the first paragraph of the essay instructions tells you what sort of text to write about. The second paragraph of the essay instructions tells you **what you are actually going to do** in your essay. Remember, if you don't do what

that second paragraph tells you to do then you aren't answering the question and you will never pass the essay. Here is the second paragraph of that essay question which we decided could suit 'Incident':

If you look at this instruction carefully, you will see that in this essay you have two main things to do:

1 **Show how** the poet treats the subject of love.

2 **Explain to what extent** you find that treatment convincing.

In fact many of the Critical Essays you will find in past papers or in the exam give you two things to do.

Now try this

You are going to see the first paragraphs of some essay instructions you have seen before. This time you will also see the second paragraphs of the instructions. From each second paragraph, pick out the two things you have to do in the main body of the essay.

Choose a poem in which the poet explores the significance of the passage of time.

Explain why the passage of time is significant in this poem and discuss the means by which the poet explores its significance.

I have to …

Then I have to …

Choose a poet who reflects on the idea of change.

Show how the poet explores the subject in one or more poems, and explain to what extent your appreciation of the subject was deepened.

Now try this continued

I have to …
Then I have to …

Choose a poem in which the poet has created a perfect blend of form and content.

Show how the poet achieves this and discuss how it adds to your appreciation of the poem.

I have to …
Then I have to …

Choose a poem in which there is a noticeable change of mood at one or more than one point in the poem.

Show how the poet conveys the change(s) of mood and discuss the importance of the change(s) to the central idea of the poem.

I have to …
Then I have to …

Choose a poem which explores either the significance of the past or the importance of family relationships.

Show how the poet treats the subject, and explain to what extent you find the treatment convincing.

I have to …
Then I have to …

Not every Critical Essay task gives you two things to do. For example, you may find one like this:

Choose a poem in which the poet creates a picture of a heroic or a corrupt figure.

Discuss the means by which the personality is clearly depicted.

In this task you don't have two different things to do, you just have to look, in a proportionate way, at the ways the poet creates a picture of that character. The important thing you must always do is read the question to find out clearly and exactly what you have to do and what you have to write about.

So, now that you know what you are supposed to do, how are you going to do it? Let's take another look at the second, instructing paragraph in the essay task that we thought would be good for 'Incident'. The words that tell you what to do have been picked out in bold.

Show how the poet treats the subject, and **explain to what extent** you find the treatment convincing.

There are two possible ways you could tackle this essay:

Method 1: You could write a number of paragraphs, maybe three or four, dealing with the first main thing, looking at how the poet treats the subject of love. That would mean doing quite a lot of analysis of the poet's techniques. Then you could write one or two more paragraphs explaining to what extent you found the treatment of love in the poem convincing. In other words you would move on to evaluating the poet's work later in the essay.

Method 2: Each paragraph in the main body of your essay could examine one way in which the poet treats the subject of love. Each paragraph would end with you evaluating how effective you found that aspect of the poet's treatment. In other words, every main body paragraph would contain both analysis of technique and evaluation of effect.

No matter which approach you choose for any particular essay:

- Every one of the main body paragraphs must help you to do what your chosen task tells you to do, and must be clearly tied in to the question.
- Every one of the main body paragraphs must use evidence from the text.

Now try this

Here's an example of a paragraph from an essay where the student has followed method 1. Read it carefully and decide:

1 Does this paragraph come from the 'Show how …' section of the essay or from the 'Say what …' section?

2 Which words in the paragraph show that this student is trying to stick to the chosen task?

3 Which words in the paragraph show the student is using evidence from the text?

The answers are at the end of the paragraph. Don't look until you have worked them out for yourself.

> One way that the poet treats the subject of love is that he shows how loving someone makes us eager to please them. He makes this clear with the line:
>
> 'Ask me, go on, ask me'
>
> The speaker's repetition of 'Ask me' makes his desperate eagerness to please very obvious to us as we read the poem. The same eagerness is shown further when the speaker shows what he would like the girl to ask him:
>
> 'to do something impossible
> something freakishly useless
> something unimaginable and
> inimitable'
>
> Repetition is key again here. The more the speaker re-uses the word 'something', the more we understand that he would actually do anything for his beloved.

Did you manage to answer the three questions?

> 1 This paragraph comes from the 'Show how …' section of the essay.
>
> 2 The words in the paragraph that show this student is trying to stick to the chosen task are:
> 'One way that MacCaig treats the subject of love is'
>
> 3 The words in the paragraph that show the student is using evidence from the text are:
> 'Ask me, go on, ask me'
> and
> 'to do something impossible
> something freakishly useless
> something unimaginable and inimitable'

Did you notice that this student once again recycled some words from the original essay question to help structure his paragraph? The words 'the poet treats the subject' are taken straight from the wording of the task. This is how the student shows that his paragraph is clearly tied in to, and is answering, the question.

If that student was using method 2 to answer that essay question, then he would go on to finish that paragraph by evaluating how effective he found that aspect of the poet's treatment of love. He might write something like this:

> MacCaig's use of repetition is highly effective here in conveying the narrator's eagerness. He's so keen to get the words and ideas out that he doesn't stop to think about varying his vocabulary, but just says over and over what matters to him, creating emphasis, perhaps unwittingly, as he goes.

Let's focus a bit more carefully on how to write the paragraphs in the main body of your essay. There are two things you should do in these paragraphs so that they will be well written and help you to achieve the task you've chosen.

1 You should begin the paragraph with a **topic sentence**.

2 You should use the **PEE structure**.

Topic sentences

Topic sentences are called this for two reasons:

1 They tie in with the topic of your essay.

2 They let the reader understand the topic of the particular paragraph you're writing.

Using a topic sentence at the start of the paragraph sets you off in the right direction.

Now try this

You're going to see again the five essay tasks you examined on pages 138–139. After the tasks you'll see a list of sentences. Each one is a topic sentence from one of the five essays. Can you decide which essay each topic sentence belongs to?

Here are the essay topics:

1 **Choose a poem in which the poet explores the significance of the passage of time.**

   Explain why the passage of time is significant in this poem and discuss the means by which the poet explores its significance.

2 **Choose a poet who reflects on the idea of change.**

   Show how the poet explores the subject in one or more poems, and explain to what extent your appreciation of the subject was deepened.

3 **Choose a poem in which the poet has created a perfect blend of form and content.**

   Show how the poet achieves this and discuss how it adds to your appreciation of the poem.

4 **Choose a poem in which there is a noticeable change of mood at one or more than one point in the poem.**

   Show how the poet conveys the change(s) of mood and discuss the importance of the change(s) to the central idea of the poem.

5 **Choose a poem which explores either the significance of the past or the importance of family relationships.**

   Show how the poet treats the subject, and explain to what extent you find the treatment convincing.

Here are the topic sentences. Can you match each one to the right essay topic?

(a) One way in which the poet shows the importance of family relationships is by his use of ambiguity when he says that the children 'expect' to be taken home.

(b) The author explores the significance of the passage of time by using 'unripe acorns' as a symbol.

(c) One way in which Browning conveys the change of mood is by the use of an end–stopped line.

(d) The writer blends form and function in the poem by using hidden verses to echo the hidden dangers in the narrator's mind.

(e) One form of change which the writer explores is physical change, and he does this by using an abstract noun in an unusually concrete way.

The PEE structure

The **PEE structure** helps you to remember what should be in each paragraph.

> P – tells you to make a **P**oint about something you can see the writer deliberately doing.
> E – tells you to give **E**vidence from the text, preferably by quoting.
> E – tells you to **E**xplain the **E**ffect of this, to show what the writer is doing to us, the readers.

The **P** part of this is also the topic sentence of the paragraph, so there's a bit of an overlap between the idea of using a topic sentence and the idea of following the **PEE** structure.

Now try this

Copy the following paragraph into your notebook. Once you've copied it out, do these three things:

1 Underline the **P** part with a straight line.

2 Underline the first **E** part with a wiggly or jagged line.

3 Draw a box round the second **E** part.

Now try this continued

One form of change which the writer explores is physical change, and he does this by using an abstract noun in an unusually concrete way. In the closing lines of the poem, as he looks at the young mothers, Larkin tells us that:

'Their beauty has thickened'

We usually think of 'beauty' as something which is an idea, an abstract, and does not have any physical substance. By making it real and concrete in this way, Larkin startles the reader and forces us to see how growing older and going through pregnancy has made the women put on weight, losing the slimmer figures they once had.

Notice that the student who wrote this **indented** his quotation – it is set in from the edges of the page to make it narrower than the rest of the essay. If you are quoting anything longer than just a single word or short phrase you should indent. It lets the marker see that you are using words from the text confidently. You should also have spotted that the student is writing in **present tense**. You should do this whenever you write about a text you have studied.

Now try this

Read the essay extract again. Pick out all the verbs that show that the student is writing in present tense.

Writing about techniques

This is where the advice in the box above each set of essay tasks comes in. The wording of this paragraph follows a pattern.

Now try this

To get you to spot the pattern of this paragraph in the essay instructions, you're going to see the advice for two different types of essay. The first one is for poetry essays, the second one is for drama essays. Read the two paragraphs and then answer the two questions below.

Answers to questions on poetry should address relevantly the central concern(s)/theme(s) of the text(s) and be supported by reference to appropriate poetic techniques such as: imagery, verse form, structure, mood, tone, sound, rhythm, rhyme, characterisation, contrast, setting, symbolism, word choice …

Answers to questions on drama should address relevantly the central concern(s)/theme(s) of the text and be supported by reference to appropriate dramatic techniques such as: conflict, characterisation, key scene(s), dialogue, climax, exposition, dénouement, structure, plot, setting, aspects of staging (such as lighting, music, stage set, stage directions …), soliloquy, monologue …

1 Which words are always used at the **start** of the advice above the essay tasks?

2 What do you always see at the **end** of the advice above the essay tasks? What do you think this means?

What this advice paragraph does is just remind you to write about some of the techniques the author uses. Remember that **a technique is anything a writer deliberately chooses to do**. While some techniques have simple names like *simile*, *metaphor*, *alliteration* and so on, anything a writer does on purpose to have an effect on the reader is a technique.

Notice that the paragraph doesn't actually specify which techniques and features you should write about. The ones named in the paragraph are just suggestions, and the three dots at the end of that paragraph show that you can write about whichever techniques and features you think are important for the text and task you have chosen.

For example, if you were writing an essay on 'Incident', and depending which essay you chose, you could pick any of the following techniques and features that we looked at as we studied the poem:

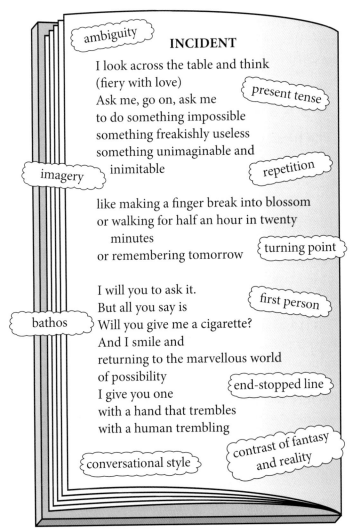

ambiguity

INCIDENT

I look across the table and think
(fiery with love)
Ask me, go on, ask me
to do something impossible
something freakishly useless
something unimaginable and
inimitable

present tense

imagery

repetition

like making a finger break into blossom
or walking for half an hour in twenty
      minutes
or remembering tomorrow

turning point

I will you to ask it.
But all you say is
Will you give me a cigarette?
And I smile and
returning to the marvellous world
of possibility
I give you one
with a hand that trembles
with a human trembling

first person

bathos

end-stopped line

conversational style

contrast of fantasy and reality

You don't actually have to force a technique into every one of your body paragraphs. It's still more important to make sure that every paragraph you write is tied in to your chosen task and helps you to answer the question. You just have to pick up and deal with appropriate techniques on your way through the essay as you answer the question.

The way that you write about techniques is all tied in with that important **PEE** structure. The

P part, remember, is where you make a point about the writer's technique. The first **E** part has you quoting an example of that technique being used by the author. When you get to the second **E** part of the structure you are explaining how the writer creates an effect, or how the writer achieves what he or she set out to.

The following words and phrases describe **what the writer does**, or **what some aspect of the text does**. They will help you to show that you are **analysing** the author's work.

has connotations of   suggests   shows
creates   mirrors   establishes
underlines   reinforces   emphasises
highlights   foreshadows   exemplifies
explains   demonstrates   echoes
reveals   hints   introduces   means
indicates   clarifies

The following words and phrases describe **how the reader feels**, or **how the text affects us** as we read. They will help you to show that you are **evaluating** the author's work.

thought-provoking   inspiring   horrifying
hard-hitting   stimulating
pivotal moment   key idea(s)   fast-paced
effective   gripping   skilful(ly)
perceptive   moving   profound
striking   important   intelligent
thoughtful   disturbing   challenging
startling

Now try this

You might want to work with a partner or group to do this. You should be quite familiar with this essay task by now. Can you think of:

- four more ways that 'Incident' treats the subject of love?
- two reasons why you find the poet's treatment of love convincing?

Compare your answers with those from the rest of the class. Agree on the best answers for building each main area of the essay.

Now try this

Your teacher needs to divide the class into six small groups. Each group should take just one of the four ways or one of the two reasons you agreed on earlier. That will mean each group has just one idea to work with. Your group should create just one, perfect, essay paragraph from your one idea.

Remember:

- Use quotations from the text and indent the words that you quote.
- Make sure you start with a topic sentence and that the topic sentence works as the **P** part of the **PEE** structure in your paragraph.
- Use some of the key words and phrases from the boxes on the previous page.

Either swap your paragraphs with another group to see what they think of them, or give them to your teacher for marking.

The conclusion

After your introduction, summary and main body, you need to finish off your essay with a conclusion. The conclusion needs to do two things:

1   Sum up and round off what you have written.

2   Give your personal response.

Summing up just means reminding the examiner what you have written about. You could try one of these approaches:

In this essay I have shown how Norman MacCaig's 'Incident' treats the subject of love and discussed how convincing his treatment of this subject is.

Clearly, Norman MacCaig's 'Incident' treats the subject of new, young love in a convincing way, showing the lover's excitement and eagerness.

In each case, the student has only written one sentence to sum up.

Now try this

Decide the answers to these two questions:

- Which summing up do you think you would find easier to write? Why?
- Which summing up do you find to be more effective? Why?

Giving your personal response takes a little more thought. Earlier in your school career your personal responses were probably a bit like this:

I liked the poem because it had a happy ending and good images.

However, at Higher level your personal response needs to be more sophisticated. Just like everything else in your essay, it should fit your chosen task, as well as fitting the text you are writing about.

This task was about the poem's treatment of love, so your personal response should say something about what you thought overall of how MacCaig tackles that subject. You could, for example, say whether you thought his treatment seemed realistic.

Now try this

Work with a partner for five minutes. Jot down two or three ideas you could use in writing the personal response part of a conclusion to this essay.

Writing a whole essay

If you've worked through this chapter you have found out step by step how to tackle Higher Critical Essays. Your teacher will give you lots of chances to practise essay writing in class.

Now try this

You're going to see the whole of the wording for that essay task on 'Incident' again.

First of all, above the essay choices for poetry, the exam paper has this wording:

> Answers to questions on poetry should address relevantly the central concern(s)/ theme(s) of the text(s) and be supported by reference to appropriate poetic techniques such as: imagery, verse form, structure, mood, tone, sound, rhythm, rhyme, characterisation, contrast, setting, symbolism, word choice …

Then you see this essay task:

> Choose a poem on the subject of love.
>
> Show how the poet treats the subject, and explain to what extent you find the treatment convincing.

Now, using all the advice from this chapter and everything you have learned, write this essay. Remember you need to have:

- an **introduction** including some indication of your **line of thought**
- a short **summary** of the text
- about five main body paragraphs beginning with good **topic sentences** and using the **PEE** pattern
- a conclusion in which you **summarise** the essay and give your **personal response**.

Check over your essay and then hand it in to your teacher for marking.

At the end of the chapter about 'Incident' you will find other essay questions that fit that text. Every other literature chapter of this book also ends with a selection of essay questions you can try.

Essays on two texts

Both the poetry and prose sections of the exam paper may contain questions asking you to write about two texts rather than just one.

Some of these questions can be very general, like this one:

> Choose two short stories in which aspects of style contribute significantly to the exploration of theme.
>
> Compare the ways in which stylistic features are used to create and maintain your interest in the central ideas of the texts.

That might seem like a very easy question. If a story is worth studying for Higher at all, then surely there must be some aspects of the writer's style which help him or her to explore a theme? But what actually makes this essay question a hard one to answer is the word **compare** at the start of the second paragraph. What the examiners are asking you to do is not just to show how each individual writer's techniques are useful in exploring themes. The examiners want you to **compare** how the writers do this, or in other words to **evaluate** what the writers do.

You can see more clearly how much evaluation matters in the essay on two texts by looking at two more sample questions:

1 Choose two poems on the same theme which impress you for different reasons.

> Compare the treatment of the theme in the two poems and discuss to what extent you find one more impressive than the other.

2 Choose two poems which explore human relationships.

> By referring to both poems, discuss which you consider to be the more convincing portrayal of a relationship.

In these questions, phrases like **more impressive** and **more convincing** show that you have to be able to evaluate what each writer does, and to give clear reasons why you find one writer to be more successful.

That's one reason why these essays are actually trickier than questions about just one text. Also, it's hard to do two texts justice in just 45 minutes. You have to know your material exceedingly well to be able to select the most useful ideas and knowledge and cover each one in what still feels like some depth.

There are two ways that you might structure essays like these:

1   After your introduction, and a brief summary of each text, you could do a couple of paragraphs about text one, then a couple of paragraphs about text two. Then you write one further paragraph in which you explicitly compare the two texts and evaluate which was the more convincing, successful, effective, or whatever the question asked you.

2   After your introduction, and a brief summary of each text, each paragraph in the body of the essay (about four or five paragraphs in all) would compare both texts. At the end, in your conclusion, you would take a step back and evaluate which of the two was, overall, the more convincing, successful, effective, or whatever the question asked you.

Now try this

Work with a partner or small group. Read the descriptions above of the two ways to tackle this sort of essay.

*   What are the advantages of each method?
*   What are the disadvantages of each?
*   Decide which pairs of texts you could use to answer each of the essay questions.

Share your answers with the class.

Now try this

Find someone different to work with.

*   Choose one of the essay questions on the previous page.
*   Work out which texts would be suitable to write about in answering it.
*   Decide which approach would be most suitable for structuring your essay.
*   Work together to create a detailed essay plan.
*   Now go back to working on your own, taking a copy of the plan with you. In 45 minutes, write the essay.

Essay writing in the exam

During the Higher course you will get lots of chances to write essays about the texts you study. At first your teacher may support you in some of the following ways:

*   getting you to work through this chapter
*   letting you see essay questions in advance
*   giving you a plan to follow
*   making a plan with the class
*   letting you plan in groups or pairs
*   letting you use your texts and/or notes while you write the essay
*   giving you as long as you need to finish the essay
*   letting you take the essay home to finish it.

However, by the time you get to the exam you need to be able to quickly choose, plan and write two essays in 90 minutes. Two things will help you with this.

First you need to know your texts and all your notes and materials about them really well before you go into the exam. That way you can pick out the right material to use in answering the essay questions you have chosen.

It's a bit like this. You probably have lots of clothes in your wardrobe so that you always have the right outfit for any situation. The clothes you would wear to go camping wouldn't be the same ones you would wear to a party. In the same way the information you use to write an essay about how an author gets you to respond to a character might not be the same information you would use to write an essay about how the writer deals with a particular theme or issue.

Secondly, you need to make a quick plan in the exam before you write each essay. It can be as simple as a list of the five key ideas you want to base your main body paragraphs on, or a mind map or spider plan with a leg for each main body paragraph. The fact that you've made it at all means you have thought about how you will answer the question.

Sometimes, students go into the exam and panic. No matter how scared you are, don't be tempted to write about the Film and TV Drama option if you haven't studied for it in class. Even if *The Godfather* is your favourite film of all time, don't write about it if you haven't been trained to. The same applies to the language section. There might well be a question in there about teenage slang, and you may be a slangy teenager, but don't try to write about it if you haven't been taught it.

Another danger in the exam is that you might write the essay you want to write, and not the one the examiners want. It's really important to learn essay skills – and that's what this whole chapter has been about – but there's no point trying to learn a particular essay off by heart, even if it's one you got a good mark for in class. You can only write about what the examiners want on that day.

Let's end with a piece of positive advice. If at all possible, you should try to make one of your two exam essays be about poetry. There's much less risk with poetry that you will fall into retelling the plot, which can sometimes happen with essays about novels or plays. Also, because poems are very short and the language in them has to work very hard, poems are stuffed with recognisable techniques. That makes it very easy for you to identify these techniques and to write about them, which immediately makes your essays more analytical, and makes you seem more clever. Their being short also makes poems easier to know, and easier to learn quotations from.

So, when you go into the exam, look at the poetry questions first. Decide if there is one that really works for the poems you know. If there is, circle it, and then look at the questions in the other sections you've studied for. Choose what your second essay will be and circle it too. Then go back and write that poetry essay, which will almost certainly be your strongest one. Don't use more than the 45 minutes available, but do go into your second essay knowing you've made a great start to the exam with your first one.

CHAPTER 9 Textual Analysis

The Textual Analysis NAB is based on an extract from a short story, novel or play, or perhaps on a whole short poem. This will be a text you haven't met before. You have to read it carefully, and then answer questions on **how** it is written – the techniques the writer uses and the effects he or she creates. If you don't pass first time you can re-sit it by trying a different passage and a new set of questions.

This NAB is actually a very easy one to pass if you do it as your final NAB and do it quite late in your Higher course, because by then you should have picked up all the skills you'll need. Your study of literature will have given you the ability to get into a text and find out what the writer is saying and how. Your practice in Close Reading, especially the **A** for Analysis questions, will equip you to analyse quickly and effectively.

Because of this, there will be no direct teaching of Textual Analysis in this chapter, but instead two opportunities for practice, one of which comes with a bit of coaching. Once you have tried these, and your teacher has gone over the answers with you, you should be ready to try the NAB. However, if you do still want more practice, you could use *Developing Skills in Textual Analysis* by Dr Susan MacDonald. This book focuses quite heavily on the analysis of poetry; do remember your NAB could also be based on prose or drama.

Now try this

The first practice task is based on a Victorian novella. You may have to work round formal and unfamiliar vocabulary and will have to navigate through some quite long paragraphs. The passage here is rather longer than you'll get for the actual NAB, so you can take a bit longer than the 45 minutes the NAB allows.

As this is your first attempt at a Textual Analysis task, most of the questions come with a little coaching. Remember, the most important advice of all is **answer the question**. Using bullet points or headings may be useful in organising some of your answers.

In this extract from a novella by Mrs Gaskell (published in 1863) Paul, the narrator, is introducing his employer and friend, Mr Holdsworth, to his cousin, Phillis.

'This is Mr Holdsworth, Phillis,' said I, as soon as I had shaken hands with her. She glanced up at him, and then looked down, more flushed than ever at his grand formality of taking his hat off
5 and bowing; such manners had never been seen at Hope Farm before.

'Father and Mother are out. They will be so sorry; you did not write, Paul, as you said you would.'

10 'It was my fault,' said Holdsworth, understanding what she meant as well as if she had put it more fully into words. 'I have not yet given up all the privileges of an invalid; one of which is indecision. Last night, when your
15 cousin asked me at what time we were to start, I really could not make up my mind.'

Phillis seemed as if she could not make up her mind as to what to do with us. I tried to help her, –

'Have you finished getting peas?' taking hold
20 of the half-filled basket she was unconsciously holding in her hand; 'or may we stay and help you?'

'If you would. But perhaps it will tire you, sir?' added she, speaking now to Holdsworth.

25 'Not a bit,' said he. 'It will carry me back twenty years in my life, when I used to gather peas in my grandfather's garden. I suppose I may eat a few as I go along?'

'Certainly, sir. But if you went to the strawberry-
30 beds you would find some strawberries ripe, and Paul can show you where they are.'

'I am afraid you distrust me. I can assure you I know the exact fullness at which peas should be gathered. I take great care not to pluck them when
35 they are unripe. I will not be turned off, as unfit for my work.' This was a style of half-joking talk that Phillis was not accustomed to. She looked for a moment as if she would have liked to defend herself from the playful charge of distrust made
40 against her, but she ended by not saying a word. We all plucked our peas in busy silence for the next five minutes. Then Holdsworth lifted himself up from between the rows, and said, a little wearily,
45 'I am afraid I must strike work. I am not as strong as I fancied myself.' Phillis was full of penitence immediately. He did, indeed, look pale; and she blamed herself for having allowed him to help her.
50 'It was very thoughtless of me. I did not know – I thought, perhaps, you really liked it. I ought to have offered you something to eat, sir! Oh, Paul, we have gathered quite enough; how stupid I was to forget that Mr Holdsworth had
55 been ill!' And in a blushing hurry she led the way towards the house. We went in, and she moved a heavy cushioned chair forwards, into which Holdsworth was only too glad to sink. Then with deft and quiet speed she brought in a little tray,
60 wine, water, cake, home-made bread, and newly-churned butter. She stood by in some anxiety till, after bite and sup, the colour returned to Mr Holdsworth's face, and he would fain have made us some laughing apologies for the fright he had
65 given us. But then Phillis drew back from her innocent show of care and interest, and relapsed into the cold shyness habitual to her when she was first thrown into the company of strangers. She brought out the last week's county paper (which
70 Mr Holdsworth had read five days ago), and then quietly withdrew; and then he subsided into languor, leaning back and shutting his eyes as if he would go to sleep. I stole into the kitchen after Phillis; but she had made the round of the corner
75 of the house outside, and I found her sitting on

the horse-mount, with her basket of peas, and a basin into which she was shelling them.

'Don't you think him handsome?' asked I.

'Perhaps – yes – I have hardly looked at him,'
80 she replied. 'But is not he very like a foreigner?'

'Yes, he cuts his hair foreign fashion,' said I.

'I like an Englishman to look like an Englishman.'

'I don't think he thinks about it. He says he
85 began that way when he was in Italy, because everybody wore it so, and it is natural to keep it on in England.'

'Not if he began it in Italy because everybody there wore it so. Everybody here wears it
90 differently.' I was a little offended with Phillis's logical fault-finding with my friend; and I determined to change the subject.

'When is your mother coming home?'

'I should think she might come any time
95 now. Don't you think you ought to go and see how Mr Holdsworth is going on, Paul? He may be faint again.'

I went at her bidding; but there was no need for it. Mr Holdsworth was up, standing by
100 the window, his hands in his pockets; he had evidently been watching us. He turned away as I entered.

'So that is the girl I found your good father planning for your wife, Paul, that evening when
105 I interrupted you! Are you of the same coy mind still? It did not look like it a minute ago.'

'Phillis and I understand each other,' I replied, sturdily. 'We are like brother and sister. She would not have me as a husband if there was
110 not another man in the world; and it would take a deal to make me think of her – as my father wishes (somehow I did not like to say 'as a wife'), but we love each other dearly.'

'Well, I am rather surprised at it – not at your
115 loving each other in a brother-and-sister kind of way – but at your finding it so impossible to fall in love with such a beautiful woman.' Woman! Beautiful woman! I had thought of Phillis as a comely but awkward girl; and I could not banish
120 the pinafore from my mind's eye when I tried to picture her to myself. Now I turned, as Mr Holdsworth had done, to look at her again out of the window: she had just finished her task, and was standing up, her back to us, holding
125 the basket, and the basin in it, high in air, out of Rover's reach.

'I should like to have sketched her,' said Mr Holdsworth, as he turned away. He went back to his chair, and rested in silence for a minute or
130 two. Then he was up again.

'I would give a good deal for a book,' he said. 'It would keep me quiet.' He began to look round; there were a few volumes at one end of the table. 'Housewife's Complete Manual,' said he, reading
135 their titles aloud. 'Berridge on Prayer; L'Inferno – Dante! In Italian too!' in great surprise. 'Why, who reads this?'

'I told you Phillis read it. Don't you remember? She knows Latin and Greek, too.'
140 'To be sure! I remember! But somehow I never put two and two together. That quiet girl, full of household work, is the wonderful scholar, then, that put you to rout with her questions when you first began to come here. What's here: a paper

145 with the hard, obsolete Italian words written out. I wonder what sort of a dictionary she has got. Baretti won't tell her all these words. Stay! I have got a pencil here. I'll write down the most accepted meanings, and save her a little trouble.'
150 So he took her book and the paper back to the little round table, and employed himself in writing explanations and definitions of the words which had troubled her. I was not sure if he was not taking a liberty: it did not quite
155 please me, and yet I did not know why. He had only just done, and replaced the paper in the book, and put the latter back in its place, when I heard the sound of wheels stopping in the lane.
160 'Oh, Paul!' said Phillis's mother coming in, 'I am so sorry I was kept. But where's your friend Mr Holdsworth? I hope he is come?'

From Cousin Phillis *by Mrs Gaskell*

1 By referring to the text of lines 1–16 show how the attitudes of Phillis and Mr Holdsworth to the meeting are conveyed. **4**

   Advice: Phillis and Mr Holdsworth's 'attitudes' are how they feel about this meeting. For each character you need to identify an attitude. Then quote from the text, and explain how the words you have quoted display the attitude you identified.

2 What can you deduce about Phillis's state of mind from the text of lines 17–22? **2**

   Advice: You will get one mark for correctly identifying Phillis's state of mind, and a second for giving evidence from the text to support this.

3 Read lines 32–44.
   (a) How does Paul perceive Mr Holdsworth's answer? (lines 32–36) **1**
   (b) How does Phillis perceive his answer? **1**

   Advice: Think about how well each of these two characters understands Holdsworth's tone.

4 Read lines 50–71.
   How does the writer's use of language reflect the contrast between Phillis's behaviour in lines 50–65 and her behaviour in lines 65–71? **4**

   Advice: This answer needs careful structuring so that you can earn all the marks. First, say how Phillis is behaving in lines 50–65 and support this answer with evidence from the text. Next, say how Phillis is behaving in lines 65–71 and support this part of your answer with evidence from the text. If you do this correctly, the contrast will be clearly implied and you will not need to state it explicitly or separately.

5 Look at the dialogue between Phillis and Paul (lines 78–97).
   By referring to these lines, show what you can deduce about each of their attitudes towards Mr Holdsworth at this point in the narrative. **2**

   Advice: Name Phillis's attitude, then quote from the text to support it. Next, name Paul's attitude and quote from the text to support it.

6 Read lines 107–130.

   (a) Show how the writer's choice of words in these lines makes clear Paul's statement that his relationship with Phillis is not a romantic one. **2**

   Advice: Quote briefly from the text, and explain how what you have quoted shows the non-romantic nature of the relationship. Do this twice.

   (b) Show, by referring to language and incident in these lines, that the reader is given the impression that Mr Holdsworth's attitude to Phillis is more romantic. **2**

   Advice: Make sure you do refer to both language and incident. That word 'incident' really just means what Holdsworth says he'd like to do.

7 Read lines 131–144.

   (a) What causes Mr Holdsworth's attitude to Phillis to change? **1**

   (b) Show how the language in these lines reveals this new attitude. **2**

   Advice: The language you quote does not have to come only from what Holdsworth says, though some of it might.

8 (a) What difficulty does Mr Holdsworth assume Phillis has after seeing her list of words inside Dante's *Inferno*? **1**

   (b) By referring to lines 147–159, show how Mr Holdsworth's reaction to finding the list of words contrasts with Paul's reaction to the situation. **2**

   Advice: This should be approached in the same way as question 4.

9 Consider the whole extract. How effectively does the writer give the reader an insight into the relationships between the each 'pair' of characters? **6**

   Advice: The large number of marks available here means that how you tackle this question can make the difference between passing and failing. There are three different relationships to consider: Phillis and Paul; Paul and Holdsworth; Holdsworth and Phillis. Within each relationship, the two people involved may not feel the same way about each other. In each case, you need to say what the relationship is like and show how the extract has made that clear. Organising your answer with headings will really help you here.

Now try this

The next practice Textual Analysis is based on a far more modern text, a poem. There are no detailed coaching tips for individual questions this time.

You should notice that in this task there are far more questions about specific techniques. You will be asked about imagery, word choice, sound, structure and ambiguity. You have learned about all of these already in your Higher course. You can look back at your notes, or at earlier chapters of this book, to revise these techniques.

WORK AND PLAY

The swallow of summer, she toils all the summer,
A blue-dark knot of glittering voltage,
A whiplash swimmer, a fish of the air.
　　But the serpent of cars that crawls through the dust
5　In shimmering exhaust
　　Searching to slake
　　Its fever in ocean
　　Will play and be idle or else it will bust.

　　The swallow of summer, the barbed harpoon,
10　She flings from the furnace, a rainbow of purples,
　　Dips her glow in the pond and is perfect.
　　　　But the serpent of cars that collapsed at the beach
　　Disgorges its organs
　　A scamper of colours
15　Which roll like tomatoes
　　Nude as tomatoes
　　With sand in their creases
　　To cringe in the sparkle of rollers and screech.

　　The swallow of summer, the seamstress of summer,
20　She scissors the blue into shapes and she sews it,
　　She draws a long thread and she knots it at the corners.
　　　　But the holiday people
　　Are laid out like wounded
　　Flat as in ovens
25　Roasting and basting
　　With faces of torment as space burns them blue
　　Their heads are transistors
　　Their teeth grit on sand grains
　　Their lost kids are squalling
30　While man-eating flies
　　Jab electric shock needles but what can they do?

　　They can climb in their cars with raw bodies, raw faces
　　And start up the serpent
　　And headache it homeward
35　A car full of squabbles
　　And sobbing and stickiness
　　With sand in their crannies
　　Inhaling petroleum
　　That pours from the foxgloves
40　While the evening swallow
　　The swallow of summer, cartwheeling through crimson,
　　Touches the honey-slow river and turning
　　Returns to the hand stretched from under the eaves –
　　A boomerang of rejoicing shadow.

Ted Hughes

1　Consider the description of the swallow in lines 1–3.
Comment fully on the effectiveness of one of the images that Hughes uses to describe her movement.　**2**

2　By referring to word choice in lines 4–8 show how Hughes, in contrast, describes the movement of the cars and their occupants.　**3**

3　Show how the imagery in lines 10 and 11 enhances the effect of sunlight on the swallow.　**3**

4　Read lines 12–18. Show how word choice, imagery and sound contribute to the generally unpleasant picture painted of the cars and their occupants.　**6**

5　Explain fully how the idea of the swallow as 'seamstress' is visually and aurally effective as a representation of a swallow's flight.　**4**

6　Choose two of the torments which afflict the holidaymakers, and show how each is made more severe by the poet's use of language.　**4**

7　Comment on ways in which the structure of the whole poem is effective in highlighting one of the central concerns of the poem.　**2**

8　To what extent would you agree with the statement that the last four lines of the poem reach a climax of beauty and wonder? Justify your opinion with close reference to these lines.　**4**

9　Comment on the ambiguity of the title of the poem.　**2**

Total marks: 30

Once you have done these two practice tasks, and your teacher has gone over them with you, you should be ready to try the Textual Analysis NAB. It should take you around 45 minutes, and if you don't pass the first time you can have another attempt with a new unseen text and a different set of questions.

CHAPTER 10
Answers to Close Reading Questions

These are the answers to the short questions in the first part of the Close Reading chapter (Chapter 2). In each case you will see the passage extract, the question, and then the possible answers. This will enable you to mark your own work and see how well you've done in answering these short questions.

In a world changing faster now than ever before, the dispossessed and the ambitious are flooding into cities swollen out of all recognition. Poor cities are struggling to cope. Rich cities are re-configuring themselves at breakneck speed. China has created an industrial powerhouse from what were fishing villages in the 1970s. Lagos and Dhaka attract a thousand new arrivals every day. In Britain, central London's population has started to grow again after fifty years of decline.

We have more big cities now than at any time in our history. In 1900, only sixteen had a population of one million; now it's more than 400. Not only are there more of them, they are larger than ever. In 1851, London had two million people. It was the largest city in the world by a long way, twice the size of Paris, its nearest rival. That version of London would seem like a village now. By the official definition, London has getting on for eight million people, but in practical terms it's a city of 18 million, straggling most of the way from Ipswich to Bournemouth in an unforgiving rush of business parks and designer outlets, gated housing and logistics depots.

Having invented the modern city, 19th-century Britain promptly reeled back in horror at what it had done. To the Victorians exploring the cholera-ridden back alleys of London's East End, the city was a hideous tumour sucking the life out of the countryside and creating in its place a vast polluted landscape of squalor, disease and crime. In their eyes, the city was a place to be feared, controlled and, if possible, eliminated.

Q1 **Read the middle paragraph of the extract. Explain two ways in which 'that version of London would seem like a village now.'**   2 U

The answer must be in your own words. 'Lifting' from the text will get you no marks.

A1 One mark each (up to a total of 2 marks) for:

1 Officially London is now a city of almost 8 million **and/or** in reality London is now a city of 18 million – much larger than the 'version' referred to (which had a population of 2 million).

2 (Because it spreads over a vast area) London is more sprawling, less definable, less cohesive than the 'version' referred to.

Teachers are giving up teaching, and youth organisations are dying because they cannot find adults prepared to run them. Everywhere good, inspirational people are turning their backs on children because they are terrified of the children and their parents turning on them, accusing them of all manner of wrongdoing. They can no longer operate, they say, in a climate of suspicion and fear.

Q2 **Why, according to the writer, are teachers and youth workers 'turning their backs on children'?** 2 **U**

The answer must be in your own words. 'Lifting' from the text will get you no marks.

A2 One mark each (up to a total of 2 marks) for:

1 They are frightened of accusation (from parents or children).

2 They are unable to give their best.

3 The atmosphere is not conducive to helping young people.

The discovery that a comet impact triggered the disappearance of the dinosaurs as well as more than half the species that lived 65 million years ago may have been the most significant scientific breakthrough of the twentieth century. Brilliant detective work on the part of hundreds of scientists in analysing clues extracted from the study of fossils, and by counting the objects in near-earth space, has allowed the dinosaur mass-extinction mystery to be solved. As a result we have new insight into the nature of life on Earth.

Q3 **According to the first sentence, what important discovery has been made about comet impact?** 2 **U**

A3 Any two of the following for 1 mark each:

1 It wiped out/destroyed …

2 … half of the existing life-forms …

3 … including dinosaurs.

Once we appreciate that impact catastrophes have shaped life as we know it, and that such events will happen again in the future, how will this awareness alter the way we see ourselves in the cosmic context? Will we let nature take its course and trust to luck that our species will survive the next violent collision? Or will we confront the forces that may yet influence the destiny of all life on Earth?

Q4 **According to the writer, what two possible courses of action are open to us with regard to future 'impact catastrophes'?** 2 **U**

The answer must be in your own words. 'Lifting' from the text will get you no marks.

A4 1 mark each for the following two answers:

1 Do nothing (and just hope no comet hits us too hard).

2 Take preventative action (so that comets or asteroids don't hit Earth).

Evolution is mostly to blame. It has designed mankind to cope with deprivation, not plenty. People are perfectly tuned to store energy in good years to see them through lean ones. But when bad times never come, they are stuck with that energy, stored around their expanding bellies.

Q5 **'Evolution is to blame.' How does the writer go on to explain this statement?** 2 U

The answer must be in your own words. 'Lifting' from the text will get you no marks.

A5 1 mark each for any two of the following answers:

1 An acceptable gloss in your own words of 'has designed mankind'.

2 Humans have the ability to survive shortages by storing reserves.

3 People become bigger and bigger in periods of continuous prosperity.

My love affair with libraries started early in the Drumchapel housing scheme in the Fifties. For the 60,000 exiles packed off from slum housing to the city's outer fringe, Glasgow Council neglected the shops and amenities but somehow remembered to put in a public library – actually a wooden shed.

That library was split in two – an adult section and a children's section. This was an early taste of forbidden fruit. Much useful human reproductive knowledge was gained from certain books examined surreptitiously in the adult biology section.

Q6 **In your opinion, does the writer think Glasgow Council gave the library in Drumchapel a high priority? Justify your answer by close reference to the lines.** 2 U/E

A6 You could argue that he does or does not think the council gave the library high priority, or argue both sides at once. Marks will depend on the quality of explanation. A single very well-explained and suitably supported comment could get 2 marks, or two simpler comments could earn 1 mark each.

Possible answers for high priority:

1 Use of 'remembered' suggests that the library, though initially overlooked, was indeed a priority.

2 Despite the fact that the area lacked shops and amenities they put in a library, which suggests it was considered more important than these.

Possible answers for low priority:

1 The high number of possible users (60,000) with the small facility ('a shed') suggests it is inadequate.

2 Use of 'remembered' suggests it was an afterthought, a last-minute idea.

3 The fact that it was a 'shed' suggests it was basic, cheap, temporary and therefore of little importance.

4 The use of 'somehow' suggests nobody was sure why the decision was taken, it just happened.

5 Tone of 'actually a wooden shed', as if amused or sarcastic, suggests an afterthought, an admission of its inadequacies.

It may well be that public demand and technical change mean that we no longer need the dense neighbourhood network of local libraries of yore. But our culture, local and universal, does demand strategically situated libraries where one can find the material that is too expensive for the ordinary person to buy, or too complex to find online. Such facilities are worth funding publicly because the return in informed citizenship and civic pride is far in excess of money spent.

Libraries also have that undervalued resource – the trained librarian. The ultimate Achilles' heel of the internet is that it presents every page of information as being equally valid, which is of course nonsense. The internet is cluttered with false information, or just plain junk. The library, with its collection honed and developed by experts, is a guarantee of the quality and veracity of the information contained therein, something that Google can never provide.

Q7 Give four reasons the writer presents in these lines in favour of maintaining traditional public libraries.   4 U

You must use your own words. 'Lifting' from the text will get you no marks.

A7 Any of the following points for 1 mark each, up to a total of 4 marks:

1 idea of accessibility ('strategically situated')

2 idea of free access

3 idea that resources are more sophisticated ('too complex to find online')

4 idea of supporting democratic responsibilities ('informed citizenship')

5 idea of community cohesion ('civic pride')

6 idea of professional support ('trained librarian')

7 idea of informed selection ('honed and developed by experts')

8 idea of high standard of materials ('quality')

9 idea of authenticity ('veracity of information')

10 idea of selectivity of information in contrast with junk online.

If you read a wonderful new book by sociologist Frank Furedi – *Paranoid Parenting* – you will see the story of a teacher who quit the profession after a school trip was cancelled. Some parents were worried the trip would involve their children in a 45-minute journey in a private car. Would the cars be roadworthy? Were the drivers experienced? Were these non-smoking cars?

Q8 How does the story told in the paragraph help you to understand the meaning of the word 'paranoid'?   2 U

A8 One mark for giving the meaning of 'paranoid': e.g. (unnecessarily) fearful or concerned; (too) anxious; suspicious of everyone; always fearing the worst. Remember you **must** give this meaning or you cannot earn the second mark for evidence from the context.

One mark for appropriate reference to parents' questions, worries or concerns.

Others are, however, convinced that it is only a matter of time before we face Armageddon. Liberal Democrat MP and sky-watcher Lembit Opik says: 'I have said for years that the chance of an asteroid having an impact which could wipe out most of the human race is 100 per cent.' He has raised his worries in the Commons, successfully campaigned for an all-party task force to assess the potential risk, and helped set up the Spaceguard UK facility to track near-Earth objects. He admits: 'It does sound like a science fiction story and I may sound like one of those guys who walk up and down with a sandwich board saying the end of the world is nigh. But the end is nigh.'

Q9 **Show how these lines help you understand the meaning of the word 'Armageddon'.** 2 U

A9 One mark for giving the meaning of 'Armageddon', e.g. total destruction, a catastrophe so great that survival is unlikely. Remember you **must** give this meaning or you cannot earn the second mark for evidence from the context.

One mark for appropriate reference to and explanations of how the context helped you arrive at the meaning, e.g.:

- 'wipe out most of the human race'
- 'the end of the world (is nigh)'
- force of the final sentence 'But the end **is** nigh'
- 'face' suggests an ordeal and may gain a mark if well explained.

Libraries have another function still, which the internet cannot fulfil. Libraries, like museums, are custodians of knowledge – and should be funded as such. It has become the fashion in recent decades to turn over our great national libraries and museums into entertainment centres, with audio-visuals, interactive displays and gimmicks. While I have some enthusiasm for popularising esoteric knowledge, it cannot always be reduced to the level of a child's view of the universe. We have a duty to future generations to invest in the custodians of our culture, in particular its literature and manuscripts.

Q10 **The writer twice calls libraries 'custodians'. What does this mean and how does its context help you to arrive at this meaning?** 2 U

A10 One mark for giving the meaning of 'custodians', e.g. guardians, protectors, people who keep something safe. Remember you **must** give this meaning or you cannot earn the second mark for evidence from the context.

One mark for appropriate reference to and explanations of how the context helped you arrive at the meaning.

It is certainly possible that the premises advanced by environmental campaigners are sound: that we are in mortal danger from global warming and that this is a result of human activity. Yet when I listen to ecological warnings such as these, I am reminded of a doomsday scenario from the past.

In his 'Essay on the Principle of Population', published in 1798, Thomas Malthus demonstrated, in what appeared to be indisputable, mathematical terms, that population growth would exceed the limits of food supply by the middle of the 19th century. Only plague, war or natural disaster would be capable of sufficiently reducing the numbers of people to avert mass starvation within roughly fifty years. This account of the world's inevitable fate (known as the 'Malthusian catastrophe') was as much part of accepted thinking among intellectuals then as are the environmental lobby's warnings today.

Q11 **What does the phrase 'doomsday scenario' mean and how does the context help you to arrive at this meaning?** 2 U

A11 One mark for giving the meaning of 'doomsday scenario', e.g. the end of the world, a global disaster, the end of humanity. Remember you **must** give this meaning or you cannot earn the second mark for evidence from the context.

One mark for appropriate reference to such phrases as 'plague, war or natural disaster', 'the world's inevitable fate', 'catastrophe'.

It seems the childcare pendulum has swung: the principal threat to children is no longer neglectful parents, but excessively protective ones who are always worrying about germs.

Frank Furedi, reader in sociology at the University of Kent, has written a book, *Paranoid Parenting*, in which he explores the causes and far-reaching consequences of too much cosseting. 'It is always important to recall that our obsession with children's safety is likely to be more damaging to them than any risks that they are likely to meet in their daily encounter with the world,' Furedi writes.

Q12 **How does the context in which it is used help you to understand the meaning of the word 'cosseting'?** 2 U

A12 One mark for giving the meaning of 'cosseting', e.g. pampering, over-protecting, spoiling. Remember you **must** give this meaning or you cannot earn the second mark for evidence from the context.

One mark for appropriate reference to such phrases as: 'excessively protective', 'always worrying (about germs)', 'obsession with children's safety'.

Is your journey really necessary? Who would have thought that, in the absence of world war and in the midst of unprecedented prosperity, politicians would be telling us not to travel? Just as working people have begun to enjoy the freedoms that the better-off have known for generations – the experience of other cultures, other cuisines, other climates – they are threatened with having those liberating possibilities priced out of their reach.

And when I hear politicians – most of them comfortably off – trying to deny enlightenment and pleasure to 'working class' people, I reach for my megaphone. Maybe Tommy Tattoo and his mates do use cheap flights to the sunshine as an extension of their binge-drinking opportunities, but for thousands of people whose parents would never have ventured beyond Blackpool or Rothesay, air travel has been a social revelation.

So, before we all give the eco-lobby's anti-flying agenda the unconditional benefit of the doubt, can we just review their strategy as a whole?

Remember, it is not just air travel that the green tax lobby is trying to control: it is a restriction on any mobility. Clamping down on one form of movement, as the glib reformers have discovered, simply creates intolerable pressure on the others. Londoners, for example, had just become accustomed to the idea that they would have to pay an £8 congestion charge to drive into their own city when they discovered that the fares on commuter rail and underground services had been hiked up with the intention of driving away customers from the public transport system – now grossly overcrowded as a result of people having been forced off the roads by the congestion charge.

Q13 Referring to specific words and phrases, show how the sentence 'So, before … as a whole?' performs a linking function in the argument. **2 U**

A13 The words 'eco-lobby's anti-flying agenda' refer back to the idea of restrictions on travel, which was mentioned in the first two paragraphs.

The words 'their strategy as a whole' (OR 'can we just review') introduce the idea of discussing and examining these proposed restrictions, which comes up in the final paragraph.

One faction has cried constantly that the countryside is in mortal danger from greedy developers whose only motive is profit; another has kept roaring that farmers are killing every wild thing in sight and threatening the very soil on which we stand through overuse of machinery and chemicals; still another has been continually heard ululating over a decline in the bird population, or the loss of hedgerows, or the disappearance of marshland, or the appearance of coniferous forest.

Q14 Show how word choice emphasises the strong feelings of those who believe the countryside is under threat. **2 A**

A The words 'cried constantly' suggest a state of permanent outrage.

B The words 'mortal danger' suggest extreme peril, something life-threatening.

C The word 'greedy' suggests they are too eager for monetary gain.

Three more possible examples of word choice to examine in that paragraph could be taken from:

1 'only motive is profit' suggests single-minded quest for gain

2 'kept on roaring' suggests persistent expression of anger, aggression

3 'killing every wild thing in sight' is use of hyperbole to suggest the scale of the destruction

4 'threatening the very soil' emphasises the extent of the menace

5 'overuse' suggests injury by excessive use

6 'continually … ululating' suggests constant loud lamentations.

The internet search engine Google, with whom I spend more time than with my loved ones, is planning to put the contents of the world's great university libraries online, including the Bodleian in Oxford and those of Harvard and Stanford in America. Part of me is ecstatic at the thought of all that information at my fingertips; another part of me is nostalgic, because I think physical libraries, book-lined and cathedral-quiet, are a cherished part of civilisation we lose at our cultural peril.

Q15 How does the writer's word choice help to convey his view of the importance of 'physical libraries'? Refer to two examples in your answer.　　2 A

A15 Remember you must quote the words you wish to analyse, and look at their connotations and suggestions. One mark for any of these answers, up to a total of 2:

1 'book-lined' suggests a large number or area of books, implying impressive, organised

2 'cathedral-quiet' has connotations of devotion, solemnity, reverence, hush

3 'cherished' suggests cared for emotionally (rather than just practically), warmth

4 'civilisation': connotation of marking us out from less civilised societies

5 'lose': sense of being deprived, bereft

6 'cultural' suggests tradition, heritage, a civilised society

7 'peril' suggests threat, risk, danger (to something precious).

Libraries also have that undervalued resource – the trained librarian. The ultimate Achilles' heel of the internet is that it presents every page of information as being equally valid, which is of course nonsense. The internet is cluttered with false information, or just plain junk. The library, with its collection honed and developed by experts, is a guarantee of the quality and veracity of the information contained therein, something that Google can never provide.

Q16 Show how the writer's word choice emphasises the contrast between his attitude to libraries and his attitude to the internet.   2 A

Remember you must quote the words you wish to analyse, and look at their connotations and suggestions.

A16 As this is a contrast question, for full marks you need to have at least one item of word choice about his attitude to libraries, and one about his attitude to the internet.

For libraries, you should make comment on the positive connotations of any of the following: 'trained … honed … developed … experts … guarantee … quality … veracity'.

For the internet, you should make comment on the negative connotations of any of the following: 'Achilles' heel … (of course) nonsense … cluttered … false … (plain) junk … never'.

Yet if you sweep away the apoplectic froth and the self-interested posturing and look at the reality, the threat to the countryside recedes dramatically. Yes, we do occupy a crowded little island. But what makes it seem crowded is that 98 per cent of us live on 7 per cent of the land. Britain is still overwhelmingly green. Just 11 per cent of our nation is classified as urban.

Q17 Show how the writer's word choice emphasises his view that the threat to the countryside is less serious than the English middle classes suggest.   2 A

Remember you must quote the words you wish to analyse, and look at their connotations and suggestions.

A17 A single very well-explained or insightful comment could get 2 marks, or two simpler comments could earn 1 mark each. Possible answers:

1 'sweep away' suggests the previous argument is weak and can be dealt with or dismissed very quickly

2 'apoplectic' suggests uncontrolled, irrational anger

3 'froth' suggests something unimportant, trivial

4 'self-interested' suggests middle classes only concerned with themselves, not the countryside

5 'posturing' suggests middle-class concern is contrived, fake, affected

6 'look at the reality' suggests truth is clear

7 'recedes dramatically' suggests rapid movement, significant diminution of threat

8 'overwhelmingly green' emphasises full extent of Britain's rural make-up

9 'classified' official-sounding term reinforces accuracy of statistic

10 use of 'you … we … us … our' is a clear attempt to make the reader share the writer's point of view.

Is your journey really necessary? Who would have thought that, in the absence of world war and in the midst of unprecedented prosperity, politicians would be telling us not to travel? Just as working people have begun to enjoy the freedoms that the better-off have known for generations – the experience of other cultures, other cuisines, other climates – they are threatened with having those liberating possibilities priced out of their reach.

And when I hear politicians – most of them comfortably off – trying to deny enlightenment and pleasure to 'working class' people, I reach for my megaphone. Maybe Tommy Tattoo and his mates do use cheap flights to the sunshine as an extension of their binge-drinking opportunities, but for thousands of people whose parents would never have ventured beyond Blackpool or Rothesay, air travel has been a social revelation.

Q18 **Show how the writer's word choice conveys the strength of her commitment to air travel for all.** 2 A

A18 Remember you must quote the words you wish to analyse, and look at their connotations and suggestions. A single very well-explained or insightful comment could get 2 marks, or two simpler comments could earn 1 mark each. Possible answers:

1 'freedoms' suggests travel offers people independence, broadens their horizons

2 'experience' suggests something life-enhancing

3 'liberating (possibilities)' suggests travel offers people a freer life

4 'enlightenment' suggests travel can result in a fundamental increase in people's knowledge or happiness

5 'pleasure' suggests enjoyment, happiness

6 '(I reach for my) megaphone' suggests strident, vocal opposition that demands to be listened to

7 'thousands (of people)' suggests the sheer number who have benefited from travel

8 '(would never have) ventured' suggests the limited nature of past experience compared with current possibilities

9 '(social) revelation' suggests a life-changing benefit.

Then there is the proliferation of action groups dedicated to stopping construction of roads, airports, railway lines, factories, shopping centres and houses in rural areas, while multifarious organisations have become accustomed to expending their time and energies in monitoring and reporting on the state of grassland, water, trees, moorlands, uplands, lowlands, birds' eggs, wildflowers, badgers, historical sites and countless other aspects of the landscape and its inhabitants.

Q19 **Show how the writer's use of tone in these lines conveys his disapproval of the 'action groups'.** 2 A

A19 The writer creates a dismissive tone. He does this by using the words 'moorlands, uplands, lowlands' which are dismissive because they suggest just any old lands.

I am fed up listening to scaremongers about the E. coli virus, telling me my child should never visit a farm or come into contact with animals. I am weary of organisations that are dedicated to promulgating the idea that threats and dangers to children lurk everywhere. I am sick of charities who on the one hand attack overprotective parents and at the same time say children should never be left unsupervised in public places.

Q20 Identify the writer's tone and explain how it is conveyed.   3 A

A20 One mark for identifying a tone of: anger, contempt, frustration etc. NOT tired or weary.

Marks for showing how the tone is conveyed will depend on the quality of comment. A single very well-explained or insightful comment could get 2 marks, or two simpler comments could earn 1 mark each. You get no marks for just making a reference to the text or for just identifying a feature.

Possible answers:

1 Repetitive structure of 'I am fed up … I am weary … I am sick' drives the point home forcefully.

2 Word choice in 'fed up … weary … sick' has exaggerated connotations of illness or depression.

3 Word choice in 'scaremongers', 'lurk' has connotations of threat.

4 Use of intensifiers 'never … everywhere … never' shows emphatic, strong commitment.

5 Balancing of 'on the one hand … at the same time' points up the contradictory illogical attitude.

Survivors of essentially random impact catastrophes – cosmic accidents – were those creatures who just happened to be 'lucky' enough to find themselves alive after the dust settled. It doesn't matter how well a creature may have been able to survive in a particular environment before an event – being thumped on the head by a large object from space during the event is not conducive to a long and happy existence.

Q21 Explain how the writer creates a slightly humorous tone.   2 A

A21 Marks will depend on the quality of explanation. A single very well-explained and suitably supported point could get 2 marks, or two simpler comments could earn 1 mark each. You get no marks for just making a reference to the text or for just identifying a feature.

Possible answers:

1 use of 'lucky', which is not usual scientific terminology, suggests a more flippant approach

2 use of 'dust settled' may be either literal or metaphorical and can be seen as humorous

3 'being thumped (on the head)' is unscientific and creates a humorous picture

4 'thumped' and 'conducive' (or any similar combination of words) are humorous because of the mix of colloquial and formal words

5 'not conducive to a long and happy existence' is ironic, understated, deliberately clichéd

6 use of inverted commas round 'lucky' suggests means of vocal delivery and creates comic effect and emphasis.

I write these sentences with the heavy heart of a class traitor, for I am a middle-class, middle-aged property owner who has smugly watched his own house soar in value as more and more young househunters desperately chase fewer and fewer properties. I am inordinately proud of my view across the green belt (from an upstairs window admittedly because of the motorway flyover in between). And I intend to spend the weekend rambling across the rural England I have loved since boyhood.

Q22 **Show how the writer's use of language in these lines creates a self-mocking tone.**

2 A

A22 A single very well-explained or insightful comment could get 2 marks, or two simpler comments could earn 1 mark each. Remember that language is not merely word choice. Possible answers:

1 'heavy heart' deliberately exaggerates his remorse

2 'class traitor' is an inflated description suggesting his opinions are some terrible act of betrayal

3 'middle-class, middle-aged property owner' has the writer deliberately making himself into a cliché or stereotype

4 'smugly watched' suggests he is complacent, self-satisfied, gloating

5 'soar in value' suggests a smug belief that his own success is both effortless and impressive

6 'inordinately proud' suggests a pride which is hard to justify or out of proportion

7 'my view' suggests smug possessiveness

8 'from an upstairs window' undercuts his pride in his view by suggesting it is limited, partial, awkward

9 'motorway flyover in between' suggests something man-made and ugly, making fun of his pride in his view

10 repetition of '(And) I' at the start of sentences suggests he is self-absorbed, pompous

11 repetition of 'I' followed by active verb suggests inflated belief in the value of his own actions or opinions

12 contrast of his self-satisfied pride with the desperation of the 'young househunters'.

The only solution – and I am just waiting for the politicians to recommend it explicitly – is for none of us to go anywhere. Stay at home and save the planet. But that would be a craven retreat from all the social, professional and cultural interactions that unrestricted mobility makes possible – and which, since the Renaissance, have made great cities the centres of intellectual progress.

Q23 **Show how, in this paragraph, the writer creates a tone which conveys her disapproval of the 'solution'.**   **2 A**

A23 A single very well-explained or insightful comment could get 2 marks, or two simpler comments could earn 1 mark each. Possible answers:

1 'and I am just waiting' suggests the writer's world-weary distrust of politicians and her feeling that their actions are inevitable

2 'none/anywhere': emphasising the extreme nature of the 'solution'

3 'craven retreat' suggests the 'solution' would be a cowardly, backward step

4 'Renaissance' is a positive reference to an enlightened, progressive, civilised time

5 'intellectual progress' suggests society moving forward in a considered, enlightened manner

6 use of parenthesis ('and I am … explicitly') is an aside to the readers about how politicians love to jump on bandwagons

7 'Stay at home and save the planet.' This parody of a slick slogan shows the writer's contempt for the quick-fix solutions of the eco-lobby

8 'social, professional and cultural' is an accumulated list of benefits made possible by mobility

9 the position of 'But that' at the start of the last sentence sets up her explicit rejection of the 'solution'

10 the dash (followed by 'and') introduces one more point to the argument, building to a powerful climax.

The most cherished credo of the English middle classes is that the verdant hills and dales of the Home Counties should remain forever sacrosanct, and that the Government's 'Stalinist' decision to impose a million extra houses on southeast England is the most hideous threat to our way of life since the Luftwaffe made its energetic contribution to British town and country planning in 1940. Thousands of green acres will be choked by concrete, as rapacious housebuilders devour whole landscapes. England's cherished green belts – the fourteen great rings of protected fields that have stopped our major cities from sprawling outward for more than half a century – will be swept away.

Q **Show how the writer's use of imagery in these lines emphasises the extreme nature of the English middle classes' view of the threat to the countryside.**

A24 Just as a 'cherished credo' is an important religious belief, so the middle classes have an almost religious faith in the importance of protecting the countryside.

A25 Just as something that is 'sacrosanct' is sacred and holy, so the middle classes believe the countryside is too special to be changed.

A26 Just as Stalin was a ruthless dictator, so the Government is evil, brutal, cruel, heartless.

A27 'choked': Just as being choked involves difficulty in breathing or strangulation, so the countryside is having the life squeezed out of it.

A28 'devour whole landscapes': Just as to devour something is to eat it up greedily, so the builders are greedy, insatiable, consuming the countryside.

A29 'sprawling outward': Just as to sprawl is to sit or lie in an awkward way, so the outward movement of towns and cities would be unattractive and untidy.

A30 'will be swept away': Just as being swept away suggests a tidal wave, so there could be a rapid and sweeping end to the green belts.

A31 'rapacious housebuilders': Just as a rapacious act is a violent and predatory one, so the builders are greedy, aggressive, plundering, destructive.

Many details referred to in our story are still controversial. Debate is particularly heated as regards the role of impacts in directing the course of human history. All of this is very exciting. The whole topic is in a state of ferment, a symptom that something significant is brewing.

Q32 Show how effective you find the writer's use of imagery in conveying the excitement of the 'debate'.

2 A

A32 Marks will depend on the quality of explanation. A single very well-explained and suitably supported comment on one image could get 2 marks, or two simpler comments could earn 1 mark each. You get no marks for just making a reference to the text or for just identifying an image.

Answers on imagery must deconstruct the image, showing an understanding of the literal root and then exploring how the writer is using it figuratively.

Possible answers:

1 'heated': Just as substances are more volatile when heated, so the debate has become loud, animated, voluble.

2 'ferment': Just as the process of brewing causes movement, fizz, explosions etc., so the debate has become lively, loud.

3 'brewing': Just as the process of brewing causes movement, fizz, etc., so the debate is developing, growing voluble, loud.

4 'symptom': Just as a symptom is an outward sign of an underlying disease, so the debate is the outward sign of an underlying controversy.

Thanks to rising agricultural productivity, lean years are rarer all over the globe. Pessimistic economists, who used to draw graphs proving that the world was shortly going to run out of food, have gone rather quiet lately. According to the UN, the number of people short of food fell from 920m in 1980 to 799m twenty years later, even though the world's population increased by 1.6 billion over the period. This is mostly a cause for celebration. Mankind had won what was, for most of his time on the planet, his biggest battle: to ensure that he and his offspring had enough to eat. But every silver lining has a cloud, and the consequence of prosperity is a new plague that brings with it a host of interesting policy dilemmas.

Q33 **How effective do you find the imagery in these lines in illustrating the writer's line of thought? Refer to two examples in your answer.** 4 A

A33 Marks will depend on the quality of explanation. A single very well-explained and suitably supported comment on one image could get 2 marks, or two simpler comments could earn 1 mark each. You get no marks for just making a reference to the text or for just identifying an image.

Answers on imagery must deconstruct the image, showing an understanding of the literal root and then exploring how the writer is using it figuratively. For this question, you also need to connect the image to the writer's line of thought.

Possible answers:

1 'won ... battle' has idea of struggle, succeeding in a difficult situation

2 'offspring' has the idea of a product and a source, suggesting the importance of the survival of the genetic line

3 'silver lining' has the idea of a bright side, the redeeming aspect of an otherwise unpleasant situation

4 'cloud' suggests a dull or dark spot, a sense of threat

5 'plague' has the idea of a deadly epidemic, potential devastation

6 'host' has the idea of a large number, threat or army (and may tie in to the battle image).

I have spent a substantial portion of my life in libraries, and I still enter them with a mixture of excitement and awe. I am not alone in this. Veneration for libraries is as old as writing itself, for a library is more to our culture than a collection of books: it is a temple, a symbol of power, the hushed core of civilisation, the citadel of memory, with its own mystique, social and sensual as well as intellectual.

Q34 **By referring to one example, show how the writer's imagery in these lines conveys the importance of libraries.** 2 A

A34 Marks will depend on the quality of explanation. A single very well-explained and suitably supported comment on one image could get 2 marks, a simpler comment could earn 1 mark. You get no marks for just making a reference to the text or for just identifying an image.

Answers on imagery must deconstruct the image, showing an understanding of the literal root and then exploring how the writer is using it figuratively.

In this question, you must choose only one image to answer on.

Possible answers:

1 'temple': Just as a temple is a place of worship and reverence, so a library deserves our respect (because of the knowledge it contains).

2 'core': Just as the core is the heart, the essential part, so a library is central to our society.

3 'citadel': Just as a citadel is a fortress, so a library provides a safeguard for something precious.

But even in this self-interested arena a representative from the US Federal Aviation Administration caused some sharp intakes of breath from the audience by showing an extraordinary map of current flightpaths etched over one another on the world's surface. The only places on Earth that are not scarred by routes are blocks of air space over the central Pacific, the southern Atlantic, and Antarctica.

Q35 **How effective do you find the writer's use of imagery in conveying the impact that flying has on the environment?**   **2 A**

A35 Marks will depend on the quality of explanation. A single very well-explained and suitably supported comment on one image could get 2 marks, a simpler comment could earn 1 mark. You get no marks for just making a reference to the text or for just identifying an image.

Answers on imagery must deconstruct the image, showing an understanding of the literal root and then exploring how the writer is using it figuratively.

Possible answers:

1 'etched (over one another)': Just as etching involves cutting into a surface, so the Earth will be permanently scarred or damaged by our flying over it.

2 'scarred': Just as a scar is a lasting mark left by a wound, so the Earth will be permanently disfigured.

London is different for all its people. They make the most of the elements in it that have meaning for them and ignore the rest. A city is an à la carte menu. That is what makes it different from a village, which has little room for tolerance and difference. And a great city is one in which as many people as possible can make the widest of choices from its menu.

Q36 **Show how the image of the 'à la carte menu' illustrates the point the writer is making in these lines.**

2 A

A36 Marks will depend on the quality of comment. A single very well-explained and suitably supported comment could get 2 marks, a simpler comment could earn 1 mark.

Answers on imagery must deconstruct the image, showing an understanding of the literal root and then exploring how the writer is using it figuratively.

Possible answer:

Just as an 'à la carte' menu lets diners make a choice from a varied and extensive list, so people in London can choose to pursue any lifestyle as there is a wide range of jobs, activities, cultures and pursuits.

A lot has been learned about the nature of cosmic collisions and this new knowledge has given a remarkable twist to the story of our origins. We now recognise that comet and asteroid impacts may be the most important driving force behind evolutionary change on the planet. Originally, such objects smashed into one another to build the Earth 4.5 billion years ago. After that, further comet impacts brought the waters of our oceans and the organic modules needed for life. Ever since then, impacts have continued to punctuate the story of evolution. On many occasions, comets slammed into Earth with such violence that they nearly precipitated the extinction of all life. In the aftermath of each catastrophe, new species emerged to take the place of those that had been wiped out.

Q37 **How does the sentence structure of these lines highlight the writer's ideas?**

A37 By beginning a number of the sentences with references to time periods such as 'originally' and 'after that', the writer creates a sequence through time which suggests that comet impacts were part of the process of evolution.

By ending the last two sentences with the phrases 'all life' and 'wiped out' the writer creates a climax that emphasises his point about the destructiveness of these impacts.

The fact that he uses the word 'impacts' three times shows how important these events have been.

One faction has cried constantly that the countryside is in mortal danger from greedy developers whose only motive is profit; another has kept roaring that farmers are killing every wild thing in sight and threatening the very soil on which we stand through overuse of machinery and chemicals; still another has been continually heard ululating over a decline in the bird population, or the loss of hedgerows, or the disappearance of marshland, or the appearance of coniferous forest.

Q38 **Show how the sentence structure here emphasises the strong feelings of those who feel the countryside is under threat.** 2 A

A38 The listing of the different subjects that factions complain about emphasises the wide range of causes of protest. Repetition of 'or' emphasises a determination to find something to complain about.

Then there is the proliferation of action groups dedicated to stopping construction of roads, airports, railway lines, factories, shopping centres and houses in rural areas, while multifarious organisations have become accustomed to expending their time and energies in monitoring and reporting on the state of grassland, water, trees, moorlands, uplands, lowlands, birds' eggs, wildflowers, badgers, historical sites and countless other aspects of the landscape and its inhabitants.

Q39 **Show how the writer's use of sentence structure in this paragraph conveys his disapproval of the 'action groups'.** 2 A

A39 The list of developments these groups wish to stop suggests that he feels they protest excessively. The list of projects they spend time and energy on suggests that they are excessively concerned about a wide range of aspects of nature.

The green-belt protectionists claim to be saving unspoilt countryside from the rampant advance of bulldozers. Exactly what unspoilt countryside do they imagine they are saving? Primordial forest, unchanged since Boudicca thrashed the Romans? Hogwash. The English have been making and remaking their landscape for millennia to suit the needs of each passing generation.

Q How effective do you find the writer's use of sentence structure in conveying his attitude to this argument from the 'green–belt protectionists'?

A40 (Look at the writer's use of repetition.)

2 A

The writer's repeated use of questions shows his disbelief in the protectionists' ideas.

A41 (Look at one other facet of sentence structure.)

2 A

His use of a single-word sentence 'Hogwash' highlights his utter rejection of their claims.

These protectionists are fond of deriding any housebuilding targets set by the Government as monstrous, Soviet-style diktats. Good grief, what on earth do they imagine that the planning laws protecting the green belts and agricultural land are, if not Government interventions that have had a huge, and often disastrous, impact not just on the property market, but on employment, on transport, on public services and on economic growth?

Q How effective do you find the writer's use of sentence structure in conveying his attitude to this argument from the 'green–belt protectionists'?

2 A

A42 and **43** Possible answers:

1 Position of 'Good grief' at start of sentence establishes his exasperated tone to follow.

2 The parenthesis 'and often disastrous' adds an additional layer of criticism.

3 The rhetorical question invites the reader to agree with him or share his beliefs.

4 Repeated use of 'on' suggests the scale and variety of problems caused by the current laws.

Everywhere you turn there is an army of professionals – ably abetted by the media – hard at work encouraging parents to fear the worst. Don't let your children out in the sun – not unless they're wearing special UV-resistant T-shirts. Don't buy your children a Wendy house, they might crush their fingers in the hinges. Don't buy a baby walker, your toddlers might brain themselves. Don't buy plastic baby teethers, your baby might suck in harmful chemicals. Don't let them use mobile phones, they'll sizzle their brains. Don't buy a second-hand car seat, it will not protect them. And on and on it goes.

Q44 How does the sentence structure of these lines emphasise the writer's feelings about the 'army of professionals'? **2 A**

A44 Marks will depend on the quality of comment. A single very well-explained or insightful comment could get 2 marks, or two simpler comments could earn 1 mark each. You get no marks for just making a reference to the text or for just identifying a feature.

Possible answers:

1 Positioning of 'everywhere' at the start of the sentence creates emphatic exaggeration.

2 Parenthesis about the media creates sneering tone.

3 String of sentences beginning 'Don't' emphasises negative, authoritarian attitude.

4 Repeated structure of command followed by reason emphasises negative, authoritarian attitude, or emphasises that the writer thinks these are weak justifications.

5 'And on and on it goes' is deliberately glib and repetitive.

When the world was a simpler place the rich were fat, the poor were thin, and right-thinking people worried about how to feed the hungry. Now, in much of the world, the rich are thin, the poor are fat, and right-thinking people are worrying about obesity.

Q45 Identify two ways in which the sentence structure in these lines emphasises the change in the concerns of 'right-thinking people'. **2 A**

A45 This question only asks you to identify; you do not need to comment or analyse. 1 mark each, up to a total of 2, for any of these 'ways':

1 Parallelism/balanced construction.

2 A series of contrasts ('when/now' … 'fat/thin' … 'feed the hungry/obesity'.

3 Repetition of 'rich … poor … right-thinking'.

There is no doubt that obesity is the world's biggest public-health issue today – the main cause of heart disease, which kills more people these days than AIDS, malaria, war; the principal risk factor in diabetes; heavily implicated in cancer and other diseases. Since the World Health Organization labelled obesity an epidemic in 2000, reports on its fearful consequences have come thick and fast.

Q46 **How does the writer's sentence structure stress the seriousness of the health problem?** 2 A

A46 Marks will depend on the quality of comment. A single very well-explained and suitably supported comment could get 2 marks, or two simpler comments could earn 1 mark each. You get no marks for just making a reference to the text or for just identifying a feature of sentence structure.

Possible answers:

1 Single dash explains/exemplifies the opening statement by introducing the main risk.

2 Semicolons separate items in a list, which emphasises the serious consequences of obesity.

3 Listing emphasises the number or cumulative effects of health-related problems.

4 Second sentence provides a summing up of the dire effects of obesity.

Speaker after speaker bemoaned how the public had somehow misunderstood the aviation industry and had come to believe that aviation is a huge and disproportionate polluter. Let's get this in perspective, said repeated speakers: this is small fry compared with cars, factories, even homes. Why are we being singled out, they cried? Why not, they said, chase after other industries that could easily make efficiency savings instead of picking on an industry that gives so much to the world, yet is currently so economically fragile?

Q47 **Show how the writer's use of sentence structure conveys his unsympathetic view of the speakers at the conference.** 2 A

A47 Marks will depend on the quality of explanation. A single very insightful point could get 2 marks, a simpler comment could earn 1 mark. You get no marks for just making a reference to the text or for just identifying a feature.

Possible answers:

1 Repetition ('speaker after speaker') emphasises the number of speakers who were of like mind in claiming their industry was being victimised.

2 Use of colon introduces the so-called justification for their case by singling out what they claim are greater or worse causes of pollution.

3 Use of questions in the last two sentences is designed to divert attention from their culpability.

You see their traces in the Spitalfields district, where a French Huguenot chapel became, successively, a synagogue and a mosque, tracking the movement of waves of migrants from poverty to suburban comfort. London's a place without an apparent structure that has proved extraordinarily successful at growing and changing. Its old residential core, sheltering in the approaches to its Tower of London fortress, has made the transition into the world's busiest banking centre. Its market halls and power stations have become art galleries and piazzas. Its simple terraced streets, built for the clerks of the Great Western Railway in Southall, have become home to the largest Sikh community outside India.

Q48 Show how the sentence structure of the paragraph as a whole emphasises the idea of change. **2 A**

A48 Marks will depend on the quality of comment. A single very well-explained and suitably supported comment could get 2 marks, simpler comments could earn 1 mark. You get no marks for just naming a feature of sentence structure. Possible answers could look at these features:

1 Parallel openings ('Its old residential core', 'Its market halls and power stations', 'Its simple terraced streets').

2 Repeated 'before and after' formula.

3 Similar verb patterns ('has made the transition', 'have become').

Any or all of these features stress the repetitive nature, widespread scale and perhaps inevitability of change.

In comparison with the more immediate threats to the continued survival of our species (acid rain, destruction of stratospheric ozone, the greenhouse effect, overpopulation), the danger of comet or asteroid impacts may seem remote. The problem with impact events, however, is that their consequences are so awesome that we can barely imagine what it would be like to be struck by a large object from space. And there would be limited opportunity for reflection following such an event.

Q49 In these lines, the writer deals with various threats to the survival of our species. Show how effective the last sentence is as a conclusion to this paragraph. **2 E**

A49 For full marks you must connect a specific aspect of the sentence with the main idea of the paragraph, which is that in comparison with other threats, comet impact is much more serious.

The following sample answer was given in Chapter 2:

> By beginning with the word 'And' the writer shows that he has reached a summing up. This summing up effect is added to by his use of a relatively short sentence. This sense of summing up or ending effectively shows that a comet could cause the end of everything.

The following answers are also possible, backed up by evaluative comment:

1 The sentence expands/reinforces the idea of widespread devastation.

2 The sentence uses understatement and irony.

3 The sentence reads like an addition or afterthought.

Astrophysics expert, Dr Alan Fitzsimmons of Queen's University, Belfast, who advises the UK NEO (Near-Earth Objects) Information Centre in Leicester, is optimistic that Earth will come through the latest asteroid scare unscathed: 'In all probability, within the next month we will know its future orbit with an accuracy which will mean we will be able to rule out any impact.'

Q50 **By commenting on specific words or phrases in these lines, show to what extent you would have confidence in Dr Fitzsimmons.** 2 A/E

A50 You may have evidence both for and against having confidence in him. Marks will depend on the quality of comment. A single insightful comment could get 2 marks, or two simpler comments could earn 1 mark each. You get no marks for just making a reference to the text.

Possible answers for confidence:

1 'Astrophysics expert', 'Dr', 'University' suggest academic ability and success

2 'advises' shows he is recognised in his field

3 'accuracy', 'rule out', 'will' suggest knowledge and precision.

Possible answers for lack of confidence:

1 'NEO (Near-Earth Objects)' vague title does not inspire confidence

2 'optimistic' idea of being hopeful is perhaps not supported by facts

3 'In all probability' is not complete certainty.

Warnings of catastrophe come and go. Whatever their validity, we cannot and should not ask people to go back to a more restricted way of life. The restrictions would not work anyway, because they are impracticable. If they were enforced, they would be grotesquely unfair and socially divisive. If we really are facing an environmental crisis, then we are going to have to innovate and engineer our way out of it.

Q51 **How effective do you find the writer's language in emphasising her opposition to placing restrictions on people's way of life?**   **2 A/E**

A51 Marks will depend on the quality of explanation. A single very well-explained or insightful point could get 2 marks, a simpler comment could earn 1 mark. Remember that language is much more than just word choice. Possible answers:

1 'Warnings of catastrophe come and go' suggests these warnings are not worthy of the current over-reaction. You might also make the case that the shortness of this sentence suggests the writer's blunt dismissal of these warnings.

2 'Whatever their validity' suggests the writer is sceptical.

3 'we cannot and should not' uses repetition to emphasise opposition

4 'more restricted way of life' suggests loss of freedom

5 'anyway' has a dismissive tone, rejecting the idea of restrictions

6 'impracticable' highlights the flaws in the proposals

7 'grotesquely unfair' suggests a monstrous travesty of justice

8 'socially divisive' suggests an attack on the very fabric of society

9 repetition of the 'If' structure in the final two sentences brings the passage towards a climax

10 use of 'we' throughout the paragraph suggests the writer is taking a stand for all of us; underlines her belief that we can solve this together rather than being dictated to by the Government.

Answers for the 30-mark, single-passage task on Privacy

These are the answers for the 30-mark, single-passage task on Privacy from the end of the Close Reading chapter (Chapter 2). Because this was a far bigger task, the answers will be dealt with in much more detail.

	passage extract
✓	straightforward acceptable answer
★	really good answer
✗	weak/misguided answer
+	other possible points
!	important advice

1 Read lines 1–22.

'If you have something that you don't want anyone to know, maybe you shouldn't be doing it in the first place.' Who said this, do you think? Stalin? J. Edgar Hoover? Well, no: in fact, it was the chief executive of Google, Eric Schmidt, who controls one of the biggest internet companies in the world. So we ought to take what he says seriously, even if – especially if – we disagree with it.

Why? Not simply because, in one blunt, bland phrase, this extremely powerful and completely unaccountable man has casually erased our right to privacy, but because 10 or 20 years from now his statement might not seem outrageous at all. It might, indeed, be considered utterly normal and unobjectionable. If our children grow up in Schmidt's brave new world – a world of CCTV cameras in classrooms and intimate revelations posted on the internet – then how will they even know what they are losing? The entire notion of privacy as a human right is being eroded, and at a speed which is frightening.

(a) Explain how lines 1–9 create an effective opening to the passage. 2 A

✓	It is effective because it starts with a quote and you don't know who said it, which creates a little suspense. The writer then suggests possible names of people who liked to control people's lives.
★	He opens with an unattributed quotation which intrigues the reader, especially since the quotation seems so sinister. He then teases the reader by offering suggestions as if he's chatting to us ('do you think?') and then giving the rather surprising answer.

	It is an effective opening because it asks if Stalin or J. Edgar Hoover said this and then telling us who did say it. It was the boss of Google. **(This is a weak answer because it merely states what the opening sentences do, with no attempt to explain what makes this effective.)**
	Comment could also be made on: • the very chatty nature of 'Well, no: in fact …' • the sense of addressing the reader directly 'you … we' • the specific ideas conjured up by the two people named: tyrant/mass murderer; the archetype of the spying profession and paranoid secrecy.
	It's important not just to *assert* that it's effective; you must try to explain *in what way* it is effective.

(b) What are the writer's main objections to Schmidt's statement? 2 U

	It shows how much our privacy is being taken away and it could lead to a situation where we don't even realise this has happened.
	He objects to the underlying belief that we have no right to privacy. Not only that, it questions our right to have any privacy in the first place.
	Schmidt has casually erased our right to privacy and the entire notion of privacy as a human right is being eroded. **(This is a weak answer because it simply quotes from the passage with no attempt to use own words.)**
	Reference could also be made to: • the deceptive simplicity of the statement • the fact that he is 'unaccountable', i.e. cannot be called to account by anyone.

(c) Show how the writer's use of language in lines 10–22 conveys his strong feelings on the subject. Refer in your answer to at least two language features such as word choice, sentence structure, imagery … 4 A

	Imagery: 'erased' is like a rubber removing pencil marks without trace, which shows he thinks our privacy will soon be gone forever; 'eroded' means literally taken away bit by bit until nothing remains – our privacy is being chipped away. Sentence structure: the rhetorical question 'how will they even know what they are losing?' shows he thinks they won't ever know and creates a tone of despair. Word choice: 'casually' suggests that Schmidt has no concern for what is happening – it means nothing to him.

The structure of 'not simply because … but because' effectively highlights the extent of his objections by drawing attention to his belief that there is more than one level of criticism, one of them deep and worrying.

The parenthetical addition of 'a world of CCTV cameras …' illustrates powerfully the intrusive nature of the invasion, referring to seemingly everyday features such as school classrooms and internet chatrooms.

The imagery of 'erased' and 'eroded' creates a sense of something being taken away by a relentless process of decay until it reaches a point when there is nothing left. He is presenting the abstraction 'privacy' as a physical object which is being systematically reduced to nothing.

His frequent use of intensifiers makes his strong feelings very clear, e.g. Schmidt is described as 'extremely' powerful and 'completely' unaccountable; it's not just the notion of privacy he sees as being threatened but the 'entire' notion.

He makes his strong feelings clear by using a rhetorical question. He also uses dashes for a parenthesis. He uses alliteration in 'blunt, bland'. His word choice is effective too: 'outrageous', 'frightening'.

(This is a weak answer because though it identifies several points on which comment could be made, it does no more than that.)

Comment could also be made on:
- 'blunt, bland' – monosyllabic and alliterative to add some punch and aggression to his criticism
- 'powerful'/'unaccountable' – presents Schmidt in a very negative, threatening way
- 'outrageous' – emphasises just how shocking this statement is
- 'utterly' – emphasises just how frighteningly 'normal' the state of affairs could be
- 'brave new world' – allusion to a (fictional) highly controlled, nightmarish society
- 'our children' – rather emotional appeal to our desire to protect the innocent
- 'human right' – sense of basic, unquestionable privileges under threat.

Analysis questions for 4 marks need a lot of work. Always try for four separate points.

For imagery, remember to state as clearly as possible the 'literal' idea behind the image.

2 Read lines 23–40.

There is a growing assumption that what has for centuries seemed an essential division between our private selves and the world at large is now vanishing – and that this is somehow a natural and irreversible process.

The assumption is false. We do not have to go down this dangerous road. But the fact that so many changes have taken place without any great debate or protest is symptomatic of its insidiousness. We are sleepwalking into a version of Orwell's *Nineteen Eighty-Four*. If we do not wake up and open our eyes, we will be living in the land of Big Brother before we know it. It is significant already that, to a whole generation, the phrase 'Big Brother' conjures not a nightmarish vision of totalitarianism, but a voyeuristic and relatively harmless reality-TV show.

(a) **How effective do you find the imagery of 'sleepwalking' to convey what the writer is saying in these lines?** 2 A/E

	If you're sleepwalking you're doing things while you're asleep so you're not really aware of what's going on around you and it could be dangerous. This is a good way of describing the way we are letting our privacy be taken away from us without us realising it.
	Someone who is sleepwalking is literally moving around and perhaps appearing normal while actually only semiconscious. The writer believes that society is behaving similarly in relation to the erosion of our privacy: we are going about our 'normal' lives while totally unaware of what is happening to our privacy. He effectively extends the metaphor by saying what it could be like when we 'wake up and open our eyes'.
	Very effective because when you're sleepwalking you don't know what's going on as you're still asleep. (This is a weak answer because although there is a good start to the answer, with a definition of the literal idea of sleepwalking, the student does not go on to look at the metaphor or to relate this to what the writer is saying.)
	The 'good' answer adds in a reference to 'wake up and open our eyes' which is not essential to score full marks, but is very impressive as it shows someone who is reading thoughtfully and has noticed that the writer is developing the image.

(b) **In what way, according to the writer, does the younger generation misunderstand the phrase 'Big Brother'?** 2 U

	They think it refers to a simple TV show when it really refers to the horrible world of Orwell's book.
	The phrase originates in Orwell's *Nineteen Eighty-Four*, which creates a horrifying picture of brutal power. Most young people think of it in terms of the reality programme on TV which is mildly intrusive but not very threatening.
	It obviously helps here if you are familiar with Orwell's book and the 'real' Big Brother, but it is not difficult to work out from the text what it is about.

3 **What, according to the writer in lines 41–48, 'needs to be questioned'?** 1 U

	The very ubiquity and triviality of Big Brother, Facebook and Twitter is what blinds us to the dangers they pose. Not that I am suggesting there is anything specifically sinister about reality TV or social networking websites; rather, it is the underlying values of a society in which they are so popular that needs to be questioned.
	He thinks society's basic morals need to be questioned.
	He believes that our fundamental standards as a society need to be questioned, because inconsequential things such as *Big Brother* and Twitter are so pervasive and have taken on such importance.
	A very straightforward question which asks simply for a 'gloss' of 'the underlying values of a society in which they are so popular'. The OK answer does enough for the 1 mark by getting the important part, but the 'good' answer takes no chances, even for 1 mark.

4 Read lines 49–87.

> The case of Facebook is worth examining in more detail. It has become a vast money-making machine with 400 million users worldwide, and recently overtook Google as the most-used website in the world. Last December, Facebook's founder Mark Zuckerberg announced new privacy settings for all its users: certain information such as profile photographs and lists of friends would now be visible to everyone, while text, photo and video updates – which had all previously been private by default (seen only by your list of friends) – now became public by default. And this is the crucial point. Everyone had the choice of changing their privacy settings, but as is usually the case, the majority of us didn't bother. By doing nothing, hundreds of millions of people suddenly went from sharing the intimate details of their lives with a circle of friends and acquaintances to sharing those details with anyone who wishes to see them.
>
> Zuckerberg's justification for changing Facebook's privacy settings was that it was simply reflecting broader changes in society. 'People have really gotten comfortable not only sharing more information and different kinds, but more openly and with more people,' he said. Again, the phrasing is bland, but in a way what Zuckerberg is suggesting is every bit as sinister as Eric Schmidt's quote at the beginning of this piece. He is claiming that the popularity of blogs, Twitter, YouTube and reality TV shows indicates a new willingness among ordinary people to make their private lives public. There is perhaps some truth to this, but it is a moot point. Whether Facebook is a symptom or a cause, the fact remains that our 'default settings' for privacy in society have been changed. And most of us aren't even aware of it.

(a) Summarise the main points the writer is making about privacy by using the example of Facebook.   **3 U**

> The writer tells how Facebook changed its default settings for privacy. Before this your personal information could only be seen by your friends. Now it can be seen by everyone with a Facebook account. This a big change to privacy. The writer thinks everyone should have more say in what is private and not have it dictated by companies like Facebook. He thinks the man in charge of Facebook is as bad as the man in charge of Google – they both think this is perfectly OK and that people don't care much about privacy. He also thinks we are to blame for letting this happen without bothering to do anything about it.

> Facebook recently changed its privacy settings so that all personal information is open to all users.
>
> The writer sees the assumption behind this as symptomatic of the general change in attitudes to privacy.
>
> He is concerned that most people don't seem to care much about this.

> Reference could also be made to the point about the alleged 'new willingness among ordinary people to make their private lives public'.

> Note how succinct the 'good' answer is: 3 marks – 3 clear points. The 'OK' answer gets there (just), but think how much time has been wasted!

(b) Show how the writer's use of language in lines 70–87 makes clear his disapproval of Mark Zuckerberg.

2 A

	He calls him 'sinister' which suggests he is a little bit evil. The word 'claiming' suggests Zuckerberg is trying to make a false case for something.
	When he says that Zuckerberg's justification 'was that it was simply reflecting', the use of 'simply' presents him as rather disingenuous, as if this was nothing to worry about. Describing his phrasing as 'bland' suggests he is deliberately disguising something quite sinister in a harmless, unobjectionable way.
	He says it is a 'moot point', which means he is saying it very quietly. (This is a weak answer because the phrase 'moot point' does not refer to Zuckerberg, and because the student has mixed up 'moot', which means something people might argue about, with 'mute', which means silent.)

5 Show how the writer's use of language in lines 88–101 increases the impact of what he is saying.

2 A

	Did you know that the United Kingdom is surveyed, 24 hours a day, by more than five million CCTV cameras – the highest proportion of cameras per citizen in the world? That most British secondary schools have at least 20 such cameras? That Google Street View now provides panoramic images of 95% of the streets in the UK? That the proposed new Communications Data Bill will require internet service providers to hand their records, currently retained for commercial purposes, to the Home Office for 'the prevention and detection of crime and protection of national security'?
	The whole paragraph is one long list of facts showing just how many ways our privacy is being invaded. Every item is structured in the same way, a question 'Did you know that …', which makes it sound as if all these things are the same type of attack on our privacy.
	The writer structures the paragraph to sound like an impassioned orator firing out points in an attempt to convince an audience of the dire threat to our privacy. The similarity of structure – a series of direct questions all stemming from 'Did you know …?' – makes it sound as if the assault on our privacy is every bit as relentless.
	He asks a lot of questions inviting the reader to answer 'no'. He says that we have more CCTV cameras than anywhere else. He also says there are 20 CCTV cameras in most schools which is really shocking. (This is a weak answer because it is mostly simply a re-statement of details from the paragraph without attempting to show how features of language add impact; the point about 'questions' is a possible *start* to quite a good answer, but it is too vague – it doesn't refer to privacy at all.)
	Reference could also be made to the following (although the structural points made in the two answers above are the really relevant ones): • the use of statistics to drive home the points about the extent of the intrusion • the idea of compulsion in the word 'require' • the general tone of indignation, anger, …

> This is a good example of a question where the features of the paragraph (the questions, the repetitive structure, the tone, etc.) are obvious to see, but where it is not all that easy to put into words *how* these add impact. This is true of all answers on structure.

6 Read lines 102–120.

> What's most worrying is that our children won't be as shocked and angry about all this as I am. They are growing up in a world where remote-controlled cameras are everywhere, where their friends post pictures of them drunk or naked on the internet, where nightly entertainment often consists of watching real people break down in tears or humiliate themselves on live television. It hardly requires much of a science-fictional leap to imagine their children's DNA, fingerprints, iris scans, hourly movements, home environments, bank details, their most intimate conversations, being monitored and recorded from cradle to grave. Our children are being desensitised to the idea of their private lives being public property. What will they answer when their son or daughter asks: 'Daddy, what does "privacy" mean?'

(a) Why, according to the writer, are young people not as 'shocked and angry' as he is about the invasion of privacy? 1 U

	It is happening all around them and they have become used to it.
	Young people have grown up in a society where features which to the writer seem intrusive are so common as to be widely accepted as the norm.
	Because there are cameras all over the place, their mates upload images of them in embarrassing situations to the internet, they spend lots of time watching TV programmes with real people making fools of themselves for the entertainment of others. (This is a weak answer because, although it is in the student's own words, it merely re-states the examples without explaining why this leads young people to be less shocked.)
	An 'Understanding' question for 1 mark can always be answered very briefly.

(b) What vision does he have of life for his grandchildren? 1 U

	He imagines them living in a world where not a single detail of their lives is private.
	He envisages a society in which every single detail of their lives is observed and kept on record. They will probably not even know what the concept of 'privacy' actually is.
	The idea of being 'desensitised' could probably be used to answer the question successfully.
	Again, a 1-mark 'U' question, so a brief answer will do. If it were for 2 marks, then both points in the 'good' answer would be needed.

7 Read lines 121–136.

Think again about Eric Schmidt's words: 'If you have something that you don't want anyone to know, maybe you shouldn't be doing it in the first place.' Well, maybe you shouldn't be making that assumption, Eric. His statement is, when you think about it, a breathtaking inversion of long-held human values: the idea that the desire for privacy is somehow sinister and suspicious. Is it really inconceivable that people might not want anyone (or, rather, everyone) to know about some aspect of their lives without that aspect being criminal or shameful?

We are halfway down a road that will take us to a place most of us don't want to go: we should turn back before it is too late.

(a) Explain why the writer thinks Schmidt's statement is 'a breathtaking inversion of long-held human values' (lines 126–128). **2 U**

Schmidt's statement makes it sound as if you're up to no good if you want privacy. It used to be that wanting privacy was what most people did.

According to the writer, a desire for privacy has, until now, been considered as normal and natural. Schmidt's statement turns that idea on its head, so that nowadays anyone wanting privacy is treated as being deviant and not to be trusted.

Schmidt means that if you want to keep something secret then people will assume that you're doing something wrong.

(This is a weak answer. It might get 1 mark and is not completely wrong as it shows a good understanding of what Schmidt is implying. However, it cannot get 2 marks as it doesn't get the idea that this is an 'inversion' of previous values.)

A successful answer should make it clear that the idea of 'inversion' has been understood.

(b) Referring to one language feature in these lines, discuss to what extent it provides an appropriate way to conclude the passage. **2 A/E**

The structure makes it an appropriate conclusion. The command to 'Think again' involves the reader (and takes the reader back to the opening of the passage) and sort of shocks us into action. Also the rhetorical question 'Is it really inconceivable …?' again involves the reader by demanding the obvious answer of No.

The 'road' imagery in the last paragraph is a good way to conclude the argument. The writer depicts society as on a journey whose destination is 'a place most of us don't want to go', i.e. the nightmare vision of Orwell's *Nineteen Eighty-Four*, with no privacy for the individual. There is, however, some hope in that we are only 'halfway' down the road and have not left our starting point (i.e. the 'old' world that the writer prefers) too far behind. Predictably, the writer urges us to 'turn back'.

Comment could also be made on:

- the 'conversational' tone of 'Well, maybe …, Eric'
- the direct address to 'Eric' – as if someone needs to stand up to him
- the word choice of 'breathtaking'.

Question 8 – 'Evaluation'

NB: The 'Evaluation' question will be dealt with slightly differently from other questions. There are examples of a weak answer, a reasonable answer and a really good answer which would get full marks. There is a brief commentary about each answer.

8 To what extent do you agree with the writer's concerns in the passage as a whole?   4 E

[1/4]

I agree with the writer that there are too many CCTV cameras and that we are being watched far too much. There is no need for all this, even though it helps to catch some criminals and stops people dropping litter.

(**A very slight answer, worth, at most, 1 mark. It deals with merely an example mentioned in the passage and doesn't touch on any of the key ideas. On the positive side, it does argue that CCTV cameras have some advantages.**)

[2/4]

I think the writer is right that we are losing our privacy, especially the way that internet sites are able to keep all our details and let other people see them without asking us. Also, the number of CCTV cameras is quite frightening. I think, however, that his vision of life for future generations is a bit extreme.

(**Sensible enough comments, which shows some understanding of key ideas (general erosion of privacy, the writer's vision of the future). A general lack of development, especially of the last point.**)

[4/4]

I agree totally with the writer's assertion that recent developments, such as Facebook's unilateral decision to change its privacy settings, are symptomatic of a change in attitude to the concept of privacy. The idea that wanting privacy is no longer the norm, but is coming to be seen almost as an admission of guilt, is a truly disturbing one. The glib statements from two giants of the internet make it seem all the more frightening.

I would, however, take issue with the writer's attitude to the younger generation. He asserts that we are all hopelessly unaware of the dangers and are in fact complicit with the developments. He bases this on the expansion of Facebook and Twitter and the current popularity of reality TV. However, I am inclined to see these as passing fads rather than steps in an unstoppable removal of our right to privacy; his Orwellian vision of the future brought on by the shortcomings of the younger generation is a little over the top. And I think young people are a little smarter than he thinks.

(**A well-written and well-developed response which shows a deep understanding of the writer's key points – and it is not afraid to challenge them.**)

Answers for the 50-mark, double-passage task on Stonehenge

These are the answers for the 50-mark, double-passage task on Stonehenge from the end of the Close Reading chapter (Chapter 2). Because this was a major task, the answers will be dealt with in detail.

📖	passage extract
✓	straightforward acceptable answer
★	really good answer
✗	weak/misguided answer
✚	other possible points
❗	important advice

Questions on Passage 1

1 Read lines 1–32.

It is generally accepted that Stonehenge, Britain's most famous Stone Age site, was built in three stages by three different groups of people over a period of about 800 years. The first stage was a circle of timbers surrounded by a ditch and bank and was constructed by what archaeologists have called the Windmill Hill people, named after their earthworks at the site of the same name. They used animal bones and antlers to dig the trench and the circle of 56 holes to hold the wooden posts of the first structure. Radiocarbon dating of these utensils has recorded a date of 3100BC.

The next stage was built by the Beaker Folk, who came from Europe at the end of the Neolithic Period, and began about 2500BC. They brought the bluestones from Prescelli Mountains in Pembroke, some 245 miles away. It was an impressive operation given that some of these stones weighed five tons and had to be hauled over land and floated up rivers.

The final, third phase of the construction occurred about 2300BC by the Wessex People, who were Bronze Age pioneers. They dug up and re-arranged the bluestones and brought in even bigger stones from Marlborough Downs some 20 miles away. These giant sandstones, called Sarsen stones, were hammered to size and shaped with carpenter's joints so that they could sit on top of each other to form the classic lintels that have made Stonehenge so unique. The hauling and erection of the Sarsen stones is an engineering miracle – some of them weigh 45 tons.

(a) Outline very briefly the three stages in the construction of Stonehenge. 3 U

The first stage was a circle of wooden posts surrounded by a trench and a mound of earth which was dug using animal remains. The second stage began about 2500BC and involved 'bluestones' from Prescelli which had to be brought over a long distance. The third stage was when huge sandstone blocks were arranged in a circle with other blocks laid on the tops of these stones.

- a ring of 56 wooden stakes inside a channel dug in the earth
- the heavy bluestones which were brought from Wales
- the circle of Sarsen stones, with stones across the top.

First the Windmill People built something, then the Beaker Folk, then the Wessex People.

(This is a weak answer because it identifies the people involved but not, as the question asked, the 'stages of the construction'.)

Not always easy to use own words, but you must make an effort.

Notice how brief and precise the good answer is; using bullet points (especially in a '**U**' question) is perfectly acceptable.

(b) Show how the writer's word choice in lines 13–32 conveys his admiration for the work on Stonehenge. 2 A

He says it was 'an engineering miracle', which suggests it was something wonderful and hard to believe. Also he says it was an 'impressive operation', which shows he thinks it was remarkable.

- 'impressive' – connotations of being extraordinary, exciting, almost inspiring
- 'miracle' – connotations of something amazing, superhuman.

His word choice is really good because he uses effective words like 'weighed five tons' which shows how heavy they were and 'unique' which shows how special Stonehenge is.

(This is a weak answer because the words chosen are not appropriate and there is no attempt to explore their connotations.)

Comment could also be made on:
- 'hauled' – suggests the writer appreciates the effort involved.

It's for 2 marks, so always go for two words. A really good comment on one word *might* score 2, but it would be wrong to assume your answer was good enough for that!

2 To what extent would you have confidence in the theory of Dr Jane Evans? Justify your answer by close reference to lines 33–48. 3 E

Little can be said with certainty about the purpose of Stonehenge, but the site was almost certainly a gathering place for many years for people from all over southern Britain and possibly Europe. Jane Evans of the British Geological Survey has found evidence for instance that people brought their own cattle to Stonehenge from as far away as Wales, or even further afield. Isotope analysis on the cattle teeth found at Durrington Wells shows that the animals were reared in a different geological place to where they were slaughtered. Dr Evans suggests it shows that there was a 'bring-your-own beef barbeque' at Stonehenge which was probably a centre for grand feasts long before the construction of the ancient stone circle.

I would have a lot of confidence in her. She works for the British Geological Survey which sounds like an important official organisation and she is a Doctor. Her methods sound scientific as she uses isotope analysis and bases her conclusions on 'evidence'.

Dr Evans appears to be well qualified (the 'Dr' is presumably a PhD in some branch of science) and she works for the prestigious British Geological Survey. She employs advanced scientific techniques such as 'isotope analysis'. As such, I would have every confidence in her. However, her rather flippant reference to a 'bring-your-own beef barbeque' might suggest she is not serious enough to command anyone's confidence.

 I would not have confidence in her because she thinks they had a big feast at Stonehenge but there is no evidence for this and I don't think it sounds likely.

(This is a weak answer because it is a very vague comment and there is no attempt to justify it – indeed there is actually some evidence to support the big feast idea.)

 It could equally be argued that her reference to the 'bring-your-own beef barbeque' shows she is down to earth and has a sense of humour, is not an aloof, distant egghead – thus gaining our confidence.

 The use of 'to what extent' in the question is usually an invitation to look at both sides. You don't *have* to, but it will give you a better chance of coming up with ideas.

3 Read lines 49–71.

(a) Outline briefly the theories described in these lines.   2 U

 There are many other speculations about Stonehenge, some of them decidedly outlandish. It is widely claimed that Stonehenge was built to celebrate or mark the summer and winter solstices, when the Sun reaches its furthest point north and south of the equator, respectively, which is denoted by the point at which the Sun rises or sets on the horizon. The alignment of the stones would appear to have been designed to mark the two solstices, and hence the points at which summer and winter reach their mid-points.

Some scholars have gone further to suggest that Stonehenge was a far more sophisticated astronomical instrument that could, for instance, be used to predict lunar eclipse, when the Earth passes in between the Sun and the Moon. They believe that the inner 'horseshoe' of 19 bluestones at the centre of the circle acted as a long-term calendar to calculate when the next lunar eclipse would occur – when, in other words, the shadow of the Earth would fall upon the Moon.

 One theory is that Stonehenge was built so that people would know by looking at the stones when it was midsummer or midwinter. Another theory is that the arrangement of the stones meant you could tell when an eclipse was about to happen.

 That Stonehenge was organised such that:
- the mid-points of winter and summer could be observed
- eclipses of the Moon could be forecast.

 According to one theory Stonehenge was built to celebrate or mark the summer and winter solstices. According to another it acted as a long-term calendar to calculate when the next lunar eclipse would occur.

(This is a weak answer because it lifts from the passage with no attempt to use own words.)

(b) Show how the writer's use of language in these lines makes clear that they are 'speculations' (line 49). 2 A

	He uses words like 'claimed' and 'believe', all of which mean there is no certainty. Also 'would appear to have been designed' is used instead of the more certain 'was designed'.
	The idea that these theories are speculative is supported by the writer's careful use of conditional verb forms such as 'would appear to have been' and 'could … be used'. The use of 'claimed', 'suggest' and 'believe' underlines the writer's point that these ideas have been proposed but never actually proved.
	He calls them 'theories' – 'theories' are things which have not been proved and are based only on what people think. **(This is a weak answer because, though it sounds good, the word 'theories' does not appear in these lines, nor does 'theory'.)**
	It would not be wrong to comment on the connotations of the word 'speculations' (e.g. they are hypothetical, just guesswork etc.), but as a general rule it is not wise to comment on words which are actually used in the question.

4 Read lines 72–94.

	Another theory is that Stonehenge was an elaborate burial site for important people. A Professor of archaeology at Sheffield University believes that the stone structure was the 'domain of the dead', whereas the nearby 'wooden henge' structure at Durrington Wells a couple of miles away was the 'domain of the living'. Durrington Wells would have been one of the biggest, if not the biggest, settlement in north-west Europe at that time. It would probably have been used as temporary accommodation for people attending Stonehenge in mid-winter and mid-summer, he said. No human burials have been found at Durrington Wells, although 29 cremation burials have been found at Stonehenge during excavations that took place in the 1920s. The Professor believes there may have been up to 240 people buried at Stonehenge during prehistoric times and that they may be the descendants of a single family – prehistoric chiefs, perhaps even ancient royalty – who over several generations were awarded the privilege of having their remains interred at the sacred site.

(a) What, according to the Professor, was the function of Durrington Wells? 2 U

	Durrington Wells was where people stayed if they were visiting Stonehenge for the special events at midsummer.
	Durrington Wells provided short-term living quarters for those attending the observance of the solstices at Stonehenge. It contrasted, according to the Professor, with Stonehenge in that it was associated with the living, while Stonehenge was a place of death.
	Durrington Wells was one of the biggest settlements in Europe. It was quite close to Stonehenge and had a wooden henge. No bodies have been found buried there. **(This is a weak answer because, though true, it does not relate to the function of Durrington Wells.)**

(b) Show how the writer's word choice in these lines adds to the idea that Stonehenge is a very special place.

2 A

	He uses 'elaborate' and 'sacred' to describe Stonehenge. 'elaborate' suggests it was detailed and complex making it sound special. 'sacred' suggests religious which makes it special to some people.
	• 'elaborate' has connotations of being sophisticated and therefore designed not for everyday use (or people) • 'sacred' has connotations of being holy or sacrosanct and therefore very special as if part of a religion.
	Comment could also be made on: • 'privilege' – as if being buried there was something allowed to only a select few • 'interred' – more upmarket than 'buried'.

(c) How convincing do you find the Professor's theory about Stonehenge? Justify your answer by close reference to the text.

2 E

	I think the Professor's theory is good. He shows that there were no burials at Durrington Wells but a lot at Stonehenge, which was a special place and so the people buried there might well be kings etc.
	His theory seems to be based on the fact that all the burials were at Stonehenge even though Durrington Wells was the populous area. This is convincing enough to show that Stonehenge was indeed a dedicated burial site. However, I can see no reason to suggest that those buried there were the chiefs or royalty, let alone members of a single family. Perhaps the relatively low number implies that it was only for the select few, but it is not very clear.
	A very difficult question. The 'good' answer is almost certainly correct to point out that the theory seems very questionable (or at least is not supported with adequate evidence), but it takes a lot of confidence to criticise a Professor! However, you would never be faced with a situation where you *had* to, so the 'OK' answer here would get the 2 marks.

5 Read lines 95–121.

	Most recently, archaeologists have excavated a small area within the site and found evidence to suggest that Stonehenge was once a centre of healing, where people would come from far and wide in the hope of being cured of their ills. The evidence for this claim is not very straightforward, but then again nothing ever is with this mysterious ancient monument. The two archaeologists, Professor Tim Darvill and Geoff Wainwright, first of all noted the abnormal number of corpses found in tombs near Stonehenge that display signs of serious physical injury or disease. One of the most famous of these is the 'Amesbury Archer' buried about two miles from Stonehenge. He is known to have originated from the Alps and had suffered a serious knee injury and a potentially fatal dental problem before he died. His history seemed to match many of the other bodies found near the site. Analysis of the mineral isotopes found in human teeth show that about half of these people were not native to the Stonehenge area. Taken together, this could suggest that some people came to the site in order to benefit from some kind of healing powers that the bluestones were perhaps supposed to have.

(a) Explain how the 'Amesbury Archer' supports the theory described in these lines.   4 U

	The Amesbury Archer supports the theory because he had come from the Alps and had an injured knee and life-threatening problems with his teeth. It might be that he had come to Stonehenge hoping to be healed because people thought the stones at Stonehenge had special powers to cure sick people.
	The theory is that Stonehenge was visited by sick and injured people seeking some kind of remedy from mystical powers in the stones. The Amesbury Archer supports this theory because his body, found near Stonehenge, showed signs of physical damage before his death. He came from hundreds of miles away, as did many others who were not born in the surrounding area and whose remains also have evidence that they were suffering from illnesses and damaged bones.
	Careful explanation is needed here. It is important to state clearly what the 'theory' is and then, by giving relevant details about the Amesbury Archer, show how these details back up the two key aspects of the theory: that people travelled to Stonehenge from a great distance and that many of them suffered from physical injuries.

(b) Show how the writer's use of language in these lines makes clear that this is a mixture of fact and speculation.   2 A

	The writer says the Archer is 'known' to have originated, which shows there is definite proof of this. However, at other times he uses words such as 'seemed' and 'supposed', which show he is saying a lot of the theory involves guesswork.
	The factual element is clear in the writer's reference to 'analysis of the mineral isotopes' which is couched in very scientific language. The idea of speculation is seen in the vagueness and uncertainty of terms such as 'seemed', 'could suggest', 'perhaps supposed'.
	Some of the theory has been proved but other bits of it are just conjecture, so it is a mixture of fact and speculation. **(This is a weak answer because it does not deal with the writer's use of language.)**
	Reference could also be made to: • factual: the quasi-statistical nature of 'abnormal number' and 'about half' • speculative: the vagueness of 'some kind of'.

6 Show how the writer makes effective use of sentence structure in lines 122–137 to highlight the points he is making.   3 A

	Intriguingly, the two archaeologists also found that about three times as many stone chippings were taken from the bluestones compared to the Sarsen stones. Did people flake off pieces of the bluestones, in order to have a little bit to take away … as souvenirs … as lucky charms? It is unlikely we will ever know the real truth behind Stonehenge – even why this particular part of southern England was deemed so important remains one of its most enduring mysteries. Although dating technology gets better all the time, and much of the site has still to be properly excavated, Stonehenge, because it represents what was in the minds of people long dead, will always be a mystery.

The use of a question ('Did people …?') emphasises the idea that there is a lot of doubt about this idea and the writer is asking a question instead of making a statement.

The dots sound as if he is pausing and making up ideas as he goes, as if anything is possible.

The dash before 'even' prepares the reader for a really important aspect of the 'real truth', that no one even knows why Stonehenge was built where it is, let alone why.

At the end of the first paragraph the writer uses ellipses to create a sense of increasing mystery, almost playfully coming up with unlikely explanations for the removal of pieces of the stones.

The last sentence is structured very effectively to emphasise the mysteriousness of Stonehenge. Two subordinate clauses come first, creating a periodic sentence, and the impact of the main clause is delayed by inserting yet another subordinate clause ('because it represents …'). The effect is to put all the emphasis on the key word 'mystery'.

The writer asks a question and uses dots to break up his ideas. The last sentence has a lot of commas to create a list of what makes Stonehenge so exciting.

(This is a classic example of a weak answer to a sentence structure question. There is lots of identification of features such as a question, dots, commas and a list. However, there is no attempt to explain the effect these techniques have at this point in the passage.)

Comment could also be made on:
- the placing of 'Intriguingly' at the start of the sentence – stresses the idea that Stonehenge is a really fascinating place
- the fact that the last word in the entire passage is 'mystery' – leaves the reader with the key point about Stonehenge: its strange and puzzling nature.

Questions on sentence structure are never easy. There's no problem in spotting obvious features (a list, important punctuation, unusual word order, etc.); what's difficult is showing what effect the feature has on the meaning or impact of what is being said – and you must always make it clear you know exactly what is being said at that point of the passage.

Questions on Passage 2

7 **Show how the writer's use of language in lines 1–14 creates a tone which is less than serious.**

4 A

There was a familiar ring to last week's media fanfare surrounding the announcement that scientists had uncovered the true purpose of Stonehenge. According to the new theory's backer, archaeologist Geoffrey Wainwright, it was really the Lourdes of the Bronze Age, a place where the sick and wounded sought cures from the monument's great bluestones which had been dragged to Wiltshire from Wales specifically because of their magical healing properties. The evidence is, apparently, in all the ancient graves in the area filled with sick and deformed people. Thus Stonehenge was really an accident and emergency ward for the south west of England.

The words 'an accident and emergency ward' make you think of doctors and ambulances and hi-tech equipment. It is a deliberately silly comparison since Stonehenge is just a circle of big stones.

The writer is mocking the theory as if the archaeologist is stupid enough to think of an ancient monument in modern terms.

Also the writer refers to Stonehenge as the 'Lourdes of the Bronze Age'. He is not being very serious here because Lourdes is a recognised and organised place where religious pilgrims go for healing.

He puts 'apparently' in parenthesis immediately after the word 'evidence' which is a bit sarcastic and casts doubt on how valid the evidence is.

The comparisons to 'Lourdes' and 'an accident and emergency ward' clearly demonstrate the writer's tongue-in-cheek tone. Both are 'modern' and it seems absurd to have a Stone Age monument compared with them.

The expression 'media fanfare' is an early indication of the lightly mocking tone as it suggests a disapproval of the media loudly proclaiming something which doesn't really deserve it.

The use of 'specifically' creates the unlikely idea that the healing properties of the stones had been carefully worked out in advance.

The insertion of 'apparently' sarcastically undercuts the impact of the word 'evidence'.

Reference could also be made to:
- the use of 'Thus' – mockingly resembles the outcome of a carefully proven proposition
- the repetition of 'was really' – sounds less plausible each time.

8 Show how the writer's use of language in lines 15–28 conveys his attitude to the media coverage of the announcement.   **2 A**

As a result, we were greeted with a cluster of headlines of the 'Revealed: the secret of Stonehenge' variety which, some readers might have noticed, had a close similarity to those that greeted the news earlier in the year that a different group of scientists had found the true purpose of the great Wiltshire stone circle: it was really a royal burial ground for an ancient dynasty of old Brits, said a group of researchers from Sheffield University. Radiocarbon dating of human remains found nearby suggested the place was used as a cemetery right from the start of construction work in 3000BC, it was argued. Not for the common folk, it must be stressed – strictly for prehistoric toffs.

The word 'cluster' suggests all the headlines were similar – he thinks the press just follow each other. The repetition of 'greeted' suggests how the press use the same kind of headlines all the time.

The writer has a very low opinion of the press coverage. He creates a typically clichéd headline – 'Revealed: the secret of Stonehenge' – to show how unoriginal their thinking is and even refers to it as a 'type'.

The predictability of their response is further hinted at in the repetition of 'greeted'.

He describes the reporting as a 'media fanfare'. A fanfare is a blast of trumpets usually announcing the arrival of an important person. In this case the important thing is another theory about Stonehenge, but the theory is not important enough to deserve a fanfare and the writer thinks the papers are too keen to make a fuss over anything.

(This is a weak answer because, although it is an almost perfect exploration of the image of a fanfare, this image does not appear in the lines students were told to look at to answer this question.)

Reference could also be made to:
- 'some readers might have noticed' – a rather tongue-in-cheek remark which probably really means it was perfectly obvious
- 'Brits' – slang term mimics media fondness for short, pithy abbreviations.

It is tempting to comment on 'strictly for prehistoric toffs', but it is not 100 per cent certain that this expression is quoted from the press coverage – indeed it seems more likely to be the writer's way of poking fun at the theory. However, in an exam, you would almost certainly get credit for an appropriate comment on this: e.g. on the inelegant juxtaposition of the formal 'prehistoric' with the slang 'toffs' etc.

9 Read lines 29–40.

And as we move back in time, the theories about Stonehenge slowly pile up: we come across news that researchers had shown the stone circles had been used as a giant computer; that others had found it was really an observatory for studying stars and predicting the seasons; that a couple of individuals had demonstrated beyond doubt that its rings had acted as a docking pad for alien spaceships; while one Canadian researcher produced the jaw-dropping idea that the great henge had been built as a giant fertility symbol, constructed in the shape of the female sexual organ.

(a) Show how the structure of this paragraph helps the writer express his ideas clearly.

2 A

The writer uses a colon to introduce a list of some of the 'theories' and the individual theories are clearly separated by a semicolon. The use of 'that' at the start of most of the theories helps the reader remember that they all follow from the words 'we come across news …'

It is all one long sentence because the writer has a lot to say. There are colons and semicolons and commas to help the writer get across his ideas about Stonehenge.

(This is a weak answer because, as with question 6, the student identifies features of sentence structure but does not explain the effects of these.)

Reference might be made to the idea that the most absurd theory is kept to the end.

(b) How does the writer convey his scepticism about any two of the theories in this paragraph? 2 A

	His use of 'observatory' shows his scepticism because an observatory suggests a modern, scientific building not a pile of stones. The last idea he thinks is so stupid that it would almost literally make your jaw drop in amazement.
	• 'stone circles had been used as a giant computer' indicates his sceptical view by contrasting the very basic 'stone' with the ultra-modern term 'computer'; the word 'giant' serves to exaggerate just how ridiculous the idea is • 'demonstrated beyond doubt' sounds very ironic beside the outrageous claim about a 'docking pad' and 'spaceships' – of which there couldn't possibly be any proof.
	Reference could also be made to: • the use of 'was really' – used three times already in the passage, and hence less convincing each time • 'a couple of individuals' – a very dismissive way of referring to people who were, presumably, scientists or academics of some kind • the self-consciously rather crude reference at the end.

10 Show how the style of lines 41–48 differs from that of lines 49–56.

	But that, of course, is the wonderful thing about Stonehenge: there are more theories about its meaning and purpose than there are stones inside it. This is a trend that goes right back to the idea, popular in the Middle Ages, that its monoliths had been assembled on Salisbury Plain by King Arthur's resident wizard, Merlin – though nobody seems to have bothered to figure out why he did so. In fact, Stonehenge took at least 1,000 years to build, starting from rings of wooden poles to its current complex status and its use clearly changed over the millenniums. Recent studies suggest it may have been 'Christianised' in the first millennium AD and at one point was used as a place of execution by the Anglo-Saxons to judge from the 7th-century gallows found there.
	Lines 41–48 are very informal with words like 'figure out' and 'goes right back'. Lines 49–56 are much more formal: 'status', 'millenniums'.
	The first of the paragraphs is written in a fairly relaxed and conversational tone: 'of course', 'thing', 'goes right back', 'bothered to figure out'. There is even a humorous reference to Merlin as a 'resident wizard'. The second paragraph is in a much more detached, almost academic style: 'current complex status', 'recent studies suggest', 'place of execution'. This is underlined by the use of specific facts and dates: '1,000 years', 'first millennium AD', '7th-century'.
	The first paragraph is about how there are lots of theories about Stonehenge, but the second one is true facts about it. **(This is a weak answer because it says nothing specific about style.)**

	Mention could be made of the use of 'In fact' to start the second paragraph, since it acts as a kind of indicator that this paragraph will 'correct' some of the outlandish notions in the previous paragraph.
	A much more straightforward question than it perhaps appears. Note that (mercifully) you are not asked to explain or suggest *why* the writer changes style so abruptly.

11 What does the writer mean by 'every age gets the Stonehenge it deserves'? (lines 61–62)

	This multiplicity of use increases opportunities for archaeologists to pin their pet theories to the great stone monument. The crucial point is, as archaeologist Jacquetta Hawkes once remarked, that every age gets the Stonehenge it deserves. Hence in medieval times, it was built by giants, while in the 1960s, at the dawn of the computing era, researchers said you could have used it as a giant calculating machine, while in more mystical New Age times, it was clearly a spaceport for aliens. In fact, you can come up with just about any idea to explain a structure like Stonehenge if you stare at it for long enough.
	Every age comes up with a different theory about Stonehenge and the theory fits in with the kind of things people believe at that time.
	He means that Stonehenge is open to so many interpretations that in the end each interpretation reflects the interest and preoccupations of the time in which it is made. Each theory says more about those who propose it and the times they live in than it does about Stonehenge itself.

12 Read lines 71–82.

	Just what that the latest flurry of Stonehenge theories says about the 21st century is less clear. I would argue that it is probably best viewed today as a monument to government prevarication and deceit. Having promised a decade ago that it would bury and realign the roads that surround and disfigure Britain's most important ancient monument, ministers now seem to have abandoned any attempt to protect the monument and restore the site to its ancient glory, for the simple reason they are too mean-spirited and short-sighted to see its value.

(a) What criticisms does the writer make of the Government?   **2 U**

	He criticises them for saying they would do something about the roads around Stonehenge, but now changing their minds. He also thinks they don't look far enough into the future.
	He is critical of their dithering and their duplicity.
	Other points could be made: • they have no respect for the importance of Stonehenge • they don't understand the importance of (monuments such as) Stonehenge • they are penny-pinching • they lack vision • they are Philistine.

(b) Show how his use of language in these lines makes clear the strength of his feelings on the subject. 2 A

	He says the roads 'disfigure' Stonehenge, which creates an impression of how much he thinks they distort and damage its appearance. He refers to its 'ancient glory', which suggests something uplifting and beautiful, which is how he sees Stonehenge.
	His strong feelings about the Government are clear in his choice of words such as 'deceit', which suggests sly, underhand, double-dealing, and 'abandoned' which emphasises the complete lack of concern in the way they have betrayed their promise. His strong feelings about Stonehenge can be seen in the unequivocal description of it as 'Britain's most important ancient monument' and his desire to have it restored to its 'ancient glory', which has connotations of magnificence and splendour.
	Comment could also be made on: • the structure 'having promised a decade ago … now seem to have abandoned' flags up the idea of saying one thing then doing another • 'any attempt' – idea that absolutely nothing will now be done • 'simple reason' – their faults are open and undisguised.
	The question doesn't make clear if it's the writer's feelings about Stonehenge or his feelings about the Government that you're being asked about. Because it's not specified, you wouldn't be penalised for doing just one (as in the 'OK' answer), but notice how the 'good' answer doesn't take any chances!

Question on both passages

NB The 'Comparison' question will be dealt with slightly differently from other questions. There is an example of a reasonably good answer, worth 3 out of 5, and of a really good answer which would get full marks. There is a brief commentary about both answers.

Some general points about tackling the Comparison question

• You should think of your answer as being a 'mini-essay': write in formal continuous prose (no notes or bullet points) and have a clear 'line of thought' as you would in a Critical Essay.

• Stick closely to the instruction in the question about whether to write about ideas or style or both; even if it's on style only (the least likely option) you have to show understanding of the main ideas in both passages – you can't simply write about random examples of tone, imagery, etc.

• Stick closely to the 'focus' in the question; it is there to help you – you are never asked just to compare the passages.

• There is no 'right' answer – you can prefer either passage and still score well – it all depends on the quality of your argument.

• These answers are not marked according to length or according to the number of 'points' made: they are judged on their overall quality.

• Don't be afraid to have a strong personal input, but make sure you base everything on the ideas or language features of the passages.

• For more detailed advice, refer to Section Two of *Higher English Close Reading* by Ann Bridges and Colin Eckford (which includes practice material dedicated to answering the comparison question) and pages 93–96 of *How to Pass Higher English* by Ann Bridges.

13 **Which passage is more effective in engaging your interest in the history and interpretations of Stonehenge?**

Justify your choice by referring to the ideas and/or style of both passages. 5 E

[3/5]

I prefer passage 2 because it was quite funny the way it described one of the theories about Stonehenge as the Lourdes of the Bronze Age. It also lists more of the silly ideas about Stonehenge than passage 1 does, such as the claim that it was used by spaceships. Passage 1 is much duller and simply describes how Stonehenge was built in three stages, although it gives a lot more detail, e.g. about where the stones came from. Passage 1 also gives a lot more detail about the 'centre of healing' idea and how the Amesbury Archer supports this idea. Passage 2 on the other hand just makes fun of the ideas. The writer of passage 2 is also critical of the way the new ideas are reported in the press.

Both passages make the point that we will almost certainly never know what Stonehenge was used for, but Passage 2 is better because it points out that all the theories are for 'archaeologists to pin their pet theories to' and that if you try hard enough it can be about anything you want. I think this is probably true.

(This response states a clear preference and sticks to it all the way through, even though it acknowledges that in some respects Passage 1 is more detailed and that at times Passage 2 'just makes fun of the ideas'. There is a clear understanding of the contrasting styles.

The main weakness here is not just the lack of detail but the absence of a clear structure. Valid points are made, but they are not well organised.)

[5/5]

Both passages cover approximately the same ground in terms of ideas, but passage 2 does so in a much more engaging style.

Connor goes into a little more detail about the three stages of construction of Stonehenge, while McKie covers this in a single paragraph. Both writers deal with the two recent theories: Stonehenge as a burial ground for royalty and as a place of healing. Both make the point that the real purpose of Stonehenge will never be known ('It is unlikely we will ever know the real truth' and 'more theories … than there are stones inside it.'). McKie, however, extends this to a discussion of the idea that 'every age gets the Stonehenge it deserves'. I find this more engaging as it presents an interesting point that theories tend to reveal more about their proponents than they do about Stonehenge itself.

McKie's final point attacking the present Government's lack of action to protect Stonehenge is not one considered by Connor, and it gives, I think, a provocative conclusion by focusing on practical action for the sake of the site itself rather than on yet more bizarre theories.

In terms of style, Connor is very straightforward. The passage is clearly structured with helpful signposts: 'The first stage …', 'Another theory …' etc. The language is mostly objective with dates and scientific findings – the furthest he goes in expressing opinion is when he describes some of the theories as 'decidedly outlandish'.

McKie, however, is much more lively and he frequently pokes fun at most of the theories, using humorous comparisons such as 'Thus Stonehenge was really an accident and emergency ward for the south west of England' and belittling the Sheffield University team's burial theory as being 'strictly for prehistoric toffs'. One claim he describes bluntly as 'jaw-dropping'. All this makes his style of writing a much more engaging way of dealing with the subject.

Best of all perhaps is that while he is scornful of nearly all the theories, his attitude to Stonehenge itself, as the final paragraph makes clear, is very serious indeed.

(This response covers both ideas and style. It is very clearly structured with an opening statement pointing out the similarity in ideas, and announcing a preference for Passage 2 because of its style of writing. There is a clear and sustained line of thought throughout the answer.

The key similarities are outlined and McKie's extension of the discussion is noted and given praise. There is a neat handling of the point at the end of Passage 2.

The contrast in styles is then dealt with in some detail and the last paragraph provides a thoughtful and insightful conclusion.)

Answers for the 30-mark Textual Analysis task on *Cousin Phillis*

These are the answers for the 30-mark, Textual Analysis task on *Cousin Phillis*. The answers will be dealt with in some detail. However, the following answers are by no means the only ones possible. There are many other variations which could be equally valid. The following key will help you use these answers:

	passage extract
✓	straightforward acceptable answer
★	really good answer
✗	weak/misguided answer
✚	other possible points

1 **By referring to the text of lines 1–16 show how the attitudes of Phillis and Mr Holdsworth to the meeting are conveyed.**　　**4**

	'This is Mr Holdsworth, Phillis,' said I, as soon as I had shaken hands with her. She glanced up at him, and then looked down, more flushed than ever at his grand formality of taking his hat off and bowing; such manners had never been seen at Hope Farm before.
	'Father and mother are out. They will be so sorry; you did not write, Paul, as you said you would.'
	'It was my fault,' said Holdsworth, understanding what she meant as well as if she had put it more fully into words. 'I have not yet given up all the privileges of an invalid; one of which is indecision. Last night, when your cousin asked me at what time we were to start, I really could not make up my mind.'
	Phillis seemed shy – 'then looked down, more flushed than ever' and Mr Holdsworth tried to deflect the blame from Paul / put her at her ease by saying 'It was my fault'.
	(Although this is correct it is not a full enough explanation to gain all 4 marks.)

Phillis seems to be a little disconcerted by his arrival – 'more flushed than ever' – and by his (to her) extremely flamboyant behaviour ('his grand formality of taking his hat off'). She also seems to be blaming Paul for not letting her know when they would arrive – 'you did not write, Paul, as you said you would'.

Mr Holdsworth tries to smooth over the problem – 'understanding what she meant as well as if she had put it more fully into words' – that she thinks Paul has been at fault by explaining that it was he who could not make up his mind about their time of arrival: 'It was my fault … I could not make up my mind'.

Phillis was shy and Mr Holdsworth tried to put both of them at their ease.

(This is a weak answer because does not refer to the text as evidence for the statements.)

2 What can you deduce about Phillis's state of mind from the text of lines 17–22? 2

Phillis seemed as if she could not make up her mind as to what to do with us. I tried to help her, –

'Have you finished getting peas?' taking hold of the half-filled basket she was unconsciously holding in her hand; 'or may we stay and help you?'

Phillis seems to be undecided about what to do next – she doesn't say anything. She seems to have forgotten the basket of peas.

There is an implied silence after Mr Holdsworth has spoken, giving the impression that Phillis does not know what to do next. Paul tries helpfully to break the silence by asking Phillis a practical question. The basket was being held 'unconsciously' in her hand as if she has forgotten what she had been doing.

3 Read lines 32–44.

'I am afraid you distrust me. I can assure you I know the exact fullness at which peas should be gathered. I take great care not to pluck them when they are unripe. I will not be turned off, as unfit for my work.' This was a style of half-joking talk that Phillis was not accustomed to. She looked for a moment as if she would have liked to defend herself from the playful charge of distrust made against her, but she ended by not saying a word. We all plucked our peas in busy silence for the next five minutes. Then Holdsworth lifted himself up from between the rows, and said, a little wearily,

(a) How does Paul perceive Mr Holdsworth's answer? (lines 32–36) 1

Paul sees that Mr Holdsworth is slightly making fun of Phillis in his answer.

Paul sees that Mr Holdsworth is teasing Phillis, by implying that she thinks he either does not know which peas to pick, or that he will eat too many of them.

Paul thinks Mr Holdsworth is half-joking.

(This is a weak answer because 'half-joking' is a phrase lifted straight from the text without any attempt at explanation or paraphrase.)

(b) How does Phillis perceive his answer?   1

Phillis thinks he might be hurt at her lack of confidence in him, but only 'for a moment' and then she realises that he was not serious.

Phillis at first thinks that he is accusing her of thinking him not capable of picking peas properly, and wants to deny it, but realises in time that she is being teased and decides to say nothing.

4 Read lines 50–71.

How does the writer's use of language reflect the contrast between Phillis's behaviour in lines 50–65 and her behaviour in lines 65–71?   4

'It was very thoughtless of me. I did not know – I thought, perhaps, you really liked it. I ought to have offered you something to eat, sir! Oh, Paul, we have gathered quite enough; how stupid I was to forget that Mr Holdsworth had been ill!' And in a blushing hurry she led the way towards the house. We went in, and she moved a heavy cushioned chair forwards, into which Holdsworth was only too glad to sink. Then with deft and quiet speed she brought in a little tray, wine, water, cake, home-made bread, and newly-churned butter. She stood by in some anxiety till, after bite and sup, the colour returned to Mr Holdsworth's face, and he would fain have made us some laughing apologies for the fright he had given us. But then Phillis drew back from her innocent show of care and interest, and relapsed into the cold shyness habitual to her when she was first thrown into the company of strangers. She brought out the last week's county paper (which Mr Holdsworth had read five days ago), and then quietly withdrew;

Words such as 'thoughtless' and 'stupid' show she is blaming herself for suggesting that he should pick peas. Given something practical to do, she goes about it silently and efficiently as is shown by 'deft' and 'quiet speed'. In contrast, later, she turns timid and withdrawn again 'relapsed into the cold shyness' and wants to get away without any more fuss – 'quietly withdrew'.

In lines 50–65 she seems quite distressed – she calls herself 'thoughtless' and 'stupid' and even wonders if he had wanted to pick peas at all or whether he was merely humouring her: 'I thought, perhaps, you really liked it.' The sentence structure of lines 50–55 combining short sentences with dashes giving the impression of hurried and broken speech, and the exclamations, further convey her anxiety. 'And in a blushing hurry' continues the idea of embarrassed action. However, she goes about practically and efficiently to help him – 'deft' and 'quiet speed' suggest that faced with a practical difficulty she is neat and quick. In lines 65–71 when he recovers she again feels awkward – she 'drew back' because perhaps she no longer had an immediate goal of helping Mr Holdsworth and she 'relapsed', turning again self-conscious, as she had been at their first meeting. 'Quietly withdrew' contrasts with the swiftness of her actions when she was anxious about his health.

Phillis was upset that she had been instrumental in making Mr Holdsworth feel faint. But she set about helping him very efficiently. When he had recovered she began to feel awkward again, and quietly left the room.

(This is a weak answer because it again does not show how the 'language' works – there is no reference to specific words or phrases or other language features.)

5 **Look at the dialogue between Phillis and Paul (lines 78–97).**

By referring to these lines show what you can deduce about each of their attitudes towards Mr Holdsworth at this point in the narrative.   2

'Don't you think him handsome?' asked I.

'Perhaps – yes – I have hardly looked at him,' she replied. 'But is not he very like a foreigner?'

'Yes, he cuts his hair foreign fashion,' said I.

'I like an Englishman to look like an Englishman.'

'I don't think he thinks about it. He says he began that way when he was in Italy, because everybody wore it so, and it is natural to keep it on in England.'

'Not if he began it in Italy because everybody there wore it so. Everybody here wears it differently.' I was a little offended with Phillis's logical fault-finding with my friend; and I determined to change the subject.

'When is your mother coming home?'

'I should think she might come any time now. Don't you think you ought to go and see how Mr Holdsworth is going on, Paul? He may be faint again.'

Paul is anxious that Phillis should like Mr Holdsworth – 'Don't you think him handsome?'

And he is annoyed when she criticises him. 'I was a little offended.'

Phillis seems to be less in admiration of him – 'Perhaps – I have hardly looked at him' and about his hairstyle – 'I like an Englishman to look like an Englishman'.

Paul wants Phillis to admire his friend. His first question assumes that Phillis will find him handsome. He does not like Phillis criticising Mr Holdsworth – 'I was a little offended' and decides to change the subject before she has time to say anything else.

Phillis affects not to have looked at him properly – her hesitation in her answer perhaps suggests that she is thinking about her answer, but it seems likely that she has looked at him quite carefully because she has noticed his hairstyle. She does not seem to be overwhelmed by his looks – she wants him to 'look like an Englishman' – and criticises his 'foreign' looks, but almost immediately remembers that he might need some assistance, showing her caring about him.

6 Read lines 107–130.

'Phillis and I understand each other,' I replied, sturdily. 'We are like brother and sister. She would not have me as a husband if there was not another man in the world; and it would take a deal to make me think of her – as my father wishes' (somehow I did not like to say 'as a wife'), 'but we love each other dearly.'

'Well, I am rather surprised at it – not at your loving each other in a brother-and-sister kind of way – but at your finding it so impossible to fall in love with such a beautiful woman.'

Woman! Beautiful woman! I had thought of Phillis as a comely but awkward girl; and I could not banish the pinafore from my mind's eye when I tried to picture her to myself. Now I turned, as Mr Holdsworth had done, to look at her again out of the window: she had just finished her task, and was standing up, her back to us, holding the basket, and the basin in it, high in air, out of Rover's reach.

'I should like to have sketched her,' said Mr Holdsworth, as he turned away. He went back to his chair, and rested in silence for a minute or two. Then he was up again.

    (a) Show how the writer's choice of words in these lines makes clear Paul's statement that his relationship with Phillis is not a romantic one.   **2**

'Sturdily' suggests that his mind is strongly made up. 'We are like brother and sister' suggests a relationship which is close but not in romantic or sexual terms. He thinks of her as quite good-looking, 'comely', but a bit gawky and lacking gracefulness, 'awkward girl'.

The word 'sturdily' suggests a strength of mind and attitude, that he will not change his mind that they are 'like brother and sister'. 'It would take a deal to make me' suggests that he is not to be moved from his position by any trivial thought.

The repetition of the word 'woman' in 'Woman! Beautiful woman!' with the exclamation marks suggests that these are not his words – he doesn't really see it, or believe it. The words 'a comely but awkward girl' suggest that although he thinks she is not bad-looking in a homely way ('comely') he does not see her as fully mature in the romantic sense, but only as a 'girl' and also shows that he is not bowled over by her looks – he sees her faults, her lack of social graces.

    (b) Show, by referring to language and incident in these lines, that the reader is given the impression that Mr Holdsworth's attitude to Phillis is more romantic.   **2**

Mr Holdsworth uses language related to romantic relationships such as 'fall in love' and 'beautiful woman'. He admires her and would like to sketch her, as if he were a romantic artist.

The words 'fall in love with' and 'such a beautiful woman' suggest that Mr Holdsworth thinks of Phillis, at least potentially, as a woman capable of being part of an adult romantic relationship. His desire to sketch her in a dramatic pose also suggests a romantic disposition, as if to fix her beauty in his mind – it also brings the artistic side of his character to the fore, reinforcing the idealised romantic situation of artist and subject.

Mr Holdsworth seems to have been bowled over by Phillis's beauty – shown by the fact that he thinks it 'impossible' not to love her, and the word 'such' emphasises the extent of her beauty.

(This is a weak answer because while it deals quite well with language, it has forgotten to do anything about 'incident' which was part of the question.)

7 Read lines 131–144.

'I would give a good deal for a book,' he said. 'It would keep me quiet.' He began to look round; there were a few volumes at one end of the table. 'Housewife's Complete Manual,' said he, reading their titles aloud. 'Berridge on Prayer; L'Inferno – Dante! In Italian too!' in great surprise. 'Why, who reads this?'

'I told you Phillis read it. Don't you remember? She knows Latin and Greek, too.'

'To be sure! I remember! But somehow I never put two and two together. That quiet girl, full of household work, is the wonderful scholar, then, that put you to rout with her questions when you first began to come here.'

(a) What causes Mr Holdsworth's attitude to Phillis to change?   1

The fact that she reads Italian literature.

He is surprised that she reads Italian and is therefore more interested in her. Perhaps this shows that he is a bit of an intellectual snob.

(b) Show how the language in these lines reveals this new attitude.   2

The phrase 'in great surprise' shows that Mr Holdsworth has to reassess his views of Phillis, and that he did not at all expect to find any intellectual pretensions in her; 'wonderful scholar' puts her on a different, much higher and more interesting level than the competent, practical girl he has seen earlier.

The exclamatory nature of his utterances 'In Italian too!', 'I remember!' and the phrase 'in great surprise' show his excitement at having found something remarkable about Phillis.

The contrast which he makes between 'that quiet girl' and 'the wonderful scholar' shows that he sees Phillis in a new light. The phrase 'put you to rout' elevates Phillis to a status above Paul, and further shows Holdsworth's admiration for her.

8 (a) What difficulty does Mr Holdsworth assume Phillis has after seeing her list of words inside Dante's *Inferno*?   1

What's here: a paper with the hard, obsolete Italian words written out. I wonder what sort of a dictionary she has got. Baretti won't tell her all these words.

Phillis has not been able to translate some of the rarer words from Italian, and it is likely that her dictionary ('Baretti') will not have these difficult words in it.

	Phillis has not been able to translate from Italian some of the harder words ('obsolete' ones that are so uncommon she would be unlikely to find their meaning easily); he thinks that the most common dictionary, 'Baretti' – the one she is likely to have – will not have these difficult words in it.
	That she is stupid. (This is a weak answer because there is no evidence given from the text to prove the statement.)

(b) By referring to lines 147–159, show how Mr Holdsworth's reaction to finding the list of words contrasts with Paul's reaction to the situation. **2**

	'Stay! I have got a pencil here. I'll write down the most accepted meanings, and save her a little trouble.' So he took her book and the paper back to the little round table, and employed himself in writing explanations and definitions of the words which had troubled her. I was not sure if he was not taking a liberty: it did not quite please me, and yet I did not know why. He had only just done, and replaced the paper in the book, and put the latter back in its place, when I heard the sound of wheels stopping in the lane.
	Mr Holdsworth was pleased to be helpful, 'save her a little trouble'. Paul wasn't sure that Phillis would automatically be pleased – 'I was not sure if he was not taking a liberty'.
	Mr Holdsworth is enthusiastic about helping Phillis – 'Stay!' suggests that the idea of helping her has just come to him as a great idea. He 'employed himself' again has the idea of 'busyness' on her behalf. Paul seems unsure as to whether Mr Holdsworth is actually doing Phillis a favour or not. Perhaps he feels that she would not have liked her ignorance of these words to have been noticed – 'taking a liberty' – or perhaps she would have preferred to puzzle it out for herself.

9 Consider the whole extract. How effectively does the writer give the reader an insight into the relationships between each 'pair' of the characters? **6**

	The reader learns quite a lot about the relationships from this extract. Mrs Gaskell shows a close relationship between Paul and Phillis, but it is not a romantic one – they are like brother and sister. Paul helps her out of tricky situations, such as not knowing what to say to Mr Holdsworth. Phillis treats Paul in a straightforward way, not particularly worrying about his feelings when she criticises Mr Holdsworth's hair. Paul and Mr Holdsworth are good friends. Paul wants people to like his friend, and tries to see if Phillis is impressed by his appearance. Mr Holdsworth likes Paul and teases him about his father's idea that Paul should marry Phillis. Mr Holdsworth is impressed by Phillis's looks and even more by her abilities to read Latin, Greek and Italian. He wants to help her with her Italian. Phillis is shy of Mr Holdsworth because she doesn't know how to handle his half-joking way of speaking, and she doesn't meet a lot of outsiders in her home. The extract suggests that all these relationships will develop in the course of the story.

This short extract tells us quite a lot about the relationships. It is effective in giving us a brief sketch of the present situation, and also suggests the possibility of further developments.

Mrs Gaskell shows us that the relationship between Paul and Phillis is essentially a close but platonic one. Phillis is not too concerned about speaking quite openly about her views on his friend's hairstyle. Paul understands her shyness and her lack of 'small talk'. He is protective of her, helping her out of awkward situations and worrying about Mr Holdsworth's invasion of her personal life as shown in her private reading. One would expect Paul always to be there to support her if things go wrong for her.

Paul and Mr Holdsworth are shown to have an easy, friendly relationship. Paul is very keen that Phillis should like his friend – he doesn't like to hear criticism of his looks. Mr Holdsworth knows Paul well enough to talk to him about very personal matters such as Paul's father's wish that Paul should marry Phillis. But Paul's worry about Mr Holdsworth's easy manner of familiarity with Phillis (and her intellectual life) suggests that future developments might show that Mr Holdsworth's sophistication might somehow not be the best thing for Phillis's simplicity and lack of experience of the wider world.

Mr Holdsworth seems to admire Phillis's good looks, to regard her as a beautiful young woman, an object of love, and a subject for art. He also is fascinated by her academic abilities, and shows a desire to help her with such difficulties as she might have. Phillis is not quite sure what to make of Mr Holdsworth. She is not used to anything other than plain and serious communication. She does not understand teasing, and is not at ease in his company. When she forgets her shyness she cares for him and his comfort, but otherwise is uncomfortable in his presence. Mrs Gaskell has laid the foundations for a future relationship which may affect Phillis more deeply than Mr Holdsworth.

Paul and Phillis are like 'brother and sister'; they like each other.

Paul and Mr Holdsworth are good friends although Mr Holdsworth is also Paul's boss.

Mr Holdsworth seems likely to fall in love with Phillis, but she doesn't seem to care for him.

(This is a weak answer firstly because it is simply too short for 6 marks. It also doesn't make any evaluative judgement and it shows little 'insight' into the relationships.)

Answers for the 30-mark Textual Analysis task on the poem 'Work and Play'

These are the answers for the 30-mark, Textual Analysis task on the poem 'Work and Play'. They will be dealt with in some detail. However, these are by no means the only answers possible. There are many other variations which could be equally valid. The same symbols as before have been used to help you follow the answers.

📖	passage extract
✓	straightforward acceptable answer
★	really good answer
✗	weak/misguided answer
⊕	other possible points

1 **Consider the description of the swallow in lines 1–3.**

Comment fully on the effectiveness of one of the images that Hughes uses to describe her movement.   2

	The swallow of summer, she toils all the summer, A blue-dark knot of glittering voltage, A whiplash swimmer, a fish of the air.
	Just as a fish swims in a darting way through the water, so a swallow flies through the air in the same sort of way, giving a good impression of fast, energetic flight.
	'A whiplash swimmer, a fish of the air' suggests that the swallow's flight is as angular and fast as a fish: that the way a fish moves through water, with sudden twists and turns, with the speed of a whip cracking, mirrors excellently the darting, convoluted flight of the swallow.
	'A whiplash swimmer' means that the swallow moves fast and gives a good picture of its movement. (This is a bad answer because there is no attempt to get at the root of either *whiplash* or *swimmer* or at how either compares with anything to do with the swallow; therefore there is no explanation of how the image works.)
	Other possible images: 'A blue-dark knot' or 'glittering voltage' or 'A blue-dark knot of glittering voltage' or 'A whiplash swimmer' or 'a fish of the air' taken separately or even 'toil'.

2 By referring to the word choice in lines 4–8 show how Hughes, in contrast, describes the movement of the cars and their occupants. 3

	But the serpent of cars that crawls through the dust In shimmering exhaust Searching to slake Its fever in ocean Will play and be idle or else it will bust.
	'serpent of cars' gives a picture of a line of slow-moving vehicles winding round the bends in the road getting nowhere fast. 'crawls' again suggests slow speed, like a baby moving on all fours, unable to walk properly. 'fever' gives the feeling of being hot and ill, uncomfortable in the atmosphere of the traffic jam.
	'serpent' demeans the car, makes it seem like a lowly, or even sinister, creature, bound to the earth, capable only of slow movement. 'crawls' also suggests a degraded posture, and a slow speed, able only to move on all fours, head down in the dust. 'slake its fever' has connotations of illness and disease. The extreme thirst suggested brings ideas of intolerable heat and torment.
	'the serpent of cars that crawls through the dust' shows that the traffic is going slowly. 'searching to slake its fever' means that everyone is thirsty and can't wait to get to the sea. (**This is a bad answer because the quotations are too long to allow exact analysis of any particular word. All that is given is the meaning of the phrases quoted.**)
	Other possibilities: 'dust', 'shimmering (exhaust)', 'idle', 'bust'.

3 Show how the imagery in lines 10 and 11 enhances the effect of sunlight on the swallow. 3

	She flings from the furnace, a rainbow of purples, Dips her glow in the pond and is perfect.
	In this image the colours of the swallow in the sun are like the sparks that are thrown out of a furnace, so bright that the swallow glows like hot metal, but when the swallow dips in the water, the brightness disappears, as a fire would be put out. This shows the effect of the sun on the swallow's feathers.

The extended image deployed here is of a furnace, possibly in a blacksmith's shop. The glow of the flames replicates the effect of sunlight on the swallow, and the sparks which would arise from the working of the hot metal are like the spraying of purple colour appearing to spurt out as the quick flight of the swallow causes the light to be reflected in different ways. The final part of the image is when the swallow flies down to the surface of the water, and the 'fire' is put out, as the white-hot metal is quenched in the blacksmith's trough of water and the colour disappears. The effects of the light are thus vividly captured by this extended image.

The effect of sunlight on the swallow is to show the purple colours of her feathers, but when the swallow dips into the water, the brightness disappears. This shows that the sunlight makes the bird seem brighter as she is flying and enhances our appreciation of her flight.

(This is a bad answer because again there is no analysis of any particular image. There is an expansion of the text, but it only deals with meaning, not with effectiveness.)

4 **Read lines 12–18.**

Show how word choice, imagery and sound contribute to the generally unpleasant picture painted of the cars and their occupants. 6

But the serpent of cars that collapsed at the beach
Disgorges its organs
A scamper of colours
Which roll like tomatoes
Nude as tomatoes
With sand in their creases
To cringe in the sparkle of rollers and screech.

'disgorges its organs': just as a stomach disgorges food so the car throws out its occupants, showing that the car is relieved to be rid of them.

'cringe' connotes shrinking in fear, which is true because the people are afraid of the cold water.

'screech' is a grating sound, suggesting high-pitched screaming, which would be hard to listen to.

'disgorges its organs' is an effective image which suggests that the occupants of the car are like the contents of the human body, such things as the liver or the entrails generally – not a pleasant concept – and that they are being spewed out as unwanted things onto the beach.

The word 'cringe' does not have particularly pleasant connotations as it suggests fear and abasement in the face of someone or something more powerful than the 'cringers' – in this case presumably the cold or force of the sea.

The sound of 'disgorges its organs' is, because of the repetition of the 'orge', 'org', a bit disgusting, as if something were stuck in the car's throat and needs to be spat out.

	'disgorges its organs' has unpleasant connotations, giving a negative feel to the scene. 'tomatoes' suggest redness which suggests an adverse effect. 'screech' has negative connotations showing the torment of the sound. **(This is a bad answer because 'unpleasant', 'adverse' and 'negative' are all words which are too generalised to be useful in making a comment on the effectiveness of the particular images and words used here. The comment on sound merely repeats the words of the question, with a vague 'negative' thrown in.)**
	Other possibilities: Imagery: 'collapsed', 'a scamper', 'nude as tomatoes'. Word choice: any of the words of the images discussed above and 'serpent', 'roll', 'sand', 'creases', 'sparkle'. Sound: (possibly) 'cringe' or sibilance in several places (but both these ideas are difficult to handle).

5 Explain fully how the idea of the swallow as 'seamstress' is visually and aurally effective as a representation of a swallow's flight.   **4**

	She scissors the blue into shapes and she sews it, She draws a long thread and she knots it at the corners.
	'She scissors the blue (into shapes)' gives the impression of the flight of the swallow carving out pieces of the sky, by delineating them with her trace, in the same way as scissors cut out pieces of blue material into angular shapes to make something.
	She 'draws a long thread and knots it at the corners' is effective in giving a very dynamic picture of the bird's flight. The long thread which one would use to sew together pieces of material represents the long swoops of the swallow, and the knots at the corners where the thread would gather the material up into tighter loops represents the flourishes with which the bird's flight changes direction, rather like an aircraft 'looping the loop'. The repetition of sibilant sounds such as 's' and 'sh' in the line 'she scissors the blue into shapes and she sews it' can be heard as if the flight of the swallow were swishing through the air, in bursts of speed.
	Alliteration of the 's' sound is effective because it gives the impression of speed. **(This is a bad answer because it doesn't say how the 's' sound gives the impression of speed. The answer merely asserts that it does, without any evidence.)**

6 Choose two of the torments which afflict the holidaymakers, and show how each is made more severe by the poet's use of language. 4

But the holiday people
Are laid out like wounded
Flat as in ovens
Roasting and basting
With faces of torment as space burns them blue
Their heads are transistors
Their teeth grit on sand grains
Their lost kids are squalling
While man-eating flies
Jab electric shock needles but what can they do?

'Flat as in ovens roasting and basting' suggests that as poultry is cooked at a high temperature in an oven, being occasionally sprinkled with hot fat, so the holidaymakers on the beach are getting very hot and burned, being covered from time to time in suncream perhaps. The image emphasises the uncomfortable nature of being on the beach.

'Their lost kids squalling' adds to the hassles of the day – the word 'kids' is rather casual, possibly suggesting that they are rather a nuisance, and 'squalling' has unpleasant connotations of a loud and continuous, high-pitched noise emphasising the discomfort of those who are lost.

'Their teeth grit on sand grains' describes the unpleasant and uncomfortable qualities of sand, especially the word 'grit' which suggests a combination of grinding and spitting – it gets everywhere, even into your mouth, and seems impossible to get rid of. The sounds used – the repeated 't' and 'g' – are hard sounds which represent the harshness of the sand and its abrasive qualities.

The imagery of 'jab … needles' makes the bites of flies and insects seem severe – heightened by the exaggeration of the phrase 'man-eating' – as a syringe hurts when it is delivering some chemical into your body. The suddenness of the attack is further emphasised by the use of 'electric shock', which suggests a quick, damaging burst of pain.

Other possibilities:

'laid out like wounded (flat)', 'space burns them blue', 'heads are transistors'. There are also other sound effects and comment could be made on the rhythm employed.

7 Comment on ways in which the structure of the whole poem is effective in highlighting one of the central concerns of the poem. 2

In each of the first three verses of the poem there are three lines on the swallow, followed by a larger number of lines describing the cars and humans. This structure helps to make the contrast between the swallow and the humans more obvious. In the last verse this procedure is reversed so that we end up with the image of the swallow, leaving a beautiful picture in our minds.

The subject of the poem, the swallow, is described in the first three lines of each of the first three verses, its beauty contrasting with the ugliness of the cars and people which take up an increasing number of lines with each verse, mirroring the length of the day and the weariness it causes to the people. The last line in each verse is longer, representing a sort of summing up of all the discomforts described in the verse. At the end of the third verse the longer line is actually a question which is answered therefore in the first line of the last stanza, allowing the people to come first, leaving the last part of the poem to the swallow and its beauty, and in this case there are four lines, not three, creating a climax which encompasses his admiration of its appearance and way of life.

The first three verses all have one sentence to describe the swallow and then another sentence to describe the cars and the people. The last verse is all one sentence which describes them both together, bringing the poem to a satisfactory close.

(This is a bad answer because the description of the structure is accurate but the comment is too general and not 'proved' in any way: again the statement is merely an assertion.)

Other possibilities:

Comment could be made about the intricacy of the rhythms in the lines describing the swallow in contrast with the rather plain and plodding rhythms in the shorter lines about the people and cars.

8 To what extent would you agree with the statement that the last four lines of the poem reach a climax of beauty and wonder? Justify your opinion with close reference to these lines. 4

The swallow of summer, cartwheeling through crimson,
Touches the honey-slow river and turning
Returns to the hand stretched from under the eaves –
A boomerang of rejoicing shadow.

I fully agree that the last four lines are the most beautiful in the poem. The colours of the evening sunset are portrayed in the 'crimson' and the glow of the 'honey' river. 'The hand stretched from under the eaves' gives a peaceful picture of the safety of the swallow's nest, to which she is returning, like a boomerang returning to the hand that threw it, and the phrase 'rejoicing shadow' shows the happiness of the bird at the end of the day.

The last four lines of the poem seem to contain the most beautiful description and imagery of the whole poem. 'Cartwheeling through crimson' suggests the acrobatics of the swallow's flight seen at sunset – touched by the red rays; the 'honey-slow river' is glowing in the light, and quite calm (suggested by 'slow') and yet laden with good ('honey' suggests not only light but also richness) for the swallow flying low over its surface. 'Turning' continues the idea of the cartwheel but seems to be more sustained and smoother, having a clear course to follow to where 'the hand stretched from under the eaves' seems to be welcoming the bird to a safe haven at the end of the day, and the 'boomerang of rejoicing shadow' shows how gladly and swiftly the swallow flies home, as a boomerang always returns to its place of origin.

8 Comment on the ambiguity of the title of the poem. 2

	The 'Work' of the swallow – who is the one who is working for her food – seems to be very pleasurable, whereas the people who are supposed to be enjoying their day of 'Play' are having to put a lot of effort into it for not much reward. So perhaps the title is reversed by the time you reach the end of the poem.
	The title 'Work and Play' seems initially to be contrasting the swallow who 'toils' (line 1) and the people in the cars who 'will play and be idle' (line 8). But throughout the course of the poem, the swallow is described as going about her business in a carefree, effortless way ('and is perfect'), whereas the people are labouring at enjoying themselves, finding many aspects of the day unpleasant ('headache it homeward'). The contrast between the people and the 'rejoicing shadow' suggests that perhaps the swallow is more nearly at play and the people are having to work very hard to cope with their day of 'leisure'.